Critical Religious Education, Multiculturalism and the Pursuit of Truth

Religion, Education and Culture

Series Editors:
William K. Kay (Bangor University),
Leslie J. Francis (University of Warwick) and
Jeff Astley (University of Durham)

This series addresses issues raised by religion and education within contemporary culture. It is intended to be of benefit to those involved in professional training as ministers of religion, teachers, counsellors, psychologists, social workers and health professionals while also contributing to the theoretical development of the academic fields from which this training is drawn.

Critical Religious Education, Multiculturalism and the Pursuit of Truth

by

ANDREW WRIGHT

UNIVERSITY OF WALES PRESS
CARDIFF
2007

British Library Cataloguing-in-Publication Data
A catalogue record for this book is available from the British Library.

ISBN 978–0–7083–2057–0

Typeset by Florence Production Ltd, Stoodleigh, Devon
Printed in Great Britain by Antony Rowe Ltd, Chippenham

For
Hannah and Alex
Jordan, Conor, Max and Harri
Alfie Joe and Yazmin

Contents

PART IV
Theory and Practice

Series editor's preface

Religious education exists in British schools in a way that is unique to the British situation. It became part of the curriculum of maintained schools in England and Wales in 1944, after the defeat of the dictatorships of the war-time era. In the years that followed, in response to cultural and educational changes, religious education gradually developed to become more multi-faith, more imaginative and more the province of professionally trained RE teachers.

By the 1980s, RE was a world away from what it had been in the 1940s. A large number of educational fashions had left their mark, though perhaps the greatest was left by the phenomenological thrust of Ninian Smart. RE became descriptive, piecemeal and, paradoxically, the bearer of the burden to induce tolerance in the minds of pupils and, from there, in British society.

In the 1990s there were further changes, as RE came to model itself on the pattern of the National Curriculum (of which it was not part). The inspection agency Ofsted (Estyn in Wales) was by then active in schools in England and Wales, and only those subjects picked out by Ofsted/Estyn inspections tended to receive the attention and funding of educational managers. In all this, RE was in danger of losing touch with the religions that were at the centre of its concerns.

Andrew Wright, who has a long and honourable record within the world of RE in Britain (and Europe), has, in this important book, asked and answered questions about the role of truth in the educational enterprise. This book, which I believe will be widely read among educators in Britain, Europe and other parts of the English-speaking world, engages with philosophical literature in a sophisticated way that stands head and shoulders above much of the theoretical writing on RE in the past.

William K. Kay

Acknowledgements

It would not have been possible to complete this book without the encouragement of my colleagues in the Centre for Theology, Religions and Culture at King's College London, and the granting of a period of study leave by the Department of Education and Professional Studies. I am also grateful for ongoing conversations with members of the Association of University Lecturers in Religion and Education (UK), and the International Seminar on Religious Education and Values. The advice and support provided by two colleagues in particular proved indispensable: Philip Barnes at King's College London made available his deep philosophical and theological knowledge of contemporary religious education, while Elina Hella at the University of Helsinki introduced me to the pedagogical theory that forms the basis of the final section of this book.

Wisdom is to speak the truth and act in keeping with its nature.

Heraclitus

Introduction

In *Landscapes of the Soul*, Douglas Porpora sets out to map the contours of religious belief in America today (Porpora, 2001). The situation he uncovers, in a series of fascinating interviews, is one of fragmentation and dislocation. He suggests that although we acquire our identities in social, moral and metaphysical space, 'sociologists and the lay public both tend to situate identity entirely in social space' (p. 57). Contemporary society, that is to say, construes identity predominantly in terms of networks of relationships with family, friends, acquaintances and work colleagues. The result is a contraction of meaning: moral space has relevance only insofar as it impacts on social space, while metaphysical space is disregarded almost completely:

> We so lack any articulated worldview that arguments about the cosmos strike us as ponderously irrelevant. Today, we shy away from thinking cosmically. In fact, we tend actively, through humour, to distance ourselves from cosmic concerns. What is the meaning of life? In answer, we quote Douglas Adams or Monty Python and laugh.
>
> (p. 58)

Such responses ignore the fact that social space is inextricably linked to moral and metaphysical space. Our social relationships require a moral perspective to give them meaning: we do not simply interact with others – rather, we interact with others through patterns of meaning that are essentially moral. Just as 'moral space is where we find moral purpose', so 'moral purpose must be emotionally and conceptually grounded in some larger worldview' (pp. 57f). Our worldviews operate in metaphysical space, providing answers to questions about the meaning and purpose of life and the ultimate order-of-things. Further, 'because worldviews make claims about what is, they ineluctably raise questions of truth', questions that 'move us into the space of critical argument' (p. 58). Porpora's research reveals 'a culturally pervasive lack of orientation in metaphysical space, an inability to place ourselves meaningfully in the cosmos' (p. 152). This leads to 'an equally pervasive void in our own sense of self': if identity is bound up with our place in the cosmos, 'then we cannot lose our place in the cosmos without losing ourselves as well' (p. 152). Whether implicitly or explicitly, we cannot avoid acting in social and moral space without some assumptions about metaphysical space. However, our ability to attend to questions of our place in the cosmos has been severely retarded by the forces of secularization that strive to remove such questions from the public sphere.

The situation is analogous to that envisaged by Alistair MacIntyre in *After Virtue* (MacIntyre, 1985, p. 1). He asks us to imagine a situation in which the general public blames a series of environmental disasters on the scientists. Widespread rioting follows, in which laboratories are destroyed, physicists lynched and scientific texts burnt. Eventually 'a Know-Nothing political movement takes power and successfully abolishes science teaching in schools and universities, imprisoning and executing the remaining scientists' (p. 1). Later a reaction sets in, and attempts are made to revive the discipline. However, there is no longer any deep holistic understanding of science, only fragments from a long-forgotten past: 'a knowledge of experiments detached from any knowledge of the theoretical context . . . instruments whose use has been forgotten; half-chapters from books, single pages from articles, not always legible because torn and charred' (p. 1). Nevertheless, these fragments are constituted into a set of practices: adults debate the theory of relativity and children learn by heart the surviving portions of the periodic table. Nobody 'realises that what they are doing is not natural science in any proper sense at all . . . [since] those contexts which would be needed to make sense of what they are doing have been lost, perhaps irretrievably' (p. 1).

As with science in MacIntyre's mind's eye; so with theology and philosophy in the cultural situation described by Porpora. Having once abandoned transcendent belief as an outmoded and dangerous superstition, Western society is currently struggling to recover it; but having only the fragments of traditional religious visions to work with, the society appears unable to produce anything more substantial than either an incoherent mishmash of New Age idealism or a range of deeply distorted versions of Western monotheism, neither of which is capable of generating profound spiritual insight or standing the test of rigorous scrutiny. Consequently, we find ourselves living in a religiously illiterate society, one in urgent need of redemption.

This book is concerned with the place of truth in religious education: its core thesis is that the subject should enable students to engage with questions of ultimate truth, and attend to the task of living truthful lives in an informed, critical and literate manner. Traditionally, religious education has provided the context in which to explore ultimate questions concerning our place in the cosmos. The shift from confessional to liberal forms of religious education in the early 1970s reflected a growing recognition that specifically Christian answers to such questions need to be considered alongside other religious and secular worldviews. However, the forces of secularization proved so powerful that the original vision of a liberal religious education committed to the open pursuit of truth in a plural context quickly imploded. In its place emerged a religious education that turned its back on metaphysical space and put its efforts into cultivating understanding and spirituality (almost) exclusively in social and moral space. This did not mean that metaphysical questions suddenly disappeared: they simply went underground for a while before reappearing – tacitly, surreptitiously and in a distinctive form. As a result liberal religious education currently inducts pupil into a specific worldview, namely that of a comprehensive liberalism that places individual human beings at the centre of the cosmos and invites them to construct their own systems of meaning and value.

What follows is a theoretical study that focuses on the teaching of religion in community schools in England and Wales: specifically, teaching oriented towards the pursuit of ultimate truth, concerned to allow pupils to live truthful lives in the light of an informed understanding of the contested question of their place in the cosmos. Despite this narrow regional and institutional focus, the core argument is transferable – albeit with certain revisions – both to faith schools in England and Wales and to religious and secular schools in other national contexts.

Part I Concepts and Context sets out the basic assumptions that underline the rest of the book. *Chapter 1 Truth and truthfulness* defends a realistic understanding of truth and identifies a truthful life as one lived in harmony with the ultimate order-of-things. *Chapter 2 Political liberalism* challenges the closed worldview of comprehensive liberalism and sets out a vision of a political liberalism concerned to enable a range of communities and traditions to pursue truth in a secure and sympathetic environment.

Part II The Nature and Task of Religious Education sets out the theory of critical religious education. *Chapter 4 Classical religious education* argues that pre-modern forms of religious education shared the common task of grappling with questions of ultimate truth and encouraging the living of truthful lives in harmony with ultimate reality. *Chapter 5 Liberal religious education* tells the story of the eclipse of concerns for truth and truthfulness in contemporary religious education. *Chapter 6 Critical religious education* seeks to justify the central importance of such concerns in the classroom.

Part III A Heuristic Framework establishes a conceptual structure designed to support the pursuit of truth and truthfulness in critical religious education. *Chapter 7 Ontology: the ultimate order of things* identifies discrete religious traditions as the primary bearers of transcendent truth claims. *Chapter 8 Semantics: the language of life* argues that such truth claims are most clearly visible in the metanarratives and worldviews owned by discrete religious traditions. *Chapter 9 Hermeneutics: understanding reality* offers a hermeneutical model of religious understanding, predicated on the notion of critical conversations between competing horizons of meaning. *Chapter 10 Epistemology: wrestling with truth* advocates a contextual epistemology in which critical judgements between conflicting truth claims are made in the holistic context of faith seeking understanding.

Part IV Theory and practice addresses questions of the implementation of the theory of critical religious education and the use of the heuristic conceptual framework designed to support it. *Chapter 11 The pedagogy of learning* eschews any simplistic transition from theory to practice, drawing of phenomenography and the Variation Theory of Learning to establish a theoretical basis for the pedagogy of critical religious education.

Part I
Concepts and Context

1

Truth and truthfulness

The central argument of this book is that religious education should enable pupils to wrestle with ultimate truth. It is, of course, a contentious thesis. Many of us are profoundly suspicious of truth claims in general, and ultimate truth claims in particular. Mention of truth conjures up secular images of totalitarianism, religious images of fundamentalism, and educational images of indoctrination. However, these are images not of truth, but of the distortion and perversion of truth. It is an impoverished society that responds to such misrepresentation by employing strategies of evasion rather than retrieval. Truth matters, and it is precisely because it is such a precious commodity that I have no interest in a religious education that imposes certain beliefs on pupils; on the contrary, given that truth is a deeply contested matter, I am proposing that we should empower pupils to *pursue* truth in an informed and critical manner. This chapter sets out an understanding of the twin concepts that are at the heart of my argument: 'truth' and its cognate 'truthfulness'. I begin by sketching the contours of a realistic understanding of truth, predicated on ontological realism, epistemic relativism and judgemental rationality. This raises questions about the meaning of life and our place in the universe, to which I respond by proposing that a truthful person is one who strives to live life in harmony with the ultimate order-of-things. I then address metaphysical issues concerning the nature, organization and meaning of reality. My aim throughout this chapter is not to defend any narrowly conceived worldview, but establish a framework for debate between different religious and secular traditions, both amongst religious educators and in the classroom itself. With this in mind, I go onto address the particular concerns of anti-realists, arguing, that despite my realistic commitments, the understanding of truth presented here is broad enough to accommodate their position. I conclude the chapter by outlining seven guiding propositions regarding truth and truthfulness, which will form the basis of the ensuing discussion.

1.1 Realism, relativism and rationality

What is truth? The question can be broken down into three further questions. What is reality? How do we experience reality? How do we judge whether such experience is authentic? In line with the philosophy of critical realism, I will defend the notions of onto-logical realism, epistemic relativism and judgemental rationality (Archer, Collier and Porpora, 2004, pp. 1ff; Sayer, 2000, pp. 10ff). Ontological realism claims that reality, the totality of all that is, exists independently of our ability to experience it. Epistemic relativism claims that our experience of reality is always limited to the particular contexts in which we find ourselves. Judgemental rationality claims that, despite such limitations, we *can* make informed judgements about our experience that enable us to lay claim to relatively secure – although never complete or absolutely certain – knowledge of reality.

According to ontological realism, a 'statement (proposition, belief . . .) is true if and only if what the statement says to be the case actually is the case' (Alston, 1996, p. 5; Devitt, 1997). Thus, the statement 'Helsinki is the capital of Finland' is true if, and only if, Helsinki is actually the capital of Finland; similarly, the claim that 'God created the world *ex nihilo*' is true if, and only if, God actually created the world *ex nihilo*. Statements are true only insofar as they relate appropriately to the ontological reality of a world that exists independently of our ability to apprehend and describe it. It is important to recognize that such statements only *bear witness* to truth: although we often refer to 'true propositions', truth itself resides primarily in the reality such propositions seek to describe, and only secondarily in the propositions themselves.

This use of the word 'truth' and its cognates to refer to the way things actually are in the real world is a familiar feature in our everyday lives. We understand what it means to claim that aspirin can help relieve pain, that Neil Armstrong walked on the moon, that the vast majority of Muslims believe in the existence of God, and that a witness in a court of law ought to tell 'the truth, the whole truth, and nothing but the truth'. Ontological realism constitutes the common-sense understanding of truth accepted by the majority of human beings in many different geographical and historical contexts. Although descriptions of the nature of reality vary enormously, there is a shared cross-cultural assumption that there is an actual reality 'out there' to account for. This immediately becomes clear if we try to imagine how people might behave if they genuinely believed there is nothing beyond their sentient minds. The world would simply be a figment of their imagination, and they would have no reason to interact with it in any way. Yet, we all – with the exception of chronically ill people in vegetative states – act on the assumption that we engage with some kind of external reality. Even the Buddhist, viewing the present life as an illusion and seeking emancipation from it, assumes that this world actually *is* ephemeral and responds to it accordingly. The solipsistic denial of ontological reality is the stuff of philosophical speculation, not ordinary life.

There is one important caveat to which we must draw attention. Talk of a 'real world out there' implies an ontological dualism between self and world. Yet, we are inextricably bound to the world we indwell and, as such, are integral parts of the reality we seek to describe. Such a non-dualistic ontology suggests that whenever we think or act, we engineer a change in the totality of the actual order-of-things. But how does this square with the claim that reality exists independently of our ability to experience it? The answer is one of degree: it is of course true that whenever I act in the world I bring about a change in the order-of-things. However, such changes are so miniscule, when read in the light of the totality of all that exists, as to be of no deep ontological significance. If I were to die tomorrow the impact, however distressful for those close to me, would not reverberate very far or for very long: I am, after all, only one of more than 6 billion people currently living on earth, a planet that orbits one of 70 sextillion *observable* stars – about ten times as many stars as grains of sand in the world's beaches and deserts. It is certainly true that when I observe an object the world changes slightly as a result; but it is equally true that, to all intents and purposes, reality exists independently of my ability to perceive it.

Our epistemic relationship with ontological reality is relative to our cultural contexts: only God can discern the totality of all that is and fully understand its nature, extent, order and purpose. The modernist dream of establishing secure and certain knowledge has not been realized: our understanding of the world is partial, contingent and often wrong. It follows that there is epistemic distance between reality and our perception of reality. Roy Bhaskar distinguishes three interrelated ontological domains: the empirical, actual and real (Bhaskar, 1977, p. 56). The *empirical domain* consists of all that we ever experience. The *actual domain* consists of the totality of objects and events in the world – including our experiences – that exist and occur, regardless of whether we are aware of them or not. The *real domain* consists of the totality of objects, events and experiences, together with the forces and mechanisms that make them possible, and which have the potential to generate new configurations of the actual world. If I get caught in a thunderstorm, I have a first-hand *empirical* experience of the weather. However, the *actual* weather is greater than that which I experience – if the sun is shining in Rome while it rains in London, it does so whether I am aware of it or not. At a deeper level, the *reality* of the weather is the result of a complex set of mechanisms – chemical reactions in the sun, temperature changes, pressure in the earth's atmosphere, etc. – that are continually generating actual weather systems.

A relatively common mistake is to commit the epistemic fallacy of identifying reality with experience and forcing the world into the straightjacket of our epistemological procedures. The classic modern example is logical positivism, which limits truth to that which is directly verifiable through our senses. Although we can verify some propositions as true by appealing to the evidence of our sense experience, others are simply unverifiable: since we cannot hear goodness, taste beauty, or see God, our moral, aesthetic and religious utterances are merely emotive expressions devoid of any cognitive connection with the real world. There is no suggestion that we may need to adjust our epistemic procedures in response to realities we encounter in the world; on the contrary, reality must conform to our pre-established ways of knowing. In effect, logical positivism reduces reality to the domain of the empirical and bypasses the domains of the actual and real. For the critical realist, on the other hand, reality is largely independent of epistemological concerns: whatever its nature and extent, the world exists independently of our ability to know it. Since 'the statement that gold is malleable is true if and only if gold is malleable', there can be 'no *epistemic* requirements for the truth of [this] statement . . .

It is not required that any person or any social group, however defined, know that gold is malleable or be justified or rational in believing it' (Alston, 1996, p. 5). Similarly, if God did indeed create the world *ex nihilo*, then the act of creation was an actual event, and whether or not human beings or any other sentient life forms are aware of this fact makes no substantial difference to its ontological reality.

We can explore this issue further by addressing the issue of the nature of language. How do propositions engage with the actual order-of-things? How can we distinguish between true and false statements? Responses to such questions must take account of our increasing awareness of the complexity of language. There is rarely a simple one-to-one relationship between words and objects: we depend on a complex web of metaphors, models and narratives to make sense of the world. Further, since we are not neutral observers seeking to describe an external world but rather active participants in reality, we use language not merely to depict our world but, more fundamentally, as a vehicle through which to live out our lives. Consequently, it is important – insofar as it is humanly possible – that our language accords with reality. Without such a connection, language will be unable to support our efforts to relate appropriately to the actual order-of-things. If we proclaim allegiance to God and seek to order our lives accordingly, we stake everything on the belief that our creed correctly identifies, however partially, divine reality: if we are wrong, we will end up basing our lives on a false premise. Although it is certainly possible to live in blissful ignorance of the way things actually are in the world, on balance it is preferable not to be duped – whether by oneself or by others – in this way: better the discontented philosopher than the contented pig (Wright, 1993, pp. 65ff). It follows that the question of the truth of the words we utter and seek to live by is fundamentally important.

It is the actual realities with which our language seeks to engage with that constitute the source and ground of truthful statements. There is a distinct danger of slipping into a semantic version of the epistemic fallacy and equating language with reality. Some forms of postmodern philosophy are particularly vulnerable to this hazard. High levels of scepticism about the extent of our knowledge lead to the belief that attempts to describe reality are nothing more than arbitrary language games, and hence to the assumption that since we can know nothing of a world beyond our linguistic constructions, language and reality must be identical. In sharp contrast, a realistic understanding of truth insists that language functions to *describe* and *respond* to reality, rather than *create* it. The fact that the ontological reality of the world is largely independent of our ability to discern it means that our statements are true only insofar as they accurately engage with actual states of affairs in the world.

This is not to suggest that we do not construct language, merely that our constructions may be either true or false. Large, bipedal, flesh-eating dinosaurs existed during the Cretaceous Period, long before the emergence of human life on earth: geologists coined the name 'Tyrannosaurus rex' to describe such creatures, not to create them. When Harvey Cormier suggests that 'we didn't make the dinosaurs, but we did make the truth about them when we generated the concept dinosaur and satisfactory beliefs involving it', he comes perilously close to embracing the epistemic fallacy (Cormier, 2001, p. 64). It is a primary *ontological truth* that 'we didn't make the dinosaurs', but only a secondary *semantic truth* that 'we generated the concept dinosaur'. The ontological reality of dinosaurs is substantially independent of the discourse of palaeontologists. It is true that we coined the term 'dinosaur', but equally true that our conversations *about* dinosaurs possess veracity only insofar as they accurately describe a previous state of affairs on earth. The label 'dinosaur' is simply a convention through which we attempt to describe one aspect of reality and the accuracy or inaccuracy of our descriptions has no impact whatsoever on the actuality of these pre-historic creatures. The fact of epistemic relativism means that we cannot limit the order-of-things to our ability to know it, or reduce reality to the sum of our true statements.

The juxtaposition of ontological realism and epistemic relativism means that we must rely on rational judgements to make sense of the world. Some philosophers read the fact that such judgements can be mistaken as an invitation to radical scepticism. If we can be wrong some of the time, how can we be sure that we are not wrong all of the time? Where modernity sought to resolve this dilemma by demanding absolute certainty of our knowledge, postmodernity responded by making a virtue of agnosticism (Wright, 2004a). If knowledge is relative to the community that produces it, and absolute certainty a criterion for knowledge, then it could be argued that we have no access to *any* knowledge of the world. However, a straight choice between scepticism and certainty is not the only response to the fact of epistemic relativism. Contra the radical sceptics, it is palpably clear that we do have relatively secure knowledge of the world: if this were not the case we would be unable to boil a kettle, perform open-heart surgery, appreciate the beauty of a sunset, or condemn genocide as evil. Contra the advocates of absolute certainty, it is equally clear that our knowledge of the world is limited and contingent. The simply fact is that we know an awful lot about the world despite being certain of very little.

Bhaskar draws an important distinction between intransitive and transitive domains of knowledge. Objects in the intransitive domain possess independent ontologically reality: human beings do not create them and they are not dependent on human action. 'If men ceased to exist sound would continue to travel and heavy bodies fall to the earth, although ex hypothesi there would be no-one to know it' (Bhaskar, 1977, p. 21). Objects in the transitive domain, on the other hand, possess epistemic reality: human beings create them and they are dependent on human action. Such objects of knowledge include the 'established facts and theories, paradigms and models, methods and techniques of inquiry available to a particular scientific school or worker' (p. 21). Bhaskar goes onto argue that it is possible to 'imagine a world of intransitive objects without science', but impossible to imagine science without both intransitive and transitive objects (p. 22). It is reasonable to suppose that gravity will continue to attract heavy objects, regardless of whether scientists seek to understand the phenomenon or not; but it is inconceivable that scientists could conduct experiments and construct theories in this particular field of enquiry without the antecedent reality of gravity itself. In other words, although both the object of study and the fruits of our enquiry possess ontological reality, the transitive domain of human thought and action is dependent on the intransitive domains of the empirical, actual and real. Knowledge, despite being relative to the observer, is reliant on some form of engagement with an independent ontological reality. Because transitive and intransitive objects of knowledge are distinct yet necessarily connected, we can make critical judgements about the relationship between transitive epistemic truth claims and the intransitive ontological reality they seek to engage with.

1.2 The practice of truthfulness

What is our place in the actual order-of-things? What is the meaning and purpose of life here on earth? Although – as we shall confirm later – the world's religions make ultimate truth claims, they also offer paths to enlightenment or salvation. Hence, a religious education concerned with truth must also address the challenge of how to live life truthfully – that is to say, in harmony with ultimate reality.

At the trial of Jesus of Nazareth, as recounted in John's Gospel, Pontius Pilate infamously asked the question: 'What is truth?' (John 18: 38). The irony is not lost on John's readers, who already know that Jesus himself is 'the way, and the truth, and the life' (14: 6). Although *alethia* ('truth') is sometimes used in the Gospel in its standard Greek sense to refer to 'that which corresponds to fact . . . more characteristically it means the Christian revelation brought by and revealed by Jesus' (Barrett, 1955, p. 139). Jesus, as the incarnate Word of God, is 'full of grace and truth' (1: 14). This identification of truth with divine mercy and grace has its source in the Hebraic notion of God's loyalty and faithfulness to his covenant people (Exodus 34: 6). There is a wealth of difference between 'truth' as a static and impersonal correspondence with reality, and 'truthfulness' as an active and personal engagement with the world. The Hebrew *yada* ('to know') identifies a dynamic personal quality: 'knowing arises not by standing back from in order to look at, but by active and intentional engagement in lived experience' (Groome, 1980, p. 141). However, *yada* was translated in the Septuagint as *ginoskein*, which carries 'a predominant meaning of "intellectual looking at" an object of scrutiny and strongly connotes objectivity' (p. 141). However, there is a danger of over-stressing the distinction between Greek and Hebraic modes of thought here. For Plato, knowledge of the truth of the ultimate order-of-things is no mere academic matter: the Platonic Forms provide the necessary guide for human action and personal flourishing. Similarly, in Hebrew scripture, the personal quality of truthfulness requires knowledge of the actual reality of God, as this is revealed in the creator's covenantal relationship with Israel. Truth and truthfulness are interdependent concepts: there is an intimate relationship between truth as objective reality and truthfulness as our subjective response to that reality.

To be truthful is to act habitually in a loyal, faithful, honest and upright manner. How might we measure this? We might say that a person is true to themselves, or to some external standard – such as the values of the community they identify with, or to the God they believe in. However, this raises fundamental problems, since paedophiles may be true to themselves, many of Hitler's henchmen were true to Nazi ideals, and suicide bombers are true to the God they worship. Hence there is no avoiding the question: Are the values against which we measure truthfulness appropriate to the actual nature of reality? If God is the ultimate source of goodness, then a truthful life ought to be one lived in harmony with the divine will; if, on the other hand, God does not exist and there is no transcendent source of value, then it appears likely that we are ultimately responsible for our own sense of goodness and that we should measure our lives against the goals we set ourselves, either individually or communally. In each case, it is our understanding of the nature of reality that informs our judgements. This suggests a close reciprocal relationship between the pursuit of truth and the practice of truthfulness: a truthful life is one lived in harmony with the way things actually are in the world.

According to Bernard Williams, contemporary society combines an intense commitment to the practice of truthfulness with a deep scepticism regarding the pursuit of truth (Williams, 2002). The practice of truthfulness has to do with the way we live out our lives in social space: the kind of people we are, the integrity of our behaviour, the way we display virtues such as honesty, sincerity and trustworthiness. The pursuit of truth, on the other hand, has to do with our particular understanding of the world: our political principles, religious commitments and metaphysical beliefs. He suggests it is increasingly commonplace to suppose that there is no necessary connection between the two, and that we can live truthful lives regardless of the precise nature of our wider beliefs and worldviews. Hence, a permissive attitude towards a broad range of beliefs stands alongside an unwillingness to give ground when assessing issues of personal integrity. We measure truthfulness against our own sincerity and the perceived sincerity of others, rather than against any broader value system.

This commitment to truthfulness is rooted in 'a pervasive suspiciousness, a readiness against being fooled, an eagerness to see through appearances to the real structures and motives that lie behind them' (p. 1). However, this fear of duplicity operates within a postmodern society sceptical of the legitimacy of truth claims and convinced that 'the Enlightenment has generated unprecedented systems of oppression, because of its belief in an externalized, objective, truth about individuals and society' (p. 4). Consequently, there is a widespread assumption that the pursuit of truth constitutes a significant threat to the practice of truthfulness: we are suspicious of any commitment to external authority because we believe it will tend to undermine personal integrity. This throws us back onto the apparently safer option of simply being true to ourselves: 'It does not matter what you believe, it is the type of person you are that matters.' Williams contends that this polarization of truth and truthfulness breeds cynicism and apathy: thus, academics who turn their backs on the pursuit of truth risk 'sliding from professional seriousness, through professionalization, to a finally disenchanted careerism' (p. 3).

Despite this, Williams insists that the divide between truth and truthfulness is impossible to sustain. Eventually we are bound to ask: 'If you do not really believe in the existence of truth, what is the passion for truthfulness a passion for?' (p. 2). Ultimately, the exercise of truthfulness requires some standard of truth against which to judge its success or failure: 'in pursuing truthfulness, what are you supposedly being true to?' (p. 2). Thus, the rejection of science as merely the exercise of power, in the belief that 'its pretensions to deliver the truth are unfounded, because of social forces that control its activities', does little to clear the way for more truthful living: on the contrary, it entails making 'the remarkable assumption that the sociology of knowledge is in a better position to deliver truth about science than science is to deliver truth about the world' (pp. 2f). The deconstruction of scientific truth does not lead to truthfulness, merely to an alternative – and far less sustainable – account of truth. Attempts to undermine truth claims in the name of truthfulness are ultimately dependent on a commitment to some form of truth, whether acknowledge or unacknowledged. In particular, the contemporary concern for truthfulness often implies the truth claim that self-determination constitutes the highest human good. There is a certain irony in the truth claim that personal integrity requires one to avoid subscribing to truth claims. Williams suggests that truth has an unavoidable role to play in our attempts to live truthful lives: 'the value of truthfulness embraces the need to find out the truth, to hold on to it, and to tell it – in particular, to oneself' (p. 13). Hence, the need to ensure that the beliefs that inevitably inform our attempts to live truthful lives are, to the best of our endeavours, in harmony with the way things actually are in the world.

We seek to understand the world and live truthfully within it as engaged participants rather than detached observers. Although reality exists independently of our awareness of it, we nevertheless participate directly and personally in it. As Colin Gunton points out, because the world transcends our capacity to fully comprehend it, it is impossible to establish 'a 'God's-eye-view' of knowledge, detached, objective and with pretensions of infallibility' (Gunton, 1983, p. 144). Nevertheless, the fact that we can still establish substantial understanding of the world suggests that '*knowledge can be contingent, fallible and partial without for that reason losing its claim to be knowledge*' (p. 145). This opens up the possibility of striving to understand our true place in the ultimate order-of-things, and live truthful lives in harmony with reality, within the constraints and opportunities afforded us by our limited experiences of reality. Such striving has an important linguistic dimension, since words are 'not mirrors of reality but the *means by which we participate in reality*' (p. 144). The accounts we give of the world carry profound consequences for the way we seek to conduct our lives, and the stories that give our lives meaning contain deep implications for our understanding of the nature of reality. The fact that we engage with reality through the medium of language breaks down the distinction between objective factual statements and subjective value-laden ones. The notion of a division between our knowledge of the world and the way we ought to conduct ourselves, between the true nature of reality and the challenge of truthful living, is largely a product of modernity; indeed, the 'divorce of the natural and moral universes is perhaps the worst legacy of the Enlightenment, and the most urgent challenge facing modern humankind' (Gunton, 1985, p. 25). This fact–value dualism is rooted in the epistemic fallacy: the result of an unwarranted distinction between the apparent objectivity of scientific knowledge and the apparent subjectivity of our value judgements. Despite this, there is no getting away from the fact that the way we understand reality has fundamental implications for the way we conduct our lives. Whether we view the natural order as a value-free, self-generating entity, or as the purposeful, meaning-laden creation of a personal God, has fundamental implications for the way we ought to conduct our lives.

The pursuit of truth and practice of truthfulness are intimately related. A fruitful way of envisaging this relationship is in terms of correct proportion or proper balance – analogous to the way in which we refer to a 'true square' in carpentry, or a 'true note' in music. If we are to live truthful lives, it is important that our beliefs and actions are in harmony with reality itself, or at the very least with the reasonable beliefs we hold about reality. If God exists, then our actions ought to be in harmony with the divine will for our lives. Similarly, if reality is ultimately nothing more than an impersonal sequence of cause and effect in the natural order, then we ought to act in harmony with the laws of nature and with the values that we – as, to the best of our knowledge, the highest beings generated by the evolutionary process – are free to create for ourselves.

1.3   The contours of reality

I am suggesting that the pursuit of truth in religious education should adopt the working assumption that there is a real world existing largely independently of our knowledge of it, and that to live truthfully is to live in harmony with the ultimate order-of-things. I now want to say a little more about reality – the totality of all that is, has been and could potentially be – by turning to metaphysical questions. If ontology is concerned with the brute fact of all that exists, metaphysics is concerned with the nature and form, structure and organization, beauty and goodness, and ultimate meaning and purpose of reality. I do not intend to fall into the trap of attempting to construct a metaphysical system here. My account will be deliberately minimal, concerned merely to establish a framework for debate.

If reality is the sum total of all that is, then we are on safe ground to posit the existence of mind and matter. Given the success of the natural sciences, it seems entirely reasonable to assume a physical reality existing within the elastic boundaries of time and space. This will include the universe we currently inhabit, together with any universes that might have existed before the Big Bang, any universes existing parallel to our own, and the potentiality for the emergence of new universes in the future. At least one planet in our universe is occupied by sentient beings; hence it is reasonable to assume the existence of minds alongside matter. We know that these minds – when highly developed – think, feel, reason, hypothesize and communicate with other minds. The emotions, thoughts, ideas and languages generated by such sentient beings themselves constitute part of the totality of things.

Moving on, it is entirely reasonable to assume the *possibility* of the existence of some form of transcendent reality beyond the immanent realm of physical and mental objects. Thus, for example, mainstream Western monotheism assumes that the physical universe is not self-generating, but rather owes its existence to the creative act of a greater self-generating reality: God. The notion of transcendent reality is not, of course, limited to forms of theism: 'transcendence, the 'infinite Real', is expressed in monotheistic religion as 'deity' (Yahweh, the heavenly Father, Allah, Vishnu, Shiva) and in non-theistic traditions as the 'absolute' (Brahman, the Tao, the Dharmakaya, Sunyata)' (Wright, 2004a, p. 79; cf. Hick, 1989, pp. 13ff).

It is reasonable, then, to suppose that reality, the totality of all things, past, present and future consists of mind, matter, and – possibly – some form of transcendent being. We must now ask the question of the order and structure inherent within reality. It would seem reasonable to posit at least a minimal level of organization: the world appears to be open to rational exploration, and our minds are apparently structured in such a way as to be able to engage in such exploration. The alternative is to posit a world of absolute chaos: a scenario that is extremely unlikely, if for no other reason than that you are currently reading what is – I trust – a reasonably coherent sentence. Bhaskar's distinction between the domains of the actual and real is important here. As we saw earlier, the actual constitutes the sum of all that actually is, while the real also includes those mechanisms and structures that generate the actual world and are capable of turning potential states of affairs into actual ones. The fact that things happen according to discernable patterns means that we can anticipate – to a greater or lesser extent – future events. What generates such events is the structure and organization inherent in the universe. Primitive science is concerned merely to identify typological patterns within that which actually exists; advanced science, on the other hand, is concerned to *explain* why things happen in the way they do. With respect to the natural world, science seeks to discern the mechanisms through which objects interrelate and events happen. This is why 'science is concerned essentially with possibilities, and only derivatively with actualities' (Bhaskar, 1977, p. 18). Similarly, the social sciences seek to discern the structures through which society is organized, while the arts seek to engage with patterns of aesthetic, moral and spiritual meaning (Bhaskar, 1998; Danermark, Ekstrom, et al., 2002; Sayer, 2000; Hanfling, 1992). Many theologians and philosophers trace the source of order and meaning in the world back to some transcendent being.

We can go a stage further still, and suggest that the various mechanisms that organize reality are complex and stratified. In seeking to understand the world, human beings have developed a range of academic disciplines in the arts, sciences and humanities. These form part of the empirical domain, but derive their power and authority from their ability to relate to the domains of the actual and real. Contra Foucault, although there is no doubt that various historical, social, cultural and economic forces impinge on the development of academic disciplines, they are far more than mere ideologically driven power structures (Foucault, 1974, 1989). The stratification and differentiation that exists between the various academic disciplines reflects intrinsic divisions inherent within reality itself. Thus, it is possible to describe and analyse a person by drawing on a hierarchical raft of disciplines: physics, chemistry, biology, anthropology, psychology, sociology, art, music, ethics, philosophy, theology, etc. That fact that each of these disciplines offers its own relatively independent set of insights suggests two things. First, such disciplines are essentially *complementary*: since they all offer valid insights into particular aspects of the same object of study, there is no need to choose between them. Second, their ability to provide complex accounts of phenomena indicates that the world itself is inherently *complex*. It is clear that some disciplines are more 'basic' than other disciplines: there can be no chemistry without physics, no biology without chemistry, no psychology without biology, etc. At the same time, however, it is a retrograde step to attempt to reduce out understanding of the world to the insights of a single basic discipline. It is true that chemical substances and reactions form part of the make-up of all human beings, and that chemistry can account for certain aspects of human behaviour. However, chemistry can provide only a partial understanding of our actions: to obtain a rich picture we must also consider, amongst others, the insights of the psychologist, sociologist, moral philosopher and theologian. If it were possible to reduce multiple perspectives to a single perspective, then our universities would be single-discipline institutions, in which we study the world exclusively from the standpoint of whatever discipline – be it physics, theology or some other candidate – is considered the most basic. This is why we should be equally suspicious of those creationists who seek to immerse science within theology, and those physicists who promise one day to discover *the* key with which to unlock the secrets of the *entire* universe.

However, the fact that we can explain the meaning of an event or object in a number of complementary and irreducible ways does not preclude us from asking questions about the meaning of reality *as a whole*: although a rich explanation ought to embrace as many disciplinary insights as possible, the question remains as to the possibility of some *ultimate* explanation. This is not the same as a reductionist explanation: it is not so much a question of affirming one disciplinary insight over all others, as of asking whether the totality of available explanations point towards some greater whole. This raises the issue of the distinction between reality and ultimate reality: the former refers to the sum of all that exists, in all its stratified and multifaceted complexity; the latter refers to the enduring principle, power, force, mind or being that grounds reality and provides it with its fundamental organizing structure, and hence its ultimate meaning, purpose and direction. In order to clarify this distinction, we will consider three contrasting accounts of the ultimate order-of-things: two religious and one secular.

First, according to the Christian worldview, the sum total of all that exists consists of two qualitatively different orders of being: God and creation. The former is absolutely necessary, the latter utterly contingent. This is why Christianity insists on the doctrine of creation *ex nihilo*: there is only one divine source of reality, and to posit some eternal pre-existent matter out of which God forms the universe is to suggest a second primary source of reality alongside God. If, in the Christian scheme of things, reality consists of God plus creation, then *ultimate* reality consists in God alone – the creator and sustainer of all that is.

Second, according to the Buddhist understanding of reality, the world consists of a recurring cycle of death and rebirth determined by the law of karma. Whether meritorious actions bring about a good rebirth or reprehensible actions a bad rebirth, the result is the same: impermanence and suffering. The ultimate goal of life is to escape the recurring cycle of death and rebirth by extinguishing illusion and ignorance through the pursuit of the ultimate goal of Nirvana: awakening, enlightenment, the cessation of desire. If, on a basic level, the Buddhist universe consists of the totality of things, including the cycle of death and rebirth, it is Nirvana that constitutes *ultimate* reality.

Third, a naturalist account of reality limits the totality of all that is to the objects and forces that make up the physical world. Of course, the evolutionary process has generated sentient beings who seek meaning and purpose for their lives – perhaps by projecting a non-existent God, establishing some form of social contract organized around shared moral values, or embarking on the pursuit of personal happiness. Although each of these options may be fundamentally important for those who embrace them, at the end of the day they are all ultimately dependent on the natural order: for the naturalist it is the brute fact of the chain of cause and effect in the physical world that constitutes the *ultimate* reality of the universe.

Once again, there is no need to choose between these, or indeed many other possible options, here. It is sufficient, for our present purpose, simply to affirm that it is reasonable to conceive reality as consisting of the totality of objects, thoughts and events in the immanent world, together with the possibility of the existence of some form of transcendent domain, and to recognize that the complex and stratified order of the universe suggests the possibility some form of ultimate explanation of the totality of all things.

1.4   Inclusivity and the challenge of anti-realism

I am attempting to establish an approach to religious education that is open to as many different religious and secular worldviews as possible. Although I do not anticipate agreement on all the details of my argument, I hope that my minimalist account of truth and truthfulness will provide a common framework for debate. In this section I explore the potential inclusivity of my approach by considering the positions of those most likely to raise objections to it, namely defenders of anti-realism. There are two basic types of anti-realism: ontological and epistemic. Ontological anti-realism denies that there is such a thing as external reality and adopts instead a thoroughgoing solipsism. Epistemic anti-realism accepts the existence of some form of external reality, but claims either that we can have no secure knowledge of it, or that such knowledge is insignificant for human flourishing. Since we have already had occasion to refer to ontological anti-realism I will deal with it only briefly here, reserving the body of the discussion for a consideration of different versions of epistemic non-realism. I will argue that anti-realists cannot avoid asserting some form of realistic truth claim and consequently have no reason to exclude themselves from our framework.

Ontological anti-realism's denial that we inhabit an actual world runs against the grain of the common-sense experience of humankind and is virtually impossible to sustain in any coherent manner. Even to express such a belief is immediately to deny it, since the very act of speaking constitutes some form of reality. To invoke an inner–outer dualism and claim that the external world is simply a figment of my inner imagination necessarily invokes the reality of the 'I' who does the imagining. As we noted earlier, ontological anti-realism is the stuff of philosophical speculation rather than ordinary life, and the closest we can come to envisaging such a situation is by contemplating the position of chronically ill people in vegetative states. It is not viable to claim such an incoherent position as the basis for public religious education, and I am unaware of a single religious educator who wishes to do so. Nevertheless, should one appear on the scene there is no reason why they should not enter the debate within our framework, since to claim that there is no such thing as external reality is to make a truth claim about an actual state of affairs, albeit one limited to individual solipsistic consciousness.

Epistemic anti-realism recognizes the existence of external reality, but claims that we are unable comprehend it in any intelligible way. Given the complexity of our experiences of the world, the plurality of incompatible worldviews, and the supposed failure of our epistemological efforts to achieve any deep and lasting understanding of reality, the only viable option is to adopt a thoroughgoing scepticism (Popkin, 1964). The world *appears* to us either as an impenetrably mystery or as essentially chaotic. Since we have no way of properly comprehending reality, we cannot legitimately judge between conflicting accounts of it. Consequently, we have little option but to treat all such accounts as equally valid, on the understanding that such validity derives from their pragmatic utility for the communities that subscribe to them, rather than from their ability to describe the real world.

According to one version of epistemic anti-realism, the fact that words cannot engage with any external reality means that language is self-referential and as such actually constitutes reality for its users. Further, since there are no external constraints on our use of language, no access to an objective world against which to measure the truth of our statements, we are free to manipulate language according to our wishes and create our own linguistic realities in order to give our lives a sense of meaning and purpose. When Jean Baudrillard claims that the Gulf War did not take place, he is not speaking as an ontological anti-realist. There is no suggestion that the events we customarily associate with the label 'Gulf War' never happened: that soldiers and civilians did not actually suffer and die (Baudrillard, 2001, pp. 231ff). Rather, he is asserting that, since none of the accounts offered by reporters, politicians and historians are capable of providing anything resembling a definitive, or even adequate, account of the events, the notion of the 'Gulf War' is itself an arbitrary construction. Baudrillard does not contest the existence of an external world; he merely rejects the possibility of possessing any secure knowledge of it. Such a position is entirely compatible with realism, although not *critical* realism. Baudrillard inhabits Bhaskar's empirical domain, and although he rejects the possibility of accessing the domains of the actual and real, he does not dispute their existence. In other words, he accepts ontological realism and epistemic relativism, but rejects judgemental rationality. This leaves him with no alternative but to live within the transient domain of the world as it appears to him, since he can know nothing of the intransient domain of the world as it is in itself. Thus, contrary to initial appearances, and despite lacking the epistemological confidence demonstrated by critical realists, Baudrillard's vision is essentially realistic.

It is illuminating to compare Baudrillard's position with that of Richard Rorty. The latter is happy to accept a naturalistic account of reality: an ongoing process of cause and effect in the physical world ultimately determines the course of our lives. However, the high level of contingency within this process means that we retain a significant level of freedom: we may be physically determined in all we do or think, but we remain free to act within this determination. Rorty insists that his account of reality 'helps us avoid the self-deception of thinking that we possess a deep, hidden metaphysically significant nature which makes us 'irreducibly' different from inkwells or atoms' (Rorty, 1980, p. 373). Given that reality possesses no deep meaning, we are free to take pragmatic responsibility for our own self-formation and use our creative imagination to give our lives direction and purpose (Rorty, 1982). In particular, we should 'regard the realization of utopias, and the envisaging of still further utopias, as an endless process – an endless, proliferating realization of Freedom, rather than a convergence toward an already existing Truth' (Rorty, 1989, p. xvi). Insofar as we construct such utopian dreams without reference to any deep truths inherent in the natural order, it is possible to interpret them anti-realistically. However, Rorty's vision as a whole is fundamentally realistic on two counts: it affirms the objective reality of the natural order and the reality of the utopian ideas constructed by human beings – as soon as I imagine a utopian world, then my act of imagination becomes part of the real world, part of the totality of all that is.

These reflections confirm the inclusivity of the approach to truth and truthfulness proposed in this chapter: since neither ontological nor epistemic anti-realism say anything to undermine a broad realistic understanding of truth, there is no need to exclude such views from the debates that our framework seeks to generate.

1.5   Truth and truthfulness: a working framework

Given that we live in a pluralistic world in which there is no consensus about either truth or truthfulness, to attempt to provide definitive answers to the perennial problems associated with these concepts, and then offer them as a foundation of religious education, would inevitably result in a return to some form of confessionalism. Hence my concern is merely to establish a viable framework designed to support and guide ongoing discussion amongst religious educators and pupils. Such a framework must be sufficiently open ended to be inclusive of a variety of different worldviews, yet focused enough to help organize and structure discussion in a feasible manner. The working framework offered here takes the form of seven propositions, offered as a stimulus to debate rather than as a set of foundational principles.

Proposition 1: Truth is the totality of all that is

Truth is simply the sum total of the reality of everything that has being, had being in the past, and possesses the potentiality for being in the future – whether in the physical world, in the minds of sentient beings, or in some transcendent realm. This reality is in the main objective, existing for the most part independently of our experience of it.

Proposition 2: Our knowledge of reality is partial and contingent

Our knowledge is limited by our particular cultural contexts and our fallibility as human beings. However, the fact that we cannot claim any 'God's eye view' of reality does not mean that we have no knowledge of the actual order-of-things.

Proposition 3: We can make critical judgements between conflicting accounts of reality

The fact that our knowledge of reality is partial and contingent does not mean that our beliefs and worldviews are entirely arbitrary. In all spheres of knowledge we can, and normally do, make informed judgements between conflicting truth claims.

Proposition 4: Reality is ordered, complex and multifaceted

There appears to be at least a minimal level of order in reality. The complexity of the various academic disciplines reflects the complexity inherent within reality itself. The fact that different disciplines can provide complementary accounts of the same phenomena suggests that reality is also multifaceted.

Proposition 5: It is reasonable to ask questions about ultimate meaning and purpose

Since some aspects of reality are more significant than others, and some mechanisms more basic than others, we have every reason to seek to identify the ultimate organizing force, structure or being that explains the parts of reality in terms of the whole: candidates for such ultimate explanations include God, some other form of transcendent reality, the natural order, shared human values and individual desires.

Proposition 6: The ultimate nature of reality is contested

Different religious and secular traditions offer a range of incompatible accounts of ultimate reality. There are often significant degrees of overlap and continuity between such accounts: Judaism, Christianity and Islam, for example, share a belief in a creator God. However, there are also significant degrees of conflict: thus, for example, despite their common monotheism, Jews, Christians and Muslims subscribe to irreconcilable understandings of Jesus of Nazareth – he may be a great moral teacher, God incarnate or a prophet of Allah, but cannot be all three simultaneously.

Proposition 7: A truthful life is one lived in harmony with ultimate reality

Though reality exists independently of our minds and bodies, we nevertheless participate in it, and seek to live within it by organizing our lives in meaningful patterns of belief and behaviour. It make sense to order our lives in harmony with that which, to the best of our ability, we discern to be the ultimate source of meaning and value, whether that be the will of God, the natural world, social conventions, or our deepest desires. We must introduce an important concluding caveat, to which we will return later: it is possible to identify the ultimate source of meaning in the universe, but still choose to reject it in an act of 'metaphysical rebellion'. Thus, a secular humanist might believe that reality is ultimately a meaningless process of cause and effect in the natural world, yet still seek to live a meaningful life while fully aware that to do so is to live against the grain of reality; similarly, it is possible for a person to believe in the existence of God, but refuse to offer worship in protest at the level of suffering in the world.

Conclusion

This chapter set out to explore the notions of truth and truthfulness in order to establish a working framework within which a religious education concerned to address questions of truth might organize its thoughts and practices. I argued for a realistic understanding of truth as the totality of all that is, and suggested that truthful living normally requires us to seek to live in harmony with that which is ultimate in reality. Having recognized that there is no consensus about the nature of reality, I suggested that different traditions discern at least a minimal level of order in the world, and provide answers to the question of the ultimate meaning and purpose of life. I then noted the inclusive intention of the framework, suggesting that it is broad enough to host non-realists within its borders. I concluded by offering a set of guiding principles regarding the nature of truth and truthfulness – principles that will inform the rest of this study.

2
Political liberalism

Since religious education always operates in specific cultural contexts, this chapter will unpack the liberal environment in which the majority of school-based religious education in Western societies is currently delivered. I do not approach the task from a neutral perspective: my reservations about liberalism are well documented and have been the subject of some criticism (Wright, 2004a, pp. 20ff). According to Robert Jackson, 'Wright's . . . critique of liberalism is flawed in the sense that he creates an unnamed generalized liberal with all the characteristics he disapproves of, and proceeds to attack that stance' (Jackson, 2004, p. 84). Although I have reservations about this representation of my position, I accept the dangers of overgeneralization and appreciate the reminder that we are dealing with a tradition that is both complex and diffuse.

At its best, liberalism struggles valiantly to resist totalitarianism, promote freedom and tolerance, create space for political activism and dissent, secure human rights, and protect the interests of the marginalized and disenfranchised. At its worst, liberalism's marriage with capitalism appeals to self-interest as the basic human instinct, reduces human relationships to the level of economic exchange, dumbs culture down to its lowest marketable denominator, oversees the secular removal of religion from the public sphere, provides succour to the imperialistic ambitions of certain Western nations, presides over levels of global inequality that lead directly to the premature and unnecessary deaths of countless men, women and children each day, and perpetuates the self-interested myth that there is no better way of organizing society. The consequence of giving capitalism free rein in this manner is, as John Hull has so admirably documented, a debased spirituality (Hull, 1998, pp. 63ff). Viewed from the perspective of my own Christian socialism, informed as it is by a high view of humanity created in the image of God and 'crowned . . . with glory and honour', liberalism presents itself as the lesser of many evils – although an evil nonetheless (Hebrews 2: 7).

Despite such reservations, it is clear that the liberal context of contemporary religious education must be acknowledged 'not because a plural society is necessarily the ideal, but because it is inescapably the kind of society we have' (Haydon, 1997, p. 127). Consequently, a key task in this chapter will be to differentiate between those aspects of liberalism capable of supporting a critical religious education committed to the pursuit of truth, and those aspects which might serve to restrict or undermine such a project. In order to tease out this distinction, I begin by outlining the basic contours of liberalism and – drawing on my earlier contrast between liberalism as a closed worldview and an open interim ethic – positing a fundamental distinction between 'comprehensive' and 'political' liberalism (Wright, 2001a, 2007a). I then critique the notion of liberalism as a comprehensive worldview and defend a political liberalism that seeks to enable different traditions, cultures and belief systems to flourish alongside one another without any loss of integrity. I end the chapter by considering the implications of political liberalism for education in general and religious education in particular.

2.1 The contours of liberalism

Florence in the fifteenth century was a divided city. On the one hand, Renaissance humanists, stirred by an unprecedented re-awakening of learning and culture, sought to cultivate an ethos of freedom and tolerance. On the other, followers of the imposing figure of Savonarola, apocalyptic seer and hell-fire preacher, sought to implement his vision of a puritanical Christian commonwealth (Martines, 2006). If the disciples of Savonarola sought to avoid any hint of moral laxity by burning their prized possessions on the infamous 'bonfires of the vanities', the advocates of Renaissance humanism preferred to luxuriate in the very best that culture could offer. The contrast here is not between religion and secularism – since religions are just as capable of cultivating generous open-minded followers as secular traditions are of producing narrow-minded zealots – but between two very different mindsets.

Liberalism, at its most basic, embraces the virtues of generosity, tolerance, benevolence, broad-mindedness and a certain laissez-faire permissiveness.

This notion of liberalism as a virtuous disposition has a long-standing relationship with education. Traditionally, a liberal education is one that seeks to cultivate character through a general broadening of the mind. According to Aristotle, such education should prepare 'the body or soul or intellect of free men . . . for the demands and activities of virtue' (Aristotle, 1962, pp. 300f). In similar vein, Cardinal Newman sets out the case for an education in which a 'habit of mind is formed which lasts through life, of which the attributes are, freedom, equitableness, calmness, moderation, and wisdom' (Newman, 1982, p. 76). In order to achieve these goals, liberal education seeks to transcend any narrowly vocational training, and strives instead to induct pupils into a broadly based understanding of themselves and the world they indwell. Hence Newman's suggestion that a liberal disposition is best cultivated through the induction of students into intellectual traditions that enable them to apprehend 'the great outlines of knowledge, the principles on which it rests, the scale of its parts, its light and its shades, its great points and its little' (p. 76). It was just such a vision that generated Matthew Arnold's aphorism that education should enable students to engage with the very best that has been thought and said in the world (Arnold, 1994). More recently, Paul Hirst has defended 'the idea of liberal education as a process concerned simply and directly with the pursuit of knowledge' (Hirst, 1965, p. 114). A curriculum based on what is true, rather than on mere opinion, will have the effect of 'freeing the mind to function according to its true nature, freeing reason from error and illusion, and freeing man's conduct from wrong' (p. 115).

In much of the contemporary world, such liberal education takes place in the context of a distinctive form of liberal politics, rooted in the principles of constitutional democracy, social contract and human rights. Political liberalism has its roots in the Renaissance, flourished at the time of the Enlightenment, and today provides the basis for the vast majority of Western-style democratic states across the globe. Supported by a rich tradition of political theory, political liberalism is driven by 'moral criticism of dictatorship, arbitrary power, intolerance, repression, persecution, lawlessness, and the suppression of individuals by entrenched orthodoxies' (Kekes, 1999, p. 3). It emerged as a political force as the notion of the absolute monarch ruling by divine right gave way to that of the constitutional monarch governing by the will of the people – a shift that paved the way for the establishment of the modern democratic nation state. For John Locke, one of the key architects of political liberalism, the role of the state was not to act as the secular arm of the church, but to protect the life, liberty and property of its citizens through the rule of law (Locke, 1993). Locke predicated his liberalism on the twin principles of freedom and tolerance: in order to pursue the good life, individuals should be free to think and act as they wish, although such freedom brings with it the responsibility to tolerate the freedom of others to do likewise. Thus, Locke subscribes to a vision of liberalism as essentially a political process, designed to free citizens of a plural society to pursue conflicting visions of the good life in a spirit of mutual tolerance.

However, as the liberal tradition developed, it began to make universal claims about human nature that transcended the realm of politics. Thus, Rousseau developed the idea of freedom in the light of his belief in the natural goodness of humanity: to be free is to act in accordance with our inner nature, and to achieve this we need protection from the coercive, restrictive and irrational power structures endemic in society (Rousseau, 1986). In similar vein, Kant's claim, that freedom lies in having the courage to think for oneself and follow codes of behaviour that are freely chosen rather than imposed from outside, was based on a distinctive philosophical understanding of human nature (Kant, 1959). We see in Rousseau and Kant the beginning of a shift away from political liberalism towards the reification of liberal values and the formation of a distinctive worldview.

In the modern era, the classical understanding of liberalism as a set of virtues to be cultivated through education gave way to the notion of liberalism as a pragmatic political system, and then to the notion of liberalism as a comprehensive worldview. Political liberalism is concerned to provide a pragmatic solution to the challenge of ordering a plural society in which there is no consensus about the ultimate nature of reality or the meaning of life, and as such functions 'independently of any wider comprehensive religious or philosophical doctrine' (Rawls, 1993, p. 223). Comprehensive liberalism, on the other hand, constitutes a total worldview that offers an all-encompassing account of the place of humanity in the world; in doing so it reifies the principles of freedom and tolerance and establishes them as ends in themselves, rather than as the means to some greater end. Generally speaking, political liberals are committed to an economy of difference: they recognize that not all accounts of the good life are valid, that the ability of citizens to pursue the good live can be restricted by inequalities deeply ingrained within society, and that the exercise of freedom and tolerance are not ends in themselves but rather the means to the greater end of pursuing the good life in a responsible and informed manner. Comprehensive liberals, on the other hand, tend to be committed to an economy of sameness: contrasting accounts of the good life are treated as equally valid, all citizens are deemed free to pursue their chosen life regardless of their particular circumstances, and the exercise of freedom and tolerance is viewed as an end in itself.

2.2 Comprehensive liberalism

The four basic liberal values – respect, freedom, tolerance and equality – began life as desirable character traits and later became the basis of the dominant political ethic of modern times. The global impact of liberal politics led, in turn, to the reification of liberalism into a comprehensive worldview. Such has been the impact of this process that comprehensive liberalism now constitutes 'the dominant ideology of our time', one that so permeates global culture that 'even its opponents now couch their defenses of the regimes they favour in evaluative terms that liberals have imposed on political discourse' (Kekes, 1999, pp. 2). Highlighting the ideological nature of comprehensive liberalism in this manner enables us to recognize it as the local product of a specific set of historical circumstances, rather than as a given universal norm. As a result, the contrast between political and comprehensive liberalism immediately become apparent: the former seeks to enable adherents of potentially irreconcilable visions of the good life to explore their differences in a climate of mutual respect and tolerance; the latter views the basic values of liberalism as *constitutive* of the good life itself.

A concrete example will help further clarify the nature of comprehensive liberalism. In October 2004, Rocco Buttiglione, Italian European Affairs minister, Professor of Political Science in Rome, and devout Roman Catholic, was forced to withdraw his candidacy as the European Union's new commissioner for Justice, Freedom and Security (BBC News, 2004). This was a direct result of his acknowledgement, during a confirmation hearing, that he fully accepts the teaching of the Roman Catholic Church that homosexual practice is sinful. The issue was not one of homophobia, which stands condemned by the Catholic Church, but of a clash between liberal and non-liberal understandings of human sexuality. For comprehensive liberals, individuals should be free to express their sexuality in whatever way they wish, provided they do not harm others in the process. For Roman Catholics, individuals ought to express their sexuality in conformity to natural law and the will of God. Despite his affirmation of Catholic teaching, Buttiglione was quick to place his personal beliefs in the context of a liberal polity of freedom and tolerance. Pledging to defend the Charter of Human Rights, which outlaws discrimination on the ground of sexual orientation, he pointed out that the theological judgement that homosexual practice is a sin is not the same as the legal judgement that it is a crime. He also insisted that his own religious principles are consonant with the view that liberal society should not attempt to prohibit homosexual practice or discriminate against homosexuals: Catholicism is committed to democracy and does not seek to impose its moral standards on others without democratic consent. Putting aside any extraneous political factors that might have impinged on Buttiglione's decision to withdraw his candidacy, the question that needs to be asked is why he was forced to do so, given his unambiguous acceptance of political liberalism. There are clearly many European citizens, both Catholic and non-Catholic, who hold similar positions on homosexuality, yet such views appear to be so offensive as to be unworthy of tolerance. This is the case even when such citizens demonstrate respect and tolerance towards beliefs they are personally unable to accept, insist on the freedom of citizens to live according to their beliefs, and demand equal non-discriminatory treatment for all under the rule of law. In effect, tolerance is offered to those who embrace the basic values of liberalism as ends in themselves, but denied to those who subscribe to alternative traditions and belief systems. Consequently, access to the public sphere is limited to those who espouse liberal values as normative for the good life, while adherents of non-liberal traditions are ostracized and forced to live as resident aliens in a closed comprehensive liberal society.

Insofar as comprehensive liberalism subscribes to a set of beliefs that provide a self-contained understanding of reality, it constitutes a specific worldview. The understanding of worldviews adopted here draws on the work of Tom Wright, who argues that they embrace deeply rooted, pre-reflective and pre-cognitive assumptions about the nature of reality and the ultimate meaning of life (Wright N. T., 1992). By way of illustration, I will apply Wright's argument to the specific political context in the United States of America, arguing that, despite their differences, many mainstream Democrats and Republicans espouse a comprehensive liberal worldview. Wright identifies four overlapping dimensions of worldviews: narratives, questions, symbols and praxis.

a) Worldviews 'provide the *stories* through which human beings view reality' (p. 123). The core narrative of American politics concerns the founding and development of a democratic nation of free and equal individuals engaged in the pursuit of happiness under the rule of law. Living under the watchword of 'liberty', the destiny of the United States constitutes a beacon of hope for freedom loving people across the globe. It is necessary to defend such freedom against forms of totalitarianism, barbarianism, irrationalism, and superstition. President George W. Bush reflects this core narrative when proclaiming that:

> Fifteen months ago, Iraq was ruled by a regime that brutalized and tortured its own people, murdered hundreds of thousands, and buried them in mass graves. Today Iraqis live under a government that strives for justice, upholds the rule of law, and defends the dignity of every citizen.
>
> (Bush, 2004)

b) Worldviews provide answers to specific questions about the ultimate meaning and purpose of life: Who am I? Where am I? What is wrong? What is the solution? By attending to the stories told by adherents of specific worldviews, 'one can in principle discover how [they] answer the basic *questions* that determine human existence' (Wright N. T., 1992, p. 123). Broadly speaking, many

American politicians answer these questions in the following manner. Who am I? A member of a nation of free and equal citizens each engaged in their own personal search for happiness. Where am I? Living in a society that is progressively realizing the dream of living the good life, as conceived in various ways by individual citizens. What is wrong? This dream is currently under threat, externally from totalitarian states and terrorism, internally either from excessive state intervention in the private lives of its citizens, or from a lack of intervention and consequent failure to combat social and economic structures that deny all citizens an equal opportunity to pursue the good life. What is the solution? Externally, the way forward is either to aggressively resist the forces of evil, or else to resist them in more subtle, effective and humanitarian ways; internally, the answer is to pursue domestic policies likely to enable all citizens to pursue the good life, either by maximizing individual freedom or by redressing inequality through a more equitable distribution of goods.

c) Worldviews are organized around distinctive cultural symbols that express their essential identity. Such symbols may be both artefacts and events: saluting the American flag, the singing of 'God Bless America' at sporting events, the celebration of Thanksgiving and Independence Day, etc. Wright's own example, written prior to the terrorist attacks on the World Trade Centre, is particularly poignant:

> In modern North America, the New York victory parade after a successful war brings together two of the most powerful symbols of the culture: the towering skyscrapers of business-orientated Manhattan, and the heroes of battle. Both, in their own fashion, demonstrate, promote and celebrate The American Way.
>
> (p. 123)

d) Worldviews embrace a distinctive praxis or 'way-of-being-in-the-world' (p. 124). Since actions often speak louder than words, 'the real shape of someone's worldview can often be seen in the sort of actions they perform, particularly if the actions are so instinctive and habitual as to be taken for granted' (p. 124). In American society, in which the pursuit of the good life is the free choice of autonomous individuals, a vast range of praxis is discernable: earn money, raise a family, obey God, be creative, fight for justice, have fun, stay off hard drugs, etc. What binds them together, however, is precisely that each individual's life style choice is – in principle at least – freely chosen, the only restriction being the obligation not to interfere with the choices of others provided they do not threaten the fabric of society.

We will return to this discussion of worldviews later in the book. For now it is sufficient to conclude with the caveat that we should not push the concept of worldviews too far: to describe a worldview is not to describe a discrete, static and clearly identifiable entity, but rather to portray significant trends, tendencies and patterns within a culture. With this qualification in mind, it is certainly possible to discern a dominant liberal worldview within Western society. It is far from clear, however, that comprehensive liberalism is able to provide a suitable home for a critical religious education committed to the pursuit of truth.

2.3 Flaws in the comprehensive fabric

Comprehensive liberalism's core principles of freedom and toler-ance are significantly underdetermined: open to a vast range of interpretations, they are incapable of providing moral guidance without further qualification.

Both principles rely on the assumption that human beings will exercise their freedom in a responsible manner. However, such an assumption cannot be taken for granted: as John Kekes observes, 'it is a remarkable feature of liberal thought that it pays almost no attention to the prevalence of evil' (Kekes, 1999, p. 23). As a race, we are more than capable of doing wrong: evil is prevalent in the world, and is often the result of deliberately wicked actions. Hence, there is good reason to distrust the optimistic judgement of the Enlightenment, that 'the first impulses of nature are always right; there is no original sin in the human heart' (Rousseau, 1986, p. 56). A more balanced judgement is to assert the co-existence of morally good and morally bad dispositions in human nature, with the proportions of each unevenly spread between different individuals.

Freedom is an underdetermined concept because the practise of autonomy can cause great harm both to oneself and to others. How might comprehensive liberals exercise their freedom, given the prevalence of evil in the world? Kekes suggests that they face a choice between three equally unpalatable options. First, to seek to maximize individual freedom will only increase the opportunities afforded the wicked to act wickedly: it is not clear 'how evil could be made less prevalent if evil doers are encouraged by liberal political programmes that increase their freedom' (Kekes, 1999, p. 44). Second, to attempt to curtail evil by restricting individual freedoms is to acknowledge tacitly the failure of the liberal project: citizens of a liberal society will still be free to act, but only in conformity to a set of externally imposed standards. Third, to ignore this predicament is to embrace a 'sentimental falsification of human possibilities' (p. 203). While it may be comforting to believe that all human beings are inherently good, such sentiment ignores the reality of the human condition and hence makes the mistake of 'trying to make the world fit the agent's feelings, rather than the other way round' (p. 198).

Tolerance is a similarly underdetermined concept: since there are many things clearly undeserving of tolerance – racism, sexism, homophobia, slavery, genocide, etc. – an indiscriminate blanket tolerance can only lend support to the perpetrators of evil. Karl Popper responds to this dilemma by invoking the 'paradox of tolerance', claiming 'in the name of tolerance, the right not to tolerate the intolerant' (Popper, 1966, p. 265). If Popper is right then tolerance can be a source of evil and intolerance a source of good: both concepts are, strictly speaking, amoral. As Liam Gearon points out, although 'tolerance and understanding are as essential to democracies as they are to religious education, hiding behind vacuous notions of tolerance and understanding . . . will not take us very far' (Gearon, 2004, p. 29).

It is clear that freedom and tolerance are not virtues in themselves, and that to become so they must be located within a more substantial moral framework. It follows that it is not sufficient to teach the abstract principles of freedom and tolerance; teachers must also help pupils make informed moral judgements about their potential use and misuse in the light of some broader moral perspective. However, this is at odds with the fact that the underlying ideal of comprehensive liberalism 'is some variant of that most invisible, because it is the most pervasive, of all modern goods, unconstrained freedom' (Taylor, C., 1992, p. 489). Such freedom constitutes 'the fundamental principle for understanding what it means to be human in the modern (and post-modern) era', and as such 'serves as the ultimate warrant for human actions, desires and interests and as the fundamental reference-point for the justification of our actions, desires and interests' (Schwöbel, 1995, p. 57).

This ideal of absolute freedom from constraint is unsustainable, since as relational creatures we are inextricably bound to a complex series of networks and associations. Freedom *from* any form of constraint is necessarily also freedom *for* some alternative relationship. Thus, in the medieval period theologians drew a contrast between freedom from sin and freedom for an appropriate relationship with God. The Enlightenment differentiated between freedom from superstition and freedom for the cultivation of rationally ordered lives. The Romantics sought freedom from rationalism and freedom for instinct, feeling and sensibility. Finally, postmodernity sought freedom from all external forces – whether religious, rational or emotive – and the freedom for absolute self-determination. Three comments on this dialectic are apposite here. The first is to note the gulf between the Enlightenment's notion of the freedom to think and act rationally, and the post-modern notion of freedom as unconstrained self-determination. Where the former leaves room for a range of different accounts of human flourishing, the latter imposes a single story – namely, that we flourish precisely *through* our freedom to do as we desire. The second is to note the gradual reification of the notion of freedom in the modern era: starting out as a simple procedural principle, it soon became *the* fundamental criteria for understanding human nature. The third is to note the synergy between this process of reification and the shift from political to comprehensive liberalism. With these observations in mind, it becomes clear that the postmodern pursuit of absolute freedom is far more than a striving for emancipation *from* all external forces; on the contrary, it is a struggle to realize a specific vision of humanity: namely, that freedom *for* self-determination constitutes *the* basic human good.

This ideal of absolute freedom cannot avoid that fact that 'long before we understand ourselves through the process of self-examination, we understand ourselves in a self-evident way in the family, society and state within which we live' (Gadamer, 1979, p. 245). Since we always exercise autonomy within a particular cultural context, 'the meaning and limits of freedom are . . .

prescribed by the fact of human interdependence' (Grimmitt, 1987, p. 76). According to communitarian liberals, 'conceptions of the good life are not defined by autonomous agents but are the products of the moral tradition into which individuals are born and whose ideals, values, conventions, and principles their moral education inculcates in them' (Kekes, 1999, p. 14; cf. Kymlicka, 1995). The notion that we can simply select our own internal criteria when making judgements about the meaning and purpose of our lives is untenable. Similarly, it is inappropriate to equate the good life with the satisfaction of our inner desires, since external factors inevitably create, inform and stimulate such desires. Hence true freedom lies not in acting with complete autonomy, but in responding appropriately to the network of relationships that help define and constitute our personhood. As Iris Murdoch argues, in *The Sovereignty of Good*, 'freedom is not strictly the exercise of the will, but rather the experience of accurate vision which, when this becomes appropriate, occasions action' (Murdoch, 1970, p. 67).

The fact that freedom and tolerance have currency only within the ebb and flow of our interpersonal relationships leads us to Graham Haydon's important distinction between liberal society and liberal morality. He defines a liberal society as one that 'leaves people free to hold different moral outlooks and different sets of beliefs' (Haydon, 1997, p. 127). A liberal morality, on the other hand, 'characteristically leads to the liberal holding certain moral and political positions rather than others: so that we know roughly what is meant by a 'liberal' position on the morality of, say, abortion or homosexuality' (p. 128). Haydon goes on to argue that a commitment to liberal morality cannot be a qualification for membership of a liberal society: 'a society which tried to exclude anyone who was not a liberal in their moral outlook would be a markedly *illiberal* society' since it would have 'no place for those who believe that abortion is murder or that homosexuality is sin' (p. 128).

Though comprehensive liberalism clearly upholds liberal morality, it is far less effective in sustaining a liberal society. This is partly because it replicates the intellectual imperialism of the Enlightenment by setting up 'its own standards as the absolute, and only valid and possible, norm' (Cassirer, 1951, p. x). The fact that its commitment to private conceptions of the good life is 'the product of one strand in the Western tradition that has emerged from the

Enlightenment' shows liberal morality to be merely one among many potentially viable accounts of human flourishing (Kekes, 1999, p. 14). Those committed to the principle of absolute freedom frequently 'fail to recognize that there are religious, tribal, ethnic, agrarian, hierarchical, and communal conceptions of the good life to which this, or indeed any, understanding of autonomy is not only foreign but inimical' (p. 15). Of course, we might still conclude that the outlook of comprehensive liberalism remain the best moral system available to us; however, in doing so we can no longer simply take its validity for granted. Since liberal morality is contested, to embrace it requires an act of reflective faith similar to that made by informed adherents of other religious and secular traditions. Comprehensive liberalism's inability to recognize its prior faith commitments, coupled with its subsequent tendency to marginalize the truth claims of non-liberal traditions, serves to confirm its status as a narrowly defined worldview.

2.4 Political liberalism

Comprehensive liberalism embraces a clear understanding of both truth and truthfulness: the autonomous person constitutes the ultimate source of meaning in the world, and actualizes such meaning through the exercise of unconstrained freedom. The abstract and underdetermined nature of its key principles, coupled with the ever present danger of colonization – of ignoring, manipulating or distorting alternative non-liberal truth claims in an effort to make them fit this liberal framework – suggest that critical religious education is unlikely to find an appropriate home here. Might political liberalism be more accommodating?

As we have already noted, political liberalism has its roots in the political and religious crisis facing seventeenth century Europe. The emergence of a pluralistic society, populated by many different traditions, value systems and sources of authority generated significant tensions in society and nurtured various forms of enthusiasm and fanaticism. The result was a divided society hovering on the brink of a descent into anarchy (Spellman, 1988). It was against this background that John Locke, a diplomat by professional, approached the question of how such a society might flourish. Differentiating between objective knowledge and subjective belief, Locke argued that we require *both* secure knowledge *and* appropriate beliefs if we are to live a good life (Locke, 1975, 1993). With regard to beliefs, he distinguished between matters of relative indifference, and matters – especially in the realms of morality, aesthetics and religion – that raise issues of enormous consequence for the well-being of society. The key problem, according to Locke, was that 'the limits of human knowledge are so narrow and the probability of error on speculative matters so great that we can never know for certain that our religious opinions are correct and all others false and heretical' (O'Connor, 1952, p. 212). The lack of any clear boundary markers between faith and reason encouraged enthusiasts to act on their speculative opinions as if they were indisputable facts. A situation that, according to Locke, 'may possibly have been the cause, if not of great Disorders, yet as least great Disputes, and perhaps Mistakes in the World' (Locke, 1975, p. 688). Hence, his advocacy of the twin principles of freedom and tolerance, which were to function as an interim ethic designed to stabilize a volatile situation until such time as fundamental disputes about the meaning and purpose of life could be resolved. In an attempt to undermine the fanatics, Locke placed two restrictions on an individual's freedom of belief. First, although it was permissible to hold beliefs that were not *demonstrable* by reason, there was to be no place for beliefs that *conflict* with the canons of reason. Second, it was illegitimate to hold beliefs that might harm others or threatened the stability of society.

Nicholas Wolterstorff has drawn on William Alston's notion of 'doxastic practice' (from the Greek *doxa*, 'belief') to help unpack the nature of Locke's interim ethic (Wolterstorff, 1996; Alston, 1989). Alston uses the concept to refer to the way in which we live out our deepest commitments. He suggests that doxastic practice involves a constellation of involuntary beliefs, habits and dispositions that are 'acquired and engaged in well before one is explicitly aware of them and critically reflects on them' (Alston, 1989, p. 7). According to Wolterstorff, Locke recognized that doxastic practice rooted in habitual belief was ultimately dependent on arbitrary authority. Realizing that such dependence on unexamined belief was no longer a valid way of conducting life in a plural society, he sought a fundamental reform of doxastic practice. Responsible living requires us to hold our beliefs in a rational manner and be accountable for our actions: 'the doxastic practice which Locke promotes . . . incorporates various types of voluntary action –

gathering evidence, appraising that evidence so as to determine probability, etc.' (Wolterstorff, 1996, p. xviii). Since it is no longer possible to take our beliefs for granted in a plural world, we must learn to live informed and responsible lives: this requires *both* appropriate schooling *and* the cultivation of an ethic of freedom and tolerance designed to establish the conditions necessary for doxastic practice to flourish (Locke, 2000).

This, then, was the original vision of political liberalism: not a comprehensive worldview, but a set of loosely connected prag-matic practices designed to allow disputes to be resolved through reasoned debate. As Alasdair MacIntyre points out, it set out to establish 'a political, legal and economic framework' that would allow 'those who espouse widely different and incompatible conceptions of the good life for human beings to live together peaceably within the same society, enjoying the same political status and engaging in the same economic relationships' (MacIntyre, 1988, pp. 335f).

As we have already seen, political liberalism accepts that the state has a positive role to play in establishing the conditions necessary for different groups to pursue contrasting visions of the good life. Isaiah Berlin's distinction between 'negative' and 'positive' liberty is important in this context (Berlin, 2000). Negative liberty is simply freedom *from* external coercion: 'I am normally said to be free to the degree to which no man or body of men interferes with my activity' (p. 194). Positive liberty is freedom *for* the practice of reflective living: 'I wish my life and decisions to depend on myself . . . to be moved by reasons, by conscious purposes, which are my own' (p. 203).

The primary concern of negative liberty is to avoid external pressure and coercion: freedom 'in this sense is simply the area within which a man can act unobstructed by others' (p. 194). Since 'coercion implies the deliberate interference of other human beings within the area in which I could otherwise act', it follows that you 'lack political liberty or freedom only if you are prevented from attaining a goal by human beings' (p. 194). Of course, other factors apart from coercion may prevent me from obtaining my goals: I am free to attempt to win an Olympic medal, although I may not actually have the talent to achieve that goal. Defenders of negative liberty are not concerned whether I achieve my targets; merely that nobody restricts my efforts to do so. For John Stuart Mill this means that 'it is morally impermissible to interfere with the actions of individuals even if they are motivated by irrational, destructive, stupid, or emotive considerations, provided only that their actions do not harm others' (Kekes, 1999, p. 3; cf. Mill, 1978). Mill's argument rests on two assumptions: first, that individuals are the best judge of what is good for them; second, that even if they are poor judges, it is better for them to make mistakes than suffer external coercion.

The primary concern of positive liberty is to establish the conditions necessary for the proactive pursuit of the good life:

> I wish to be the instrument of my own, not of other men's, acts of will
> . . . I wish, above all, to be conscious of myself as a thinking, willing,
> active being, bearing responsibility for my choices and able to explain
> them by reference to my own ideas and purposes.
>
> (Berlin, 2000, p. 203)

According to defenders of positive liberty, mere freedom from coercion is not enough: we must also cultivate the art of reflective living and develop the capacity to think and act wisely.

Berlin rejects positive liberty because he believes it to be surreptitiously coercive. His justification of this claim proceeds through three main steps. First, the notion of encouraging pupils to live reflective lives implies the presence of some normative understanding of selfhood, and therefore suggests that positive liberty will inevitably embrace some pre-established account of human nature. Second, positive liberty requires the state to provide citizens with the goods necessary for reflective living: knowledge, habits, virtues, skills, capacities, etc. Inevitably, the state's provision of such goods – through education, social welfare, health care, sponsorship of the arts, etc. – will reflect some preconceived notion of the good life. Third, in providing these goods, the state will inevitably embark on a coercive path that leads, ultimately, to state control and tyranny. Positive liberty claims that it is justifiable 'to coerce men in the name of some goal (let us say, justice or public health) which they would, if they were more enlightened, themselves pursue, but do not, because they are blind or ignorant or corrupt' (p. 204). Once I accept this principle, 'I am in a position to ignore the actual wishes of men or societies, to bully, oppress, torture them in the name, and on behalf, of their "real" selves' (p. 205).

Berlin's critique of positive liberty is vulnerable on four points. First, negative liberty is far from value free: it holds a specific understanding of human nature predicated on the sovereignty of personal autonomy, and as such is itself open to the charge of coercion. Second, positive liberty is not necessarily committed to any substantial understanding of human nature, merely to the lesser assumption that enabling citizens to think and act wisely is an important prerequisite for the pursuit of the good life. Third, Berlin fails to take proper account of the fact that individuals lack freedom if they are ruled by 'compulsion, addiction, irrational prejudices, or uncontrolled and misdirected passions and if the genuine choices they make are informed by ignorance, stupidity, manipulation and propaganda' (Kekes, 1999, p. 7). Fourth, the logical outcome of Berlin's position is the de-schooling of society: if schools seek to change pupils in any way then they will inevitably be coercive, and if they do not seek to do so there is no reason for them to exist.

This suggests the state has a responsibility to protect citizens from coercion by providing a positive education designed to enable them to approach life in an informed and intelligent manner. This, broadly speaking, is the conclusion reached by John Rawls in his influential *A Theory of Justice* (Rawls, 1971). He defends a form of egalitarian liberalism based on the principles of equal liberty and opportunity, and driven by the notion of distributive justice. Rawls presents a thought experiment in which a group of fair-minded citizens plan a new society while unaware of the status they will hold within it. He argues that under such circumstances they would agree on three core principles: equal liberty, equal opportunity, and equal distribution of resources in a manner that benefits the disadvantaged. Although the state should remain neutral about different conceptions of the good life, it cannot remain neutral on the issue of the fair distribution of resources if it wishes all its citizens to flourish. In an unequal society, the just distribution of goods must benefit the disadvantaged. Such distribution cannot be limited to material goods: there must also be an equitable distribution of intellectual goods in order to maximize the opportunities of all citizens, especially those most disadvantaged, to live rational lives and actively pursue the good life. Despite Berlin's reservations, a positive liberty along the lines suggested by Rawls appears to be the best way of fulfilling the original vision of political liberalism, and as such promises a suitable home for religious education.

2.5   Liberalism and education

These two versions of liberalism generate different conceptions of the task of education. Where comprehensive liberalism is committed to maximizing the autonomy of citizens, political liberalism seeks to provide the intellectual and cultural goods necessary if they are to exercise their freedom to pursue the good life in an informed and intelligent manner. As we have already seen, liberal education has historically been committed to the task of aiding the personal and social development of pupils by a general broadening of their minds achieved through the transmission of appropriate knowledge. This liberal tradition forms the basis of the 1988 *Education Reform Act*, according to which education should promote the 'spiritual, moral, cultural, mental and physical development' of pupils and prepare them for the 'opportunities, responsibilities and experiences of adult life' (HMSO, 1988, p. 1). This is to be achieved through the transmission and exploration of knowledge as set out in the Basic Curriculum, which consists of the National Curriculum together with locally determined forms of Religious Education.

In the context of the present discussion, one of the key dimensions of knowledge is that of the various accounts we give of the place of humanity in the ultimate order-of-things, accounts that have fundamental implications for our understanding of the nature of the good life. According to comprehensive liberalism, the material content of the good life consists simply of our freedom for self-determination: it does not matter which particular life-style choices we make, provided we do so freely. Political liberalism, on the other hand, recognizes that we should be free to choose intelligently between conflicting visions of the good life, not all of which are necessarily equally valuable or true to the actual order-of-things. Hence, the pursuit of knowledge takes on added urgency: it is important that we make responsible choices, and one of the primary tasks of education is to provide pupils with the knowledge and skills necessary for this to happen. Where comprehensive liberalism transmits knowledge of a pre-determined account of the nature of human flourishing, political liberalism is open to the exploration of a range of different possibilities. The choice here is between a confessional induction into a narrow liberal worldview, and an open – and hence genuinely *liberal* – exploration of a plurality of possibilities.

In a plural society, the question of personal identity – of the people we are and might become – is inevitably the subject of intense debate. Comprehensive liberalism gives a clear answer to this question: the height of human achievement is simply to be free *from* coercion and hence free *for* the task of striving to satisfy personal desires and aspirations, whatever these may be. At first glance this vision of self-determination appears liberating, especially when compared to various religious and secular forms of confessional education that seek to induct pupils into a pre-packaged understanding of personal identity. However, on closer inspection it clearly constitutes a deeply paternalistic vision that imposes a singular, limited and ultimately incoherent vision of human identity. The vision is singular, because the identification of the good life with autonomous self-determination effectively brackets out the potential insights of a range of non-liberal traditions; limited, because the principle of autonomy is seriously under-determined; incoherent, because the notion of absolute freedom is an unrealizable ideal. Once again, we can see clearly that the core problem with comprehensive liberal education is that it is simply another form of confessionalism: despite its rhetoric of freedom, it actually sets out to induct students into a narrowly defined understanding of personhood. In sharp contrast, political liberalism accepts the contested nature of human identity, and embraces the challenge of empowering students to grapple with a range of contrasting and conflicting visions of what it means to be authentically human. It seeks to achieve this by providing pupils with the necessary intellectual and cultural goods that will enable them to better understand themselves and their place in the ultimate order-of-things.

The basic liberal solution to the problem of tensions within society is to cultivate an ethos of tolerance, grounded in an empathetic sensitivity towards different traditions. For comprehensive liberalism, the reified principle of tolerance is paramount. However, as we have already seen, tolerance is an underdetermined principle that remains morally vacuous unless supplemented by a more substantial ethical vision. It is by no means clear that comprehensive liberalism is capable of offering such a vision, since it views tolerance as an end in itself rather than as a means to the greater end of encouraging substantial ethical debate. Political liberalism, on the other hand, is committed to engaging with a diverse range of ethical systems, and in doing so opens up a range of contrasting accounts of appropriate ways of exercising tolerance. Rather than impose a blanket – and, as we have seen, necessarily vacuous – regime of tolerance, it invites pupils to consider the grounds on which different religious and secular traditions distinguish between that which is, and is not, worthy of tolerance.

This suggests that political rather than comprehensive liberalism offers the more appropriate framework upon which to ground liberal education. It promises to provide students with access to a broad range of conceptions of the good life, together with the means of engaging with them in an informed and intelligent manner. In doing so, it provides a way of avoiding the narrow confessionalism implicit in comprehensive liberalism's singular vision of the good life. This is not to say that comprehensive liberalism has no place in such a liberal education system. However, its place will be that of one amongst many different secular and religious accounts of the good life available for exploration in the classroom, rather than that of the foundational framework within which learning must be organized.

How might we apply this argument to religious education? Which of our two readings of liberalism offers the more viable foundation for a liberal religious education committed to the personal and social development of students through the broadening of their knowledge and understanding of religion?

In autumn 2004 the British Government published *Religious Education: The Non-Statutory National Framework* (DfES/QCA, 2004). It identifies 'learning about religion' as the first of the subject's two core attainment targets. Pupils should enquire into the nature of religion; explore the beliefs, teachings, practices, ways of life and forms of expression of a variety of religious and secular traditions; identify and develop an understanding of ultimate questions and ethical issues; and cultivate the skills of interpretation, analysis and explanation (p. 34). This concern to establish religious literacy clearly requires a high degree of openness and empathy, especially when approaching religious worldviews that predate – and in many cases remain relatively untouched by – the Enlightenment. Failure to achieve this runs the risk of assimilating such worldviews within the intellectual framework of modern Western thought. Comprehensive liberalism is extremely vulnerable to this charge, since its notion of autonomous self-determination as the highest human good is clearly at odds with religious traditions that locate the source of the good life in some ultimate or transcendent reality. Indeed, it is difficult to see how an education system committed in advance to the proposition that the ultimate meaning and purpose of life is that of self-realization could possibly do justice Islam's commitment to submission to the will of Allah or the Christian vision of self-sacrificial service, to take but two examples. Political liberalism, on the other hand, is far better equipped to resist such reductionism, since it refuses to affirm any substantial vision of the good life beyond that of the virtue of exploring a range of possibilities intelligently.

The National Framework identifies 'learning from religion' as the second of the subject's two core attainment targets. Pupils should reflect on and respond to their own experiences in the light of their developing understanding of religion. In particular, they should interpret, evaluate and seek to apply to their lives that which they learn about religion, 'particularly questions of identity and belonging, meaning, purpose, truth, values and commitments' (p. 34). Once again, comprehensive liberalism faces a major problem: given its identification of the good life with self-realization, the actual substance of the religious and secular beliefs that pupils encounter in the classroom is immaterial – all that is required is that pupils hold their beliefs freely. It follows that there is no logical connection between comprehensive liberalism's account of the good life and the truth claims of various religious and secular traditions. This immediately rules out the possibility of the study of religion having any substantial impact on the personal development of students. For political liberalism, on the other hand, the freedom to engage with conflicting beliefs places the truth claims of various religious and secular systems centre stage. Although it is important that pupils respond freely, it is equally important that their responses are wise ones, and that they have reasonable grounds for affirming the truth of the understanding of reality upon which they base their lives.

Although religious education's responsibility for contributing to the social development of students is not one of the core attainment targets, the National Framework is clear about the subject's responsibility in this area. Thus, for example, religious education should contribute to citizenship education by developing pupils' knowledge and understanding of 'the diversity of national, regional, religious and ethnic identities in the United Kingdom and the need for mutual respect and understanding' (p. 15). Both political and comprehensive liberals are committed to nurturing respect and tolerance, and seek to contribute to the well-being of Britain's multicultural society. The claim of the Swann Report (1988), that religious education has a vital role to play in 'preparing pupils for life in today's multi-racial society . . . challenging and countering the influence of racism . . . [and] laying the foundations for [a] genuinely pluralist society', is clearly fundamentally important to both liberal traditions. The key question, however, is which form of liberal religious education is best equipped to fulfil this task. A rich understanding of tolerance must certainly transcend the grudging acceptance of 'alien' communities by seeking a deep empathetic engagement with them. It is here, however, that we begin to recognize the limitations of comprehensive liberalism. In the first place, its reified notion of tolerance is in constant danger of encouraging toleration of that which is undeserving of tolerance. Secondly, its claim that we should treat all beliefs as equally valid tends to reduce empathy to the level of an engagement with relatively superficial cultural expressions, rather than encourage any substantial encounter with deeply held truth claims.

At the time of writing in 2006, the publication in Denmark of blasphemous cartoons of the prophet Mohammed has led to worldwide Muslim protests. Some demonstrators in London carried placards glorifying the recent bombings in the capital and calling for the killing of the 'enemies' of Islam. The British government simultaneously condemned publication of the cartoons and offered their support to the police should they decide to bring charges against the protestors. Asghar Bukhari, chair of the Muslim Public Affairs Committee, unequivocally condemned the protestors: 'The placards and chants were disgraceful and disgusting . . . these people are less representative of Muslims than the [extremist right-wing] British National Party are of the British people' (BBC News, 2006). The situation raises fundamental questions about freedom of speech and the nature and level of tolerance afforded minority communities. Although this is not the place to attempt to deal with them in any detail, three comments are apposite here. First, it highlights the limitations of tolerance as a blanket principle: most would agree that the issuing of death threats is intolerable, others would go further and argue that the orchestrated insulting of a religious community in the name of free speech is similarly reprehensible. Whatever view one takes, it is clear that we need to make informed judgements about such matters. Second, such judgements require a deep understanding of the beliefs and commitments that drive adherents of both secular liberalism and Islam. Third, such understanding requires a level of openness to religious adherents that is sensitive to the possibility that their belief systems might actually be true. It is to political liberalism that we must look to provide the appropriate environment within which to cultivate judgement, nurture understanding, and attend to contested questions of truth.

2.6 Conclusion

This chapter sought to contextualize religious education's pursuit of truth within a liberal environment in the light of the distinction between comprehensive and political liberalism. I suggested that comprehensive liberalism constitutes a closed worldview that embraces self-realization as the greatest of human goods and is committed to forms of education that seek to maximize autonomy by protecting individuals from external coercion. Political liberalism, on the other hand, functions as an interim ethic designed to enable adherents of various religious and secular traditions to pursue contested visions of the good life in an atmosphere of mutual respect and support. The coherence of this latter tradition, together with its openness to a range of non-liberal worldviews, suggests that it offers a viable framework for critical religious education. Consequently we will assume the framework of political liberalism throughout the rest of this study.

Part II
The Nature and Task of Religious Education

3
Classical religious education

In Part I, I set out an understanding of the concepts 'truth' and 'truthfulness' and defended a political liberal polity through which religious education might empower pupils to live flourishing lives by teaching them to grapple with questions concerning the ultimate nature of reality and the meaning of life. The intimate relationship between truth and truthfulness suggests the organic unity of religious education: the search for truth and pursuit of truthful living ought to form twin aspects of a single process. However, this has not always been the case in liberal religious education, which has often struggled to account for the nature of the relationship between 'learning about' and 'learning from' religion – in the terminology adopted here, between exploring the ultimate order-of-things and learning to live truthful lives in harmony with reality. This situation has not been helped by contemporary religious education's tendency to distance itself from its historical roots by distinguishing sharply between confessional and liberal approaches to the subject. In this chapter I will explore the suggestion that liberal religious education still has much to learn from its confessional past, not least in the area of the relationship between pursuing truth and striving after truthfulness. I will offer three historical case studies of classical religious education: in ancient Israel, the Platonic Academy and the early Christian Church. Despite their very different contexts, all three traditions were committed to supporting the personal and social formation of pupils by enabling them to engage in transformational interactions with ultimate reality.

3.1 Wisdom in ancient Israel

Our knowledge of the wisdom tradition of ancient Israel derives largely from a corpus of literature: of particular importance are the canonical texts *Proverbs*, *Job* and *Ecclesiastes*, together with the apocryphal books of *Ecclesiasticus* and the *Wisdom of Solomon*. The literature has links with popular folk wisdom, in the form of proverbial sayings designed to guide the everyday lives of various individuals and groups. There also appears to be some connection with a more developed and sophisticated tradition associated with the courtly wisdom of professional sages; as such, the corpus has parallels with – and occasionally draws directly on – other Ancient Near Eastern cultures, especially those of Egypt and Babylon. The book of *Proverbs* identifies itself as a collection of the sayings of Solomon, intended to be useful for 'learning about wisdom', 'understanding words of insight', and 'gaining instruction in wise dealing, righteousness, justice and equity' (Proverbs 1: 1ff). The central focus of the literature is on the struggle to live a virtuous life:

> When pride comes, then comes disgrace;
> but wisdom is with the humble.
> The integrity of the upright guides them,
> but the crookedness of the treacherous destroys them.
>
> (11: 2f)

In this context, a central aspiration is for the possession of wisdom:

> Happy are those who find wisdom,
> and those who get understanding,
> for her income is better than silver,
> and her revenue better than gold.
>
> (3: 13ff)

The wisdom literature offers a holistic vision of personal formation, and as such reflects the assumption that 'education involves the entire person, the totality of his or her life, and it affects all of that person's relationships – with self, with others, with things and with ideas' (Melchert, 1994, p. 49). In the Judaeo-Christian context this centres on a person's relationship with God: 'to understand God is to have a kind of wisdom or *sapientia*' that embraces contemplation, action, discursive reasoning and the affections (Kelsey, 1992, p. 34). Experience and discernment enables the wise person to establish self-mastery and respond to life's challenges by living in harmony with the world and its creator. *Proverbs* draws a dualistic distinction between two very different ways of life: wisdom

v. foolishness, diligence v. sloth, self-control v. emotivism, humility v. pride, caution v. rashness, etc. The wise person is receptive to instruction and discipline, and exercises generosity and honesty. Such wisdom brings positive rewards: 'Those who are attentive to a matter will prosper / and happy are those who trust in the LORD' (Proverbs 16: 20); 'The reward for humility and fear of the LORD / is riches and honour and life' (22: 4). Although the development of wisdom certainly involves the transmission of knowledge, its basic concern is for personal and social formation through the development of character and virtue: 'Proverbs are not simply 'knowledge' in the contemporary sense of a list of things one might know or have in one's head . . . knowing proverbs is not itself the point' (Melchert, 1998, p. 29).

If the thesis of an intimate relationship between truth and truthfulness is correct, then the striving for truthful living envisaged in the wisdom tradition can only be effective if it requires the learner to wrestle with ultimate truth: in ancient Israel, this meant engaging with the reality of God as he reveals himself within his creation and to his chosen people. Since wisdom was widespread across many Ancient Near Eastern cultures, the crucial issue here is whether Israel's assimilation of the tradition embraced a specific Hebraic worldview and theological understanding. If it did, then this will vindicate our claim that the religious education of ancient Israel did not separate the pursuit of theological truth from the cultivation of truthful living.

At first glance, the evidence in support of this thesis is not especially favourable. The style, form and content of Hebraic wisdom literature differ markedly from the corpus of historical, legal and prophetic texts. There are few explicit references to divine laws, prophetic proclamations, salvation history and the Temple cult. Although the notion that 'the fear of the LORD is the beginning of knowledge' plays an important role, specific references to God are infrequent, and the nature of God can be established only by inference (Proverbs 1: 7 et seq.). 'As a consequence a significant aspect of the interpretation of the wisdom books has been concerned with the problem of relating the distinctive interests and ideas contained in them to the major religious trends of ancient Israel' (Clements, 1983, pp. 122f).

One school of thought sees the Hebraic wisdom tradition as having only a partial and transient relationship with the theological worldview of ancient Israel (Melchert, 1998, pp. 7f). According to this view, it is God's actions – as revealed primarily in the historical and prophetic corpus of Hebrew Scripture – that constitute the definitive source of Israel's understanding of reality. It follows that the wisdom literature is peripheral to this mainstream theological tradition: assimilated from the culture of surrounding nations for social and political reasons, it lacks any deep religious significance (Bright, 1967; Wright, G. E., 1952). Thus, Eichrodt assesses wisdom as being 'only loosely connected with religious faith', while Preuss goes as far as to dismiss wisdom as 'theologically illegitimate . . . a foreign body within the Old Testament' (cited in Melchert, 1998, pp. 7f). If this school of thought is correct, then wisdom has much to do with truthful living, but enjoys at best only a fragmentary relationship with theological truth.

The traditional explanation of this state of affairs is that the wisdom tradition developed at a relatively late stage in ancient Israel's religious history. As heirs of the prophetic tradition, the authors of the wisdom books 'took the great moral principles of justice and of the divine government of the world revealed by the prophets, and applied them to the more mundane and everyday experiences of life' (Clements, 1983, p. 123). In doing so, they came to focus on the pragmatic task of cultivating virtuous living in a manner that lacked any substantial engagement with the core theological concerns of the Hebrew prophets. However, scholars have questioned this hypothesis on two main fronts. First, form criticism has demonstrated that the distinctive structure and characteristics of wisdom sayings are such that they can no longer be seen as mere offshoots of prophetic proclamation; rather, 'they must have emanated from a special class of wise men who were concerned with education and man's general progress and advancement in life' (p. 124). Second, the widespread presence of wisdom literature across the Ancient Near East at a relatively early stage in the development of Hebrew culture suggests that wisdom played a significant role in the *early* development of Israel's self-understanding. The discovery of the wisdom teaching of the Egyptian Amen-em-Opet, and the subsequent recognition of a direct literary connection with sections of the book of *Proverbs*, helped reinforce this view (Pritchard, 1958, pp. 237ff; Proverbs 22–24; cf. Clements, 1983, pp. 125f). Although these twin considerations makes the hypothesis that the wisdom tradition was a relatively late addition to the corpus of Hebrew literature that had little impact on Jewish self-understanding unlikely, this still leaves open the question of the precise nature of the relationship between Israelite wisdom and Israelite theology.

There is evidence of an underlying assumption in much of the wisdom corpus that to live truthfully requires obedience to the Torah. First, the early chapters of *Proverbs* refer to wisdom in language normally reserved exclusively for God's law:

> My child, keep my words
>> and store up my commandments with you . . .
> bind them on your fingers,
>> write them on the tablet of your heart.
>>>> (7: 1ff; cf. 3: 1ff, 6: 20ff)

Second, in the epilogue of the book of *Ecclesiastes* the connection between wisdom and Torah is explicit: 'The end of the matter; all has been heard. Fear God, and keep his commandments; for that is the whole duty of everyone' (Ecclesiastes 12: 13). Third, *Deuteronomy* repays the complement: Moses, having received the Torah from God, identifies obedience to the law with wisdom:

> See, just as the LORD my God has charged me, I now teach you statutes and ordinances . . . You must observe them diligently, for this will show your wisdom and discernment to the peoples, who, when they hear all these statutes, will say, 'Surely this great nation is a wise and discerning people!'
>> (Deuteronomy 4: 5ff)

Fourth, in some texts wisdom is personified as a transcendent reality closely associated with God – a move that reinforces the notion that to act wisely is to do the will of God:

> The LORD created me at the beginning of his work,
>> the first of his acts long ago . . .
> when he marked out the foundations of the earth,
>> then I was beside him, like a master worker;
> and I was daily his delight,
>> rejoicing before him always,
> rejoicing in his inhabited world
>> and delighting in the human race.
>>>> (Proverbs 8: 22ff)

Fifth, in the apocryphal wisdom literature, the identification of wisdom and Torah becomes even more explicit. In *Ecclesiasticus* (*Ben Sira*), for example, obedience to the Torah is seen as the culmination and fulfilment of wisdom: 'If you desire wisdom, keep the commandments'. (Ecclesiasticus 1: 26)

The implication is that the wisdom tradition, rather than being a late moralizing offshoot, is actually intimately bound up with the prophetic, historical, cultic and theological traditions of Israel. Charles Melchert, following Walter Brueggemann, suggests a way of understanding the nature of this relationship: 'when God is discerned only in the disruptions that come upon us in history, the side effect is to "devalue" ordinary daily living and human culture' (Melchert 1998, p. 29; cf. Brueggemann, 1972, p. 27). If the primary role of the prophetic and historical traditions is to reveal the divine 'disruptions' in Israel's history – the call of Abraham, exodus from Egypt, entry into the Promised Land, establishment of the Temple, Babylonian exile, etc. – then the task of wisdom is to guide ordinary everyday life in the light of these disruptions. Wisdom, that is to say, constitutes an educational tradition that takes up and interprets the covenantal relationship between God and his chosen people and applies it to the context of ordinary life. If this is so, living wisely depends on obedience to the will of God, and such obedience in turn requires an appropriate relationship with God. Thus for Hebraic religious education, truthfulness is dependent upon truth: the practice of wisdom involves living in harmony with the creator and his creation.

This reading is supported by Gerhard von Rad's interpretation of wisdom as Israel's response to the saving actions of God; a response that entails embracing the creator's covenantal relationship with his people and living a righteous life in 'fear of the LORD'. 'The thesis that all human knowledge comes back to the question about commitment to God is a statement of penetrating perspicacity', containing 'in a nutshell the whole Israelite theory of knowledge' (Von Rad, 1972, p. 67). Wisdom functions pedagogically to alert Israel to the mystery of God and the fallibility of humanity, and to call the people to commitment and obedience. The recognition that 'one becomes competent and expert as far as the orders of life are concerned only if one begins from knowledge about God' constitutes the major contribution of Israel to the universal quest for human wisdom (p. 67).

Across the Ancient Near East, the perception of recurrent patterns in nature made it possible to formulate principles of conduct in harmony with them. Although this normally involved a religious dimension, Israel was distinctive in tracing the order inherent in creation back to the creator God who established a covenantal relationship with his chosen people. If Israel's wisdom literature expresses a sense of wonder at God's creation, then it does so by offering the divine creator thanks and praise. Broadly speaking, polytheistic societies in the Ancient Near East tended to think in terms of a recurrent cycle of order emerging from, and descending back into, chaos. Israel, on the other hand, understood the created order in terms of a linear progression towards the eschatological fulfilment of God's purposes.

This creation theology links Israelite wisdom directly to the prophetic, legal and historical traditions, which told the story of the developing covenantal relationship between God and his chosen people. In *Ecclesiastes*, wisdom reveals that everything has its appropriate time: 'For everything there is a season, and a time for every matter under heaven: a time to be born, and a time to die; a time to plant, and a time to pluck up what is planted' (Ecclesiastes 3: 1f). Von Rad argues that this notion of living wisely in harmony with God's plan for creation is especially evident in the relationship between wisdom and apocalyptic literature (Von Rad, 1972, pp. 263ff). Thus, for example, the book of Daniel combines stories of wise men embodying the virtues of wisdom with apocalyptic accounts of the unfolding of the future according to God's divine plan.

The wisdom tradition also links the challenge of living wisely under the law of God with a concern for the consequences of people's actions: 'Be assured, the wicked will not go unpunished, /but those who are righteous will escape' (Proverbs 11: 21). However, there is a significant level of ambivalence here: Job's struggle with the problem of innocent suffering lacks the Egyptian concept of *Maat* – right, justice, order – that provided the cosmos with its moral order (Von Rad, 1972, p. 72). For Israel, the moral order is rooted in the will of its holy and seemingly baffling creator. Since God's activity in the world transcends human understanding, 'Israel was obliged to remain open, in a much more intensive way, to the category of the mysterious' (p. 73). This is why Israelite wisdom has no interest in rewards and punishments distributed according to any measure of human achievement; rather the consequences of actions are judged in terms of the 'fear of the LORD'. Such fear – which has to do with awe and reverence rather than terror – required both deep humility in the face of divine majesty and an acceptance that the rewards of living a wise life are entirely dependent on God's mercy.

Thus, in *Proverbs*, wisdom is not a human possession, but rather a reality that – in personified form – calls to human beings from beyond their own limited horizons, promising the gift of life, security and divine favour (Proverbs 1: 20f). Israelite wisdom, that is to say, is rooted in faith:

> The experiences of the world were for her always divine experiences as well, and experiences of God were for her experiences of the world . . . in proverbial wisdom, there is faith in the stability of the elementary relationships between man and man, faith in the similarity of men and their actions, faith in the reliability of the orders which support human life and thus, implicitly or explicitly, faith in God who put these orders into operation.
>
> (Von Rad, 1972, p. 62f)

Israel clearly understands wisdom in terms of the ultimate God-given order of reality. The Hebrew Scriptures take up the wisdom tradition of the surrounding nations and recast it within a specific theological framework. Rather than being merely a useful pragmatic tool enabling human beings to live successful lives here on earth, wisdom is equally a divine attribute, a divine gift, and a witness to God's dealings with his chosen people. If good will ultimately be rewarded and evil punished, this will not be in accordance with human expectations but in harmony with God's will for his creation – the will of that divine wisdom which transcends human understanding. It follows that the living out of truthful lives is dependent on the pursuit of knowledge of the reality of God. But what exactly does this pursuit entail?

The three great Abrahamic faiths – Judaism, Christianity and Islam – all share a deep understanding of the sovereignty of God and the fallibility of humanity. Consequently, there is a constant temptation to adopt forms of theological quietism: if we really are so insignificant in the face of God's majesty then we have no choice but to abandon ourselves to divine mercy, grace and providence. Occasionally this leads to forms of libertinism: thus Paul, in his letter to the church in Rome, squares up rhetorically to the misplaced theological conclusions extrapolated from his suggestion that the greater the sin, the greater the grace of God in forgiving it: 'Should we continue in sin in order that grace may abound?' (Romans 6: 1). More often however, such warped theological logic nurtures forms on legalism, fundamentalism and anti-intellectualism. Given Israel's focus on wisdom as a divine attribute rather than human possession, we are bound to ask the question of the nature of the relationship between the sovereignty of God and personal formation in the wisdom literature.

It is certainly true that Israel's 'focus on covenant with Yahweh and obedience to his will as enshrined in the Law, can leave the impression that there was little room among the people of God for the exercise of the human intellect' (Wilson, 1997, p. 1276). However, the reality is very different: the covenantal relationship between God and his chosen people carried with it a clear imperative: 'Be wise, my child' (Proverbs 27: 11). The ambiguities inherent in the distinction between human fallibility and divine wisdom called Israel to wrestle with her God. This required 'studious investigation into the workings of the world and human nature' and an ongoing struggle 'to know, understand, and appreciate what God is about' (Wilson, 1997, pp. 1276f). As a result, Israel was forced to address the problem of human suffering with a rigour rarely encountered amongst her neighbours. The willingness 'to acknowledge pain where it exists and to probe and question the workings of divine purpose that so often remain hidden from our view' resulted in a series of 'human quests for understanding [that] often border on the cynical or pessimistic and occupy at times the dark hinterlands of faith' (p. 1276). The fact that 'canonical Scripture can allow such alternate visions of life and the world to stand in tension with the demands of obedience and duty is a tribute to the vitality and insight of the Wisdom tradition in Israel' (pp. 1276f).

In an oral culture, wisdom sayings serve to preserve the experiences and insights of previous generations rather than transmit self-explanatory packets of knowledge: 'One does not learn *from* them but *by means of* them' (Melchert, 1998, p. 29). Their function is to guide the learner's attempts to 'try to "make sense of" the puzzles and mysteries of human and divine behaviour' (p. ix). Consequently, the pedagogic role of wisdom literature transcends the merely didactic: 'these texts offer a remarkable array of literary styles, devices, forms, and patterns that often are designed to elicit or evoke in the readers the substance of the issue the author is seeking to address' (p. 2). As such, they offer an antidote to both 'the conventional, childish religion and ethic so endemic in the West' and the 'isolated [academic] specialties that seem to have little to do with learning how to live one's daily life in the real world' (p. 2). Melchert argues that one of the key tasks of the wisdom tradition is to encourage Israel's reception of divine revelation in an informed, responsible and adult manner. The Torah certainly offers instruction in the form of imperatives –'thou shalt not' – that invite the analogy of a child responding to the authoritative instruction of a parent. However, the role of the wisdom tradition is more deliberately pedagogic:

> after the child has moved out into the world on her own, she cannot depend solely on the authority of parent or baby-sitter. Now she must learn from her own experience, not just from listening to others or reading books. As the years go by, her experience grows. She learns directly about the real world from her successes and from her mistakes. Then when she has learned something, she does not repeat the 'god's' words, nor does she transmit another's word. Now she knows what she herself has learned directly, and she says, 'I say to you . . .' If she has learned well, she speaks what is true. That is like the way of wisdom.
>
> (p. 6)

Despite Melchert's rich insight into the pedagogical task of wisdom, he appears to overplay his hand towards the end of this passage. The confidence of the learner who can now speak authoritatively – 'I say to you' – comes perilously close to the modern ideal of human freedom and self-sufficiency apart from God. Indeed, the choice of language reflects those passages in the Christian Gospels where Jesus speaks with divine authority: 'You have heard that it was said. . . . But I say to you' (Matthew 5: 17). This allusion, coupled with Melchert's advocacy of the reader-response theories of Fish and Iser, implies that the successful assimilation of wisdom places the learner on an equal footing with God (Melchert, 1998, pp.12f). Although there is certainly a call to responsibility in the wisdom texts, it is clearly a call for responsible living in harmony with the ultimate truth of God's reality, rather than a call for self-determination.

3.2 Platonic religious education

'You will know the truth, and the truth will make you free' (John 8: 32). According to Rudolf Bultmann, the *Gospel of John* reflects tensions between Greek and Hebraic modes of thought (Bultmann, 1971, pp. 433ff). The truth spoken of here is not that associated with the Greek quest for rational knowledge, for a comprehensive vision of reality, for objective understanding transcending mere opinion and appearance. Rather, the Johannine conception of truth is distinctly Hebraic: one oriented towards the existential question of the meaning of life, towards the subjective question of 'the authentic being of the man who is concerned about his life', towards the theological question of what it means to be a creature created in the image of God (p. 434). Ultimately it is God's truth 'which alone is reality because it is life and gives life'; the existence of fallen humanity is false 'because it is a reality contrived in opposition to God, and as such is futile and brings death' (p. 434). To apprehend the truth through the obedience of faith rather than disinterested rational investigation is to receive the promise of that true life which is 'the illumination of existence in that authentic self-understanding that knows God as its Creator' (p. 435).

If Bultmann's distinction between Greek and Hebraic modes of thought is accurate, then our hope of discovering a close connection between the pursuit of truth and personal formation in Plato's vision of religious education would appear to be misplaced, all the more so given the received wisdom that abstract 'academic' knowledge makes few existential demands. There is certainly a different emphasis in the two cultures with regard to their general understanding of the nature of knowledge. The ancient Greeks tended to approach knowledge introspectively, as a possession of the mind that the knower has assimilated internally and which she is able to recall from memory. In contrast, the ancient Hebrews tended to externalize knowledge and understand it relationally, as something the knower has direct experience of – as, for example, in the archaic use of 'to know' as a euphemism for sexual intercourse. However, although there is a certain merit in distinguishing between Greek and Hebraic approaches to truth, the contrast requires careful qualification. As we shall see, Plato assumes an intimate and necessary connection between the pursuit of truth and the living of truthful lives: his ethics and politics flow directly from his metaphysics and epistemology.

Pre-Socratic philosophy had a significant influence on Plato's understanding of ultimate truth, in particular the tension between the respective positions of Parmenides and Heraclitus, which – perhaps not entirely coincidentally – bears a remarkable resemblance to contemporary philosophical debates between realists and anti-realists. Parmenides offers an explicitly realistic understanding of truth as being itself, the ultimately real, that which actually is. He views the totality of reality – the 'All' or the 'One' – as self-generating, homogeneous, undividable, enduring and unchanging, and contrasts this with our perceptions of the world of everyday experience, distinguishing between 'the steadfast heart of persuasive truth' and 'the beliefs of mortals, in which there is no true trust' (Parmenides, 1984, p. 53). Heraclitus, on the other hand, bears all the traits of an anti-realist; the world is an amalgam of loosely connected parts in a state of constant flux and change: 'Just as the river where I step / is not the same, and is, / so I am as I am not' (Heraclitus, 2003, p. 51). The question of whether Heraclitus is an ontological anti-realist denying the reality of anything beyond his perceptions, or simply a sceptical epistemic anti-realist denying the possibility of knowing external reality, need not detain us here. What is of concern is the way in which Plato rejects Heraclitus' pluralistic commitment to the 'many' in favour of Parmenides' monistic concern for the 'one', and in doing so, seeks to explore the tension between the world as it is and the world as it appears to be.

Plato's response to this tension between perception and reality developed, in part at least, in reaction to the Sophists. Professional itinerant teachers, they offered instruction in philosophy and rhetoric with a pragmatic edge, designed to enable the student to speak well and be successful in public affairs (Kerferd, 2003). Protagoras, the most famous of such teachers in Plato's time, embraced an epistemological scepticism similar in many ways to the outlook of Heraclitus. He proclaimed the impossibility of penetrating beyond the realm of perception to establish knowledge of the real world. Consequently, we can know nothing about the gods: the epistemological problems are too complex for fallible human beings to grapple with successfully. Given this situation, Protagoras sought to make a virtue out of a necessity in proclaiming that 'man is the measure of all things, of those that are that they are, of those that are not that they are not' (Copleston, 1946,

p. 87). This resulted in an epistemology that viewed perceptions of reality as relative to the subjective opinions of individual thinkers. Accepting the priority of opinion over knowledge, Protagoras' pragmatic concern was to enable his students to live successful lives by altering their opinions to bring them into line with their needs. As such, he was notorious for urging them to strive for success even if this means making the weaker argument the stronger. Plato rejected both Protagoras' epistemic scepticism and his pragmatic ethics, arguing instead that it is possible to establish true knowledge of reality and to live a virtuous life in harmony with the actual order-of-things.

As an idealist, Plato drew a dualistic distinction between the physical and mental realms, viewing the former as ephemeral and subject to constant change and decay, and finding in the latter a path to an eternal and stable world of ideas. Plato first developed his doctrine of ideal abstract objects or 'Forms' in the *Phaedo*. To describe a person, a landscape, or a painting as 'beautiful' is to imply some independent standard of reference against which we measure them. Plato has no time for a subjectivism that reduces the apprehension of beauty simply to the mere opinions of individual observers; rather, all beautiful objects and events in the world participate in the objective and transcendent Form of Beauty. Similarly, the observation of sticks of equal length invokes not just the idea of equality, but also – and more fundamentally – the idea of the Form of Equality and hence 'knowledge of absolute equality' (Plato, 1961, p. 57). Plato continues: 'Our present argument applies no more to equality than it does to absolute beauty, goodness, uprightness, holiness, and, as I maintain, all these characteristics which we designate in our discussions by the term 'absolute'' (p. 58). He conceives the Forms realistically, as objective, eternal and incorporeal entities existing independently of human perception. As such, they constitute *the* ultimate reality, transcending the contingent realm of appearances.

How does Plato's doctrine of the Forms relate to his theology? It is here that the differences between Greek and Hebraic approaches to the world become significant: Plato's understanding of God is very different from that of ancient Israel. Rather than a personal being acting in creation to bring about the salvation of humanity, Plato's God functions as the principle of order on the universe. As a result, Plato's theology is natural rather than revealed: he knows God not through his actions in the world, but through inferences drawn from the order of nature. Plato's Forms are rooted in the notion of *archē* – the principle of a final causal explanation of the totality of reality. In the *Republic*, we encounter 'Plato's recognition of the theoretical desirability of unifying Forms by positing an *archē* of them' (Gerson, 1994, p. 57). This leads him to posit the Form of the Good, to make all other Forms subordinate to it, and to present it as the source of all truth and meaning:

> This reality, then, that gives their truth to the objects of knowledge and the power of knowing to the knower, you must say is the idea of good, and you must conceive it as being the cause of knowledge, and of truth in so far as known.
>
> (Plato, 1961, p. 744)

Plato views the Form of the Good as divine: the *Timaeus* represents the Forms as the thought of God and argues that that God created the universe using them as the template. In doing so, he developed the 'hypothesis of the uniqueness of god as *archē*' (Gerson, 1994, p. 7). Against Protagoras, he argues that 'it is God who is, for you and me, of a truth the "measure of all things", much more truly than, as they say, "man"' (Plato, 1961, p. 1307).

If for Israel the gulf between God and humanity is the result of sin, then for Plato it is due to ignorance. Plato's God is the eternal source of truth: 'altogether simple and true in deed and word, [he] neither changes himself nor deceives others' (p. 630). The Platonic dualism between the transcendent realm of eternal Forms and the immanent realm of change and decay carries with it a tension between, on the one hand true knowledge, and on the other hand ignorance, deception, illusion and false perception. What 'men would least of all accept', according to Plato, is 'deception in the soul about realities . . . [to] have been deceived and to be blindly ignorant' (p. 629). His famous analogy of the cave draws a distinction between the inadequate knowledge of those who, shackled in the cave, are unable to perceive more than mere shadows of reality, and the true insight and understanding of those who, on escaping from the cave, are able to gaze directly into the face of reality itself. Plato calls us to free ourselves from the chains of ignorance, so that we may comprehend reality and have our minds illumined by truth. Once an individual is freed in this way, will he not recognize 'that what he had seen before was all a cheat and an illusion, but that now, being nearer to reality and turned toward more real things, he saw more truly?' (p. 748).

However, Plato recognizes that the full glare of reality can be blinding: on emerging from the cave into the light, the pupil's eyes might 'be filled with its beams so that he would not be able to see even one of the things that we call real' (p. 748). Hence, he views education as a process of habituation: of gradually inducting and nurturing students into a true understanding of the order-of-things. The danger of such habituation is that, initially at least, it rests on opinions of others. It is, however, preferable to possess true knowledge on the basis of some external authority than false knowledge derived from one's own mistaken opinions. In the *Meno*, he introduces a distinction between knowledge and correct opinion: although both correspond to the truth, the former is to be preferred because it requires the student to provide a rational explanation of the truth they encounter, rather than merely accept the opinions of others. This raises fundamental educational questions, to which we must now turn our attention.

Plato's *Republic* is essentially a blueprint for the reformation of Athenian schooling, offering an idealized picture of education as a process of cultural induction designed to enable citizens to live virtuous lives within a just and harmonious city-state. Such truthful living is dependent on a commitment to truth. Since the essence of virtue (*arête*) is goodness, 'to be shaped by *arete* simply *is* to know the Good'; further, 'knowing the Good involves not only knowing the divine but also a deep knowing of one's own humanity' (Kelsey, 1992, pp. 66f). For Plato, education must strive to inculcate in pupils a love of truth, rather than content itself with merely transmitting prevailing norms and opinions. Hence his rejection of the teaching methods of the Sophists: in seeking to enable students to behave in a particular way, they failed to provide them with an underlying understanding of the reasons behind such actions. The philosopher-rulers – the envisaged recipients of the ideal education described in the *Republic* – were to undergo a process of enculturation designed to establish a shared vision of the good life. This vision was not reducible to some form of pragmatic insight into the likely effects of different political decisions on the well-being of the citizens of Athens. Rather, it was dependent on knowledge of the Form of the Good: knowledge that would enable the philosopher-rulers to grasp the first principles of all that is virtuous and true, and use them to guide their political decision making. Given that knowledge of the Good is simultaneously knowledge of the divine, and that its successful assimilation is dependent on the ability to distinguish between appearance and reality, it is appropriate to categorize Plato as a defender of a form of critical religious education.

How might students distinguish between appearance and reality? How is the transition from opinion to knowledge possible? In the *Phaedo*, Plato describes knowledge as reminiscence: 'what we call learning is really just recollection' (Plato, 1961, p. 55). This is the doctrine of *anamnesis*, 'by which all learning and inquiry is interpreted as a kind of remembering' (Kierkegaard, 1967, p. 11). According to Plato all that 'we recollect now we must have learned at some time before, which is impossible unless our souls existed somewhere before they entered this human shape' (Plato, 1961, p. 55). Hence, our immortal souls existed in another state before entering their physical bodies; Plato contends that the Form of the Good provided the original pattern for our souls, and that consequently they retain a spark of the divine latent within them. It follows that knowledge of ultimate truth is innate: 'every human soul has, by reason of her nature, had contemplation of true being' (p. 496). However, since we have, for the most part, forgotten such knowledge, the world we inhabit has all the characteristics of a cave that disperses the light of truth into deceptive reflections and shadows.

In this situation, the primary pedagogic task is to stimulate students to recollect their latent knowledge of the Good, rather than transmit truth to them from outside. In the *Theaetetus*, Socrates describes himself as a midwife entrusted with the role of helping students give birth to their innate knowledge: 'my concern is not with the body but with the soul that is in travail of birth' (p. 855). His maieutic task is 'to prove by every test whether the offspring of a young man's thought is a false phantom or instinct with life and truth' (p. 855). This Platonic notion of innate knowledge is not a turn to subjectivism: there is no suggestion that human beings are the measure of reality, and certainly no equation of knowledge with the expression of personal preference. Rather, the knowledge innate in the mind is objective knowledge of ultimate reality: it is the Form of the Good, or the divine, that is the only true measure of reality.

Recollection requires effort on the part of the student: 'the true lover of knowledge must, from childhood up, be most of all a striver after truth in every form' (p. 722). This entails a process of rational reflection and self-examination, in which we weigh and test opinion in the ongoing quest for knowledge. Socratic dialogue provides a key means of pursuing this quest: the teacher asks questions that require students to reflect on their beliefs, clarify them, identify contradictions, consider alternatives, draw inferences, and make judgements. The combination of recollection and critical reflection leads to an apprehension of the truth, and ultimately to a direct mystical encounter with the Form of the Good. Despite his stress on rational reflection, Plato recognizes the presence of a deeply rooted emotional or spiritual motivation driving the pursuit of truth. In the *Symposium*, he identifies love as the source of moral, spiritual, aesthetic and intellectual inspiration. The desire to apprehend and possess God, or the Good, motivates the search for that which we once knew but cannot now properly recall. It takes the form of an intellectual and spiritual pilgrimage that progresses through physical love, the contemplation of souls, apprehension of the Form of Beauty, to an encounter with the Form of the Good itself.

This pursuit of truth is both an end in itself, and a path to personal and social well-being. Human beings seek happiness, and find it in a virtuous life lived in the light of the reality of God. Truth and truthfulness, for Plato, enjoy an intimate relationship with one another: both knowledge and wise actions participate in the Form of the Good. 'Could you find anything more akin to wisdom than truth?' (p. 722). The core virtues of justice, wisdom, courage and temperance show themselves in our behaviour: we make use of our virtuous dispositions, and the 'the right user is the mind of the wise man, the wrong user the mind of the foolish' (p. 373). Personal formation and the establishment of a just society are both dependent on knowledge of the ultimate order-of-things. It is knowledge of the Form of Good that enables Plato's philosopher-rulers to discipline their emotions and govern justly, and *phronesis* – practical reason, wise judgement, prudence – that links contemplation of the divine with those truthful actions that enable persons and societies to flourish (Dunne, 1997).

Despite the theological gulf dividing Plato and ancient Israel, the different forms of religious education they envisage have at least three traits in common: a concern for ultimate truth, an acceptance of the intimate connection between knowledge and virtue, and an acknowledgment that the pursuit of truth and practice of truthfulness require strenuous effort guided by appropriate education.

3.3 Religious education in the early church

Religious education in the early church took up and developed the concept of 'paideia', whose roots ran deep into the soil of Greco-Roman culture, extending back as far as Plato himself (Jaeger, 1986). The term refers to teaching, learning and personal formation. However, it developed a broader meaning that pointed not so much 'to the principles and practices of teaching as to the formative task of transmitting a cultural heritage in order to school virtue and cultivate character' (Walker and Wright, 2004, p. 58). 'Its aim was to form in the souls of the young the virtue or arête they needed to function as responsible citizens' (Kelsey, 1992, p. 65). For Aristotle, virtues are potentialities inherent in human nature that need to be drawn out by engaging with the best that culture has to offer. Hence, 'the aim of paideia is to shape persons in such a way that they are literally "in-formed" by virtue' (p. 68). Since one of the highest virtues is the ability to reason, paideia sought to develop the capacity to make informed judgements; consequently, the cultivation of paideia was at the same time the cultivation of *phronesis* or practical wisdom (Dunne, 1997, pp. 237ff). Following in the tradition established by Plato, such judgements were dependent on knowledge of the ultimate order-of-things: an 'essential feature of Greek paideia . . . is that it not only contemplated the process of development in the human subject but also took into account the influence of the object of learning' (Jaeger, 1961, p. 91). Hellenistic culture departed from Plato in making the vision of human nature presented by Homer and the poets, rather than that established by the philosophers, central to the curriculum. This resulted in a humanistic education, grounded in the arts and humanities, which came to dominate schooling to such an extent that eventually paideia came to mean simply the tradition of Greek literature. This Hellenistic appropriation of paideia gradually took a more distinctly religious turn, so that 'by the third century AD it was a practice focused not on shaping virtuous political agents, but rather on preparation for that conversion of soul which would bring religious knowledge of the divine' (Kelsey, 1992, p. 69).

The first Christians adopted and transformed the classical notion of education as paideia. The early Church, in 'calling Christianity the paideia of Christ', sought 'to make Christianity appear to be a continuation of the classical Greek Paideia' (Jaeger, 1961, p. 12). At the same time, in 'making Christ the centre of a new culture' they clearly sought to imply 'that the classical paideia is being superseded' (p. 12). Thus, in his *Paedagogus* Clement of Alexandria argues that 'Christ in his role as the divine educator . . . transcends anything of this kind that has appeared before in human history' (p. 60). Jaeger suggests that the Christian appropriation of paideia 'marks the beginning of a decisive development in the aspiration of the Christians towards the goal of a Christian civilization' (p. 61). For the first Christians, the transformation of the human race through Christian paideia promises to fulfil the potential inherent in both Judaism and Hellenism. The providential development of the history of both cultures culminates in the new understanding of God revealed in the incarnation: an understanding that is salvific rather than merely intellectual, one grounded in the transmission of a Christian culture that draws on both Hellenistic paideia and Hebraic wisdom.

The roots of Christian paideia are clearly visible in the New Testament. According to Paul, 'All scripture is inspired by God and is useful for teaching, for reproof, for correction, and for training [*paideian*] in righteousness' (2 Timothy 3: 16). Such training is to ensure that 'everyone who belongs to God may be proficient, equipped for every good work' (3:17). *Hebrews* quotes with approval from the book of *Proverbs*: 'do not regard lightly the discipline [*paideias*] of the LORD . . . for the LORD disciplines [*paideuei*] those whom he loves' (Hebrews 12: 5f; cf. Proverbs 3: 11f). The exhortation continues: 'Endure trials for the sake of discipline [*paideian*]. God is treating you as children; for what child is there whom a parent does not discipline?' (12:7). Further, 'discipline [*paideia*] always seems painful rather than pleasant at the time, but later yields the peaceful fruit of righteousness to those who have been trained by it' (12:11).

Kelsey identifies four key features of the Platonic understanding of paideia taken up and developed by the first Christians (Kelsey, 1992, pp. 66f). First, Plato's understanding of the virtues was oriented towards the essence of virtue itself, the Form of the Good: 'to be shaped by *arête* simply *is* to know the Good' (p. 66). Similarly, Paul's list of virtues in Galatians – love, joy, peace, patience, kindness, generosity, faithfulness, gentleness and self-control – flow directly from the nature, actions and gift of God's Holy Spirit (Galatians 5: 22f). Second, 'the understanding of Plato that early Christians inherited assumed that the goal and deep foundation of paideia was knowledge of the divine' (p. 66). The Platonic identification of the Form of the Good with God, and of God as the highest rational principle of the universe, was not of course sufficient for the first Christians: the nature of God needed further clarification, and it received this in the Christian tradition through the identification of God with the man Jesus of Nazareth. Third, according to Plato, it is not possible to teach virtue directly; rather it develops indirectly, although an encounter with the Good that occurs when we recollect and call to mind that spark of divinity lying dormant within ourselves. The latent Christian doctrine of original sin already ruled out the possibility of encountering God through contemplation of an innate divine spark dormant within human beings; instead, according to Christian teaching, God approaches us in a chain of historical acts mediated through the preaching of the Gospel. Nevertheless, the role of the Christian preacher was similar to that of the Socratic midwife: not to impart truth directly, but to act as the mediator of an encounter between God and his creatures. Such an encounter 'involves not only knowing the divine but also a deep knowledge of one's own humanity' (p. 67). Fourth, Plato understood the recollection of knowledge of the Good as a form of conversion: 'the wheeling round of the "whole soul" toward the light of the Idea of the Good, the divine origin of the universe' (p. 67, quoting Jaeger, 1986, Volume 2, p. 295). Similarly, for the early Christians knowledge of God required a turning aside from sin and submission to the discipline of an extended period of divine education.

This baptized understanding of Greek paideia became so deeply rooted in Christian consciousness that for Clement of Alexandria the Christian faith is not 'like' paideia, but rather 'Christianity *is* paideia, divinely given in Jesus Christ and inspired Christian scriptures, focused in a profound conversion of soul, and divinely assisted by the Holy Spirit' (p. 69). As head of the Christian catechetical school in Alexandria, Clement pioneered the appropriation of

Hellenistic paideia into a Christian theological framework (Clement of Alexandria, 1994a, 1994b). Pannenberg argues that his theology, as set out in the *Paedogogus* and *Stromata*, adopts a view of providence as possessing 'systematic importance for the interpretation of salvation history as divine education of the race' (Pannenberg, 1994, p. 36). Clement sought to interpret classical philosophy in the light of this Christian vision, employing philosophical reflection 'to support a positive religion that was not itself the result of independent human search for the truth . . . but took as its point of departure a divine revelation contained in a holy book, the Bible' (Jaeger, 1961, p. 47). In doing so, he sought to move Christian converts from an 'unself-conscious reliance on pagan paideia . . . to the *conscious* ideal of a Christian education and culture as something integral to the Christian thing itself' (Kelsey, 1992, p. 68).

Like Justin Martyr and Irenaeus before him, Clement welcomed certain aspects of Greek philosophy as a kind of 'propaedeutic by which men's minds are trained to receive the full truth' (Lampe, 1997, p. 64). Hellenistic philosophy

> comprehends not the whole extent of the truth, and besides is destitute of strength to perform the commandments of the Lord, yet it prepares the way for the truly royal teaching; training in some way or other, and moulding the character, and fitting him who believes in Providence for the reception of the truth.
>
> (Clement of Alexandria, 1994b, p. 318)

As Karl Barth observes, the 'royal teaching' that Clement refers to is derived not from natural knowledge rooted in human effort and will, but from 'God's revelation, by which we are authorised and commanded to view and conceive Him according to the measure of our incapable capacity' (Barth, 1957, p. 200). For Barth, it is clear that Clement understands the true source and foundation of paideia to be God as revealed in Christ. For Clement the Christian virtues of love, faith and knowledge 'are not matters of formal instruction and are not gained like wisdom that is implanted by teaching – they derive through communion with God and arise in the soul as it is kindled in that union with him' (Torrance, 1995, p. 167).

Proclaiming Christianity as 'true gnosis', Clement gave short shrift to the speculative systems of his Gnostic opponents, in particular rejecting any subordination of ordinary believers to those elite

Gnostic-inspired theologians who claimed access to some hidden, secret, salvific knowledge. '*Gnosis* is the fashionable word for this trend to transcend the sphere of *pistis* [faith], which in Greek philosophical language always has the connotation of the subjective' (Jaeger, 1961, p. 53). For Clement, it is only possible to know God through faith, which is not mere subjectivity but rather a saving encounter with the objective reality of God. Further, faith is no private esoteric matter: it is public knowledge available to all who choose to listen. As such, the content of faith constitutes an objective reality, albeit one that can only be properly appropriated subjectively although personal assent rather than rational specu-lation. Insofar as the Greek tradition of paideia embraced both a search for objective truth and a striving for subjective truthfulness, it was ripe for assimilation within a specifically Christian framework. This was Clement's achievement: in effect, he stripped Hellenistic paideia of its pre-Christian ontology, and gathered what remained into 'a bouquet of the best and finest that he has found in the religions of all peoples, to lay at the feet of the Word made flesh' (Von Balthasar, 1984, p. 25).

In Clement's *Paedagogus*, the 'tutor' or 'instructor' from whom the book takes its title 'is the holy God Jesus, the Word, who is the guide of all humanity' (Clement of Alexandria, 1994a, p. 223). He rescues us from the customs of the fallen world in which were first reared, and trains us for salvation through faith in God. His instruction is hortatory, 'engendering in the kindred faculty of reason a yearning for true life now and to come' (p. 209). Its inten-tion is practical, concerned 'to improve the soul . . . and to train it up to a virtuous, not an intellectual life' (p. 209). The overriding metaphor employed by Clement is medical: the tutor sets out to cure the whole person, 'strengthening our souls, and by His benign commands, as by gentle medicines, guiding the sick to the perfect knowledge of the truth' (p. 209). Just as 'for those of us who are diseased in body a physician is required', so 'those who are diseased in soul require a pedagogue to cure [their] maladies' (p. 209). Where human wisdom seeks knowledge the tutor seeks to nurture faith, although this is not to suggest that faith does not have a cognitive dimension. Since 'one who is ill, will not therefore learn any branch of instruction till he is quite well', the tutor 'first exhorts to the attainment of right dispositions and character, and then persuades us to the energetic practice of our duties' (p. 209). Such enculturation into a Christian lifestyle is a prerequisite for formal didactic theological education (p. 209).

Clement sees Christian education as the training of children in the innocence and simplicity of faith: 'perfection is with the Lord, who is always teaching, and infancy and childishness with us, who are always learning' (p. 213). Through the incarnation, God beholds the laughter, thanksgiving and endurance of his children, and as a result of divine instruction we 'who are infants, no longer roll on the ground, nor creep on the earth like serpents as before, crawling with the whole body about senseless lusts' (p. 213). Instead,

> stretching upward in soul, loosed from the world and our sins, touching the earth on tiptoe so as to appear to be in the world, we pursue holy wisdom, although this seems folly to those whose wits are whetted for wickedness.
>
> (p. 213)

Though Christians learn as children, their education should enable them to grow in maturity and intelligence. The Christian life is a 'lifelong spring-time, because the truth that is in us, and our habits saturated with the truth, cannot be touched by old age' (p. 214).

The perfection promised by Christ takes place through baptism, which immediately regenerates and perfects us as God opens our minds to know him. 'Being baptized, we are illuminated; illuminated, we become sons; being made sons, we are made perfect; being made perfect, we are made immortal' (p. 215). By grace, baptism cleanses us from those sins 'which obscure the light of the Divine Spirit', leaving 'the eye of the spirit free, unimpeded, and full of light, by which alone we contemplate the Divine, the Holy Spirit flowing down to us from above' (p. 216). However, although baptism perfects us the full realization of this new reality must wait until eternity. In the interim, the Christian life must be one of disciplined obedience. Such discipline is primarily a gift from God, whose praise and blame are essential medicines (p. 233). Praise is necessary, since 'by encouragement he assuages sin, reducing lust, and at the same time inspiring hope for salvation' (p. 232). Blame is necessary, since the passions that divide us from God 'are, as it were, an abscess of the truth, which must be cut open by an incision of the lancet of reproof' (p. 225). Such acts of censure are a mark of the divine goodwill, instilling in us a godly fear reflective of the reverence citizens show good rulers rather than the hatred slaves show hard masters. The tutor always invites rather than coerces, since 'as far as piety is concerned, that which is voluntary and spontaneous differs much, nay entirely, from what is forced' (p. 231). Hence, we have both the freedom and responsibility to strive after the path of salvation. The majesty of God demands not passivity but a proactive engagement with the pursuit of truth and truthful living, one that demands the effort, insight and wisdom of the whole person.

3.4 Conclusion

The worldviews of ancient Israel, Plato and the early Church are fundamentally different. Nevertheless, there is a remarkable consensus concerning the basic task of religious education. First, religious education must shape and form the whole person, impacting emotionally and intellectually on all they think, say and do. Second, such formation must be guided by, and responsive to, that which is ultimate in the actual order-of-things. Third, pupil should engage actively in their learning, discerning and assimilating truth in a self-consciously responsible manner. This raises a fundamental question, to which we must turn in the next chapter: Has this classical tradition of religious education anything to offer to liberal forms of religious education operating in contexts in which the nature of the ultimate order-of-things is a deeply contested matter?

4

Liberal religious education

The three case studies presented in the previous chapter suggest a close link between classical forms of religious education and questions of ultimate truth. This is undoubtedly also the case for modern forms of confessional education, in which faith communities set out to nurture pupils within a specific worldview and seek to enable them to live lives in harmony with a particular vision of the ultimate order-of-things. However, for post-confessional forms of liberal religious education, in which state-sponsored public education programmes seek to take account of a range of different traditions and belief systems, the issue of ultimate truth inevitably becomes more problematic.

In a number of previous publications, I have offered an analysis of how liberal religious education in England and Wales has dealt with issues of truth and truthfulness since its emergence in the early 1970s (Wright, 1993, 1998a, 2000, 2004a). The growth of secularism and pluralism, I suggested, placed the issue of religious truth in an ambiguous position as the traditional assumption, that religion stands 'at the centre of our understanding of our humanity, of our society, of the ultimate questions of purpose, meaning and truth that the universe forces upon us', was increasingly questioned (Wright, 1993, p. 9). For an influential minority, religion had become 'a mere irrelevance, a superstitious remnant of a past age that the intelligent and sophisticated have outgrown, but which the timid and frightened continue to cling to' (p. 9). This suspicion of the truth claims of religions coincided with a crisis within religious education itself, as its place within the curriculum came under increasing scrutiny: if we can no longer be certain that religions offer true descriptions of the order-of-things, what justification is there for retaining religious education in the curriculum of public schools?

Given the contested nature of religious truth claims, the most effective way of justifying the subject's place in the curriculum was to reconstruct it in a form compatible with the prevailing norms of liberal society. Consequently, some sought to validate the subject on the grounds of its contribution to the social, personal – and later spiritual – well-being of the nation: attempts to engineer a harmonious multicultural society could not afford to ignore the problems and possibilities raised by religious belief. Here was a *raison d'être* for the subject that even the most cynical despiser of religious education should be able to identify with. As this moral turn took root, so attention shifted to religion as a sociocultural phenomenon, one best explored by social scientists rather than theologians, and as a result questions of ultimate truth were marginalized still further. If it was legitimate for teachers to promote tolerance by describing a variety of religious belief systems and encouraging sympathetic appreciation of them, there was an underlying anxiety that to engage with their truth claims as serious and substantial options threatened to highlight ideological differences and hence destabilize society.

My own response to this situation was to suggest that the contested nature of ultimate truth claims ought to become the key focus and driver of liberal religious education. Given that our place in the ultimate order-of-things is the subject of fundamental dispute, religious education has a duty not to neutralize the controversy but to engage with it directly:

> Put bluntly, the process of denying the ambiguity of religion denies pupils access to any depth of understanding of the complexity and ambiguity of our diverse religious and areligious heritage, it denies them the right to wrestle with the issues for themselves.

(p. 11)

In short, the plurality of accounts of truth and truthfulness demands active engagement rather than passive avoidance.

In reiterating this basic argument here, I will take the opportunity to further refine and qualify it. The adjustments in my thinking are best approached via the apparently oblique route of a brief reflection on Michael Foucault's *The History of Sexuality* (Foucault, 1990). Foucault argues that the Victorian era's increasingly reserved attitude towards sexuality was nevertheless accompanied by the proliferation of discourses *about* sex. The reference here is not to any increase in 'illicit' counter-cultural discourses designed to undermine the new code of decorum through deliberate vulgarity. Rather, these emergent discourses spoke freely about sexuality in order to reinforce the new puritanical code of conduct. Foucault viewed such sex-talk as an exercise in power, aimed not at repression but at control: Victorian society was, in equal measure, simultaneously fascinated and fearful of sex, and as such constructed a discourse designed to limit and control the extent and nature of sexual activity.

What is the relevance of this for religious education? My suggestion is that the simultaneous fascination and fear shown by late-modernity towards issues of ultimate truth has lead to the proliferation of discourses designed to ring-fence and control discussion of religious truth claims. Contra my earlier argument, contemporary religious education has not merely marginalized the issue of truth; rather, it has sought to neutralize and contain it within a wider discourse about truthfulness. As a result, many religious educators are now more concerned to equip pupils to live truthful lives within a liberal polity than engage with questions about their place in the ultimate order-of-things. The underlying assumption is that there is no necessary connection between truth and truthfulness, between learning about religion and learning from religion: instead, there is a tacit understanding that it does not matter what you believe, provided you do so with integrity. This, in effect, marks the triumph of comprehensive liberalism over political liberalism.

I begin this chapter by charting the transition from confessional to liberal forms of religious education, and tracing the genealogy of the standard distinction between 'learning about' and 'learning from' religion. I then explore the relationship between learning *about* religion and the pursuit of truth, and between learning *from* religion and the cultivation of truthfulness, as these are envisaged by liberal educators. I conclude by offering a critique of their failure to uphold classical religious education's holistic vision of a unitary relationship between these two dimensions of the subject.

4.1 From confessionalism to liberalism

John White has suggested that the primary task of religious teaching in schools is to attend to 'ethical and moral issues as part of children's general education', and argues that this perception of the subject as a subset of moral education 'is in line with the tradition of religious education in this country' (White, 2004a, p. 13). However, it is not possible to defend a historical reading of the subject that reduces traditional confessional religious education to a type of moral education in this manner. The 1944 *Education Act* certainly envisaged religious education having a major role to play in the reconstruction of a society devastated by the Second World War (HMSO, 1944). However, it sought to achieve this through the recovery of the specifically *Christian* roots of society: this accounts for its insistence on a daily act of collective worship and on the responsibility of schools to nurturing pupils in the Christian faith. Contra White, the mainstream tradition of religious education in this country is historically rooted in the affirmation of Christian truth claims; there is little evidence of any intention to use religious education instrumentally as a mere tool for a general moral education. Such instrumentalism did not emerge until the advent of liberal religious education in the 1970s, when questions of truth became dislocated from questions of morality as the humanistic virtues of freedom and tolerance gradually eclipsed the theological virtue of obedience to the will of God.

The confessional consensus that informed the 1944 *Education Act* certainly felt little tension between the pursuit of doctrinal truth and the nurturing of truthful Christian lives. As the Bishop of Bristol, in his preface to the 1947 *London Agreed Syllabus for Religious Education*, made clear, to learn about the Bible in a confessional context is to engage directly with what it claims to be: the revealed word of God rather than merely a literary collection of ancient documents or a historical record of past events (London County Council, 1947, p. 18). The syllabus assumed an intimate relationship between the moral teachings of the Bible and the Christian understanding of the ultimate order-of-things: it was simply not possible to separate the moral wheat from the doctrinal chaff. The combination of religious instruction, collective worship and nurture within the Christian ethos of the school provided a holistic learning experience – one in which learning about Christianity was inseparable from the process of religious formation. Confessional religious education, designed as it was to 'quicken the spirits of the children who take part in it, fixing their roots in the Christian faith, and giving them direction and inspiration in life', saw little tension between truth and truthfulness (p. 26). According to Archbishop William Temple, 'we are not training children according to their own true nature or in relation to their true environment unless we are training them to trust in God . . . education should throughout be inspiring faith in God and find its focus in worship' (Temple, 1942, pp. 69, 73).

The first hints of a division between truth and truthfulness emerged in the era of implicit religious education of the 1960s. It was Harold Loukes who first identified the emerging gap between the worldview of Christianity as taught in religious education, and the ordinary lifeworld experiences that pupils brought with them to the classroom (Loukes, 1961, 1965). Significantly, his response to this problem was *not* to attempt to redefine the content and aims of religious education: the Christian agenda was to remain firmly in place. However, teaching the Bible and Christian doctrine is wasted effort unless pupils 'attain a point of view from which they may, if they will, make judgements on the personal and public moral situation' (Loukes, 1965, p. 48). For Loukes, there was no underlying tension between contested perceptions of truth and truthfulness. Rather, he believed the problem lay elsewhere: in inadequate teaching methods that failed to make explicit to pupils the direct link between the truth claims of Christianity and the personal, social and moral dilemmas they encountered in their daily lives. Hence, Loukes' advocacy of a child-centred pedagogy that started out from the ordinary experiences of pupils and sought to build experiential and linguistic bridges between their lifeworlds and Christianity. However, this proposed solution failed to recognize that the real problem facing confessionalism was not its inappropriate subject-centred teaching methods, but its failure to recognize the true extent and nature of the pupils' dislocation from institutional Christianity. The increasing impact of pluralism, secularism and liberalism in the 1960s, together with a significant increase in merely nominal allegiance to Christianity, meant that it was no longer possible to simply assume the truth and authority of the Christian worldview. Consequently, many pupils struggled to discern any existential relevance in Christian teaching and experienced attempts of persuade them to acknowledge such relevance as an indoctrinatory imposition on their freedom. With the benefit of hindsight, Loukes' belief that the gulf between pupils and Christianity could be bridged merely by introducing new child-centred teaching methods appears remarkably naive. The ethos of the 'permissive sixties' had effectively plunged Christianity into a crisis of legitimation, and in such a situation it was unfortunate that religious educators did not have the insight to address the contested nature of religious truth openly in the classroom, but instead sought surreptitiously to persuade pupils of the truth of Christianity by offering pre-packaged Christian solutions to their moral and existential dilemmas.

The option of engaging directly with contested worldviews in the classroom was taken up in the 1970s by liberal religious education – albeit only in the early stages of its development. Recognizing the disputed nature of religious truth claims in an increasingly pluralistic and secularized society, it sought to recast religious education in a liberal framework predicated on the twin virtues of freedom and tolerance. Crucially, this transition from confessional to liberal religious education did not, initially at least, lead to any diminishing of interest in questions of truth and truthfulness. On the contrary, it saw the liberal virtues of freedom and tolerance not as ends in themselves, but as means to the greater end of exploring diverse worldviews in the classroom. Thus, in its early stages liberal religious education embraced a political, rather than comprehensive, understanding of liberalism.

Hence Ninian Smart, one of the key instigators of liberal religious education, argued that 'religious education must transcend the informative . . . in the direction of initiation into understanding the meaning of, and into questions about the truth and worth of, religion' (Smart, 1968, p. 105). It is noteworthy that this concern for truth continues to influence contemporary liberal religious educators. Robert Jackson, for example, argues that 'young people should have the right to study and reflect on *different* views of truth represented within and across religious traditions as well as considering the functions of religious activity in people's lives' (Jackson, 1997, p. 126). However, as we shall see, this desire to engage with questions of ultimate truth has rarely been realized in any deep, consistent or meaningful way. Instead, a gradual shift from a political to a comprehensive understanding of liberal society has had a significant impact on contemporary religious education.

Perhaps the clearest evidence of liberal religious education's original commitment to the pursuit of religious truth is contained in *Religious Education in Secondary Schools: Schools Council Working*

Paper 36 (Schools Council, 1971). Authored by Smart himself, it advocates an open 'phenomenological' or 'undogmatic' approach to religious education, and in doing so discards two alternatives: a 'confessional' or 'dogmatic' approach that 'begins with the assumption that the aim of religious education is intellectual and cultic indoctrination', and an 'anti-dogmatic' approach that ignores religious truth claims, treats religion merely as a dimension of human culture, and thereby 'rules out the subjective element in religious education and conceives it as an academic exercise, dispassionate and objective' (p. 21). The alternative 'undogmatic' approach advocated by Smart was guided by educational concerns: committed to the tools of academic scholarship, it sought to promote religious understanding by enabling pupils to enter into an empathetic experience of the worldviews of a range of different religious traditions. In doing so, 'it does not seek to promote any one religious viewpoint but it recognises that the study of religion must transcend the merely informative' (p. 21).

The crucial issue facing liberal religious education, according to Smart, was that of the relationship between subjectivity and objectivity in the study of religion. In terms of the former, he held that 'every form of religion involves passionate commitment' and is concerned with that which 'a person, or a community, regards as supremely valuable' (p. 22). It follows that 'if religion cannot properly be understood apart from subjectivity, then any satisfactory concept of objective study must somehow include that subjectivity' (p. 22). Crucially, subjectivity for Smart entails far more than private emotions: on the contrary, human beings have a capacity for self-transcendence that enables them to participate in the subjectivity of others. Such 'imaginative self-transcendence is the foundation of all scholarly objectivity and the presupposition of any intellectually responsible education' (p. 22). It follows that academic scholarship is bound up with issues of commitment, and that the critical study of religion should enable pupils to grapple with their core beliefs. This entails bringing the subjectivity of pupils into conversation with the objective truth claims of a range of religions and secular traditions. 'Teaching is not objective when one interpretation is presented as though it were absolute and unquestioned fact', rather genuinely objective teaching entails a willingness to 'admit the possibility of alternative patterns of interpretation' and present evidence for beliefs 'so that they may be accepted or rejected freely and intelligently' (p. 24):

> It is not sufficient to parade alternatives before the eyes of the imagination and to leave it at that, as if there were no objective ways of judging their relative truth or adequacy. The special function of academic communities is to create schemes for the critical evaluation of interpretations originating in non-academic communities, whether the interest be economic, social, military, political, or religious.
>
> (p. 26)

The possibility of such a subjectively committed and objectively rational search for religious truth rests on the cultivation of academic freedom in the classroom. 'In every other subject children are encouraged to question and explore, to take nothing to be true until they can see it to be truth' (p. 27). Hence, religious education should also enable students to participate in the search for 'true knowledge and understanding' in a way that becomes 'part of [their] interior mental life and convictions' and which is arrived at through 'personal discovery' (p. 28).

We have seen that the transition from confessional to liberal religious education was not initially concerned to establish a divide between truth and truthful living, marginalize religious truth claims, or reduce the subject to a form of moral education. Rather it sought to affirm the traditional unity of religious education by retain a focus on both truth and truthfulness, but in doing so it also sought to recognize – contra confessionalism – that these are contested issues that demand the critical engagement of pupils with a plurality of different religious and secular traditions. Smart's account of a critical liberal religious education is close to the one I will advocate in the next chapter; our immediate task, however, is to explore the demise of his vision in the recent history of the subject.

4.2 Truth and truthfulness in liberal religious education

As we noted earlier, the non-statutory National Framework for religious education identifies two complementary attainment targets for religious education: 'learning about' and 'learning from' religion (DfES/QCA, 2004). The process of learning about religion involves an 'investigation of the nature of religion' – including 'identifying and developing an understanding of ultimate questions' – that will challenge pupils 'to reflect on, consider, analyse, interpret and evaluate issues of truth' (pp. 7, 34). Similarly, the process of learning from religion involves pupils' 'reflection on and response to their own experiences and their learning about religion' in a manner that engages with 'questions of identity and belonging, meaning, purpose and truth and values and commitments' (p. 34).

It is clear that the National Framework accepts both the central importance and essential unity of the twin tasks of learning about and learning from religion as they relate to issues of religious truth and spiritual truthfulness. As such, it presents an agenda close to the concerns of the present book and reflects Smart's initial vision of the task of liberal religious education. This suggests that the dislocation of truth from truthfulness – in educational terms, the disruption of the unity of learning about and learning from religion – may not constitute a major problem for contemporary religious education. This, however, is not the case. It was the earlier Schools Curriculum and Assessment Authority (SCAA) *Model Syllabuses for Religious Education* that first explicitly introduced the terminology of 'learning from' and 'learning about' (SCAA, 1994). This was motivated in part by the tendency of phenomenologically based teaching to reduce learning to the accumulation of factual knowledge at the expense of any existential engagement with the ultimate questions raised by religion. This was never the intention of phenomenological syllabuses, which sought to balance an objective description of religious phenomenon with an empathetic engagement with the lifeworlds – and, by implication, truth claims – of religious adherents. However, the fact that the SCAA syllabuses felt the need to redress the balance reflected an ongoing uncertainty about the relationship between studying religion in a plural context and personal formation. Indeed, back in 1985, David Day had identified a 'permanent identity crisis' in religious education (Day, 1985). On the one hand, explicit forms of religious education sought to describe the phenomena and truth claims of religious traditions; on the other, implicit forms of religious education sought to develop the social, cultural, moral and spiritual lives of pupils. The crisis lay in the absence of any clear understanding of the connection between the two. In order to understand why this situation developed, we must dig deeper into the recent history of liberal religious education in England and Wales.

In the early 1970s, the abandonment of a 'closed' Christian confessionalism in favour of an 'open' liberalism led to a re-conceptualization of the relationship between truth and truthfulness. Defenders of the so-called 'new religious education' initially had no interest in abandoning the intricate connection between studying religion and personal formation: religious education was to be just as holistic as it had always been. However, it was no longer possible to predicate the unity of the two on the basis of a specifically Christian understanding of reality. Consequently, there was an urgent need to show how the exploration of a plurality of religious and secular worldviews could remain *intrinsically* bound up with a process of spiritual development. This, however, was not forthcoming. The desire for neutral representations of religion that avoided any hint of confessionalism had the effect of dislocating the exploration of religious truth claims from the task of enabling pupils to live truthful lives. What emerged instead was the explicit identification of these two parallel concerns, accompanied – as a direct result of the failure to provide an adequate account of their interrelationship – by a general strategy of seeking to retain a *balance* between the two. The subsequent consolidation of this strategy led ultimately to the identification of two distinctive attainment targets for the subject.

Commenting on this emerging situation, Edwin Cox drew a distinction between 'understanding religion' and 'religious understanding' (Cox, 1983). The former involves 'a relatively detached knowledge of the externals of faith . . . accessible to any rational being . . . objective, academic . . . it will probably not significantly alter the student's lifestyle' (p. 5). The latter

> is more penetrating, requiring experience of the quality of a faith's beliefs and practices, an emotional response to its cult objects, and an ability to perceive and respond approvingly to its ultimate function . . . those who so involves themselves say that their understanding of their religion is of a different quality from those who stand outside and look on.
>
> (p. 5)

Although Cox understood this distinction as a problem to be overcome, subsequent religious educators began to treat it as normative. Thus, Michael Grimmitt developed a pedagogy predicated on a distinction between 'experiential' and 'dimensional' approaches to the subject (Grimmitt, 1973). The former sets out

to use the feelings, actions and experiences of pupils as a spring-
board into the exploration of questions of existential meaning, while
the latter is concerned with the presentation of explicit religious
phenomena – mythology, ritual, ethics, doctrine, etc. As we shall
see later in this chapter, Grimmitt was concerned to balance these
two approaches on the basis of a distinctive anthropology. Raymond
Holley, on the other hand, gave spiritual development clear priority
over the study of religion:

> religious education is not primarily concerned with the Bible . . . nor is
> it simply concerned with imparting information about the religions of
> the world . . . religiously educational activities [should] provoke intellec-
> tual understanding of the spiritual personality in all its extensiveness
> and dynamism.
>
> (Holley, 1978, pp. 65f)

John Wilson went a stage further, insisting on a basic discontinuity
between questions about the nature of ultimate reality and the
spiritual formation of pupils: 'the metaphysical or doctrinal superstructure [of religion] is, in one very real sense, unimportant in
itself: it is the kind of emotions to which it has been witness that
we have to detect and educate' (Wilson, 1971, p. 171).

This unresolved tension between learning about and learning
from religion was bound up with the recognition of a plurality
of contested religious and secular worldviews. With the demise of
Christian confessionalism, there was no longer any universally
acceptable account of the nature of reality or of the truthful life
stances that might flow from it. This opened up two possibilities:
either to abandon a concern for the relationship between morality
and ontology and concentrate instead on the cultivation of liberal
values as ends in themselves, or to develop a form of religious education concerned to enable pupils to engage in the critical pursuit
of truth and develop appropriate life stances in the light of that
process. These possibilities directly parallel the distinction, outlined
in Chapter 3, between comprehensive and political liberalism. Our
next task is to explore how liberal religious educators followed up
these two options. In the following two sections, we will examine
the response of those who tended to embraced comprehensive
liberalism as they dealt, respectively, with questions of truth and
truthfulness. The final section will explore the approaches of
religious educators whose preference was to ground liberal religious

education in a political liberalism concerned to pursue questions of truth and truthfulness.

4.3 The eclipse of truth

How did the transition from confessional to liberal religious education impact on the process of 'learning about' religion? How was the question of ultimate truth dealt with in this new context? Perhaps the greatest challenge was that of religious particularity: the fact that different religious and secular traditions offer mutually exclusive accounts of the ultimate order-of-things. For political liberals, this challenge could be treated as a positive opportunity to engage with contested truth claims. For comprehensive liberals, on the other hand, the challenge of particularity was seen as a scandal urgently in need of resolution. This scandal had two dimensions: first, the intellectual scandal of traditions claiming exclusive, yet apparently unverifiable, access to knowledge of ultimate reality; second, the moral scandal linked to the arrogant tribalistic attitudes perceived to underlie such claims. Such intellectual and moral audacity was seen as a direct threat to the well-being of liberal society, since it appeared to undermine the core liberal values of freedom and tolerance. To assert an exclusive truth claim in the face of the deeply held beliefs of adherents of other traditions, without apparently having any grounds for doing so beyond that of personal conviction, was to risk further dividing an already fragmented society. Hence a major task facing comprehensive liberal religious educators was to find ways of dissipating the threat of particularity.

One solution to this problem was simply to deny its existence, either by dissolving particular religious traditions into a greater whole or by breaking them down into their constituent parts. According to the former option, particular religious traditions constitute relatively insignificant local manifestations of the universal generic phenomenon 'religion'; according to the latter, they are relatively arbitrary constructions that reify the spiritual experiences of individuals. Whether one focuses on the generic unity or the atomistic parts of the world's religions, the net effect is the same: the eclipse of the distinctive identities of discrete religious traditions and consequent avoidance of the scandal of particularity. These alternatives reflect the philosophical debate between essentialism and nominalism: according to essentialists, reality is structured around fixed universal categories, while for nominalists reality consists of atomistic parts whose relationship with one another is fluid and arbitrary. Phenomenological religious education tended to advocate an essentialist understanding of religion, treating particular religious traditions as diverse manifestations of the common generic category 'religion'. It suggested that discrete religious traditions share a common phenomenological structure and originate in the same universal experience of transcendence. As a result, particular religious traditions could be represented as culturally relative expressions of a single entity, their distinctive truth claims fading into insignificance when viewed in the light of the greater whole. Contextual forms of religious education, on the other hand, tend to reflect nominalistic interpretations of religion. Thus, Robert Jackson rejects the characterization of religious traditions as rigid and bounded systems. Since ethnographic research has exposed the 'contested representations' and 'disputed borders' of discrete religious traditions, it is no longer possible to offer an understanding of religions in which 'the fuzzy edges of real life are trimmed off, and the personal syntheses and multiple allegiances revealed by ethnographic study . . . are interpreted as deviations from doctrinally pristine religious narratives' (Jackson, 2004, pp. 81f). He views the notion of discrete religions enjoying clearly demarked boundaries as a social construction, and argues that it is better to view them as a fluid and ever-changing amalgams of the spiritualities of individual adherents. Whether religious educators opt for essentialism or nominalism, the result is the same: the scandal of particularity is circumvented and the comprehensive liberal commitment to the basic values of freedom and tolerance secured.

A second strategy for avoiding the scandal of particularity was to bracket out contested truth claims by treating religious traditions as merely sociocultural phenomena. Here the focus of attention shifts from crucial doctrinal differences to relativity insignificant cultural practices: thus learning about the particularity of Christian and Islamic dress codes appears less socially divisive to the comprehensive liberal than examining the particularity of irreconcilable truth claims about Jesus of Nazareth. As a result of this strategy, phenomenological religious education came to mean 'in the minds of many, a concentration on external, public "phenomena" as part of an "objective" study of religion' (Hammond, Hay, et al., 1990, p. 6). This implies a distinction between objective knowledge and subjective opinion: because religious truth claims are unverifiable they should be treated as private beliefs rather than contested public knowledge. There was no disputing the fact that within a liberal polity individuals are free to believe whatever they like, provided that such beliefs do not bring harm to others. Further, the assumption that religious truth claims are not open to rational debate did not rule out *describing* the beliefs of religious adherents objectively: to assert that Muslims believe in the existence of Allah is simply to state a publicly accessible fact. However, it was not considered either appropriate or possible to engage in theological and philosophical discussion about the substantial truth of such claims. One can discuss the beliefs of religious adherents, but not the truth and falsehood of the realities lying behind such beliefs. Once again the scandal of particularity is avoided: not by rejecting the claim that discrete religious traditions put forward specific truth claims, but by denying the possibility of engaging critically with them.

A third strategy for dissipating the scandal of particularity was to reject the received notion that a key role of religious language is to describe the ultimate order-of-things. It was Schleiermacher who gave an initial momentum to this option by suggesting that the roots of religion are to be found in 'neither a knowing, nor a doing, but a modification of feeling' (Schleiermacher, 1976, p. 5). In ruling out the option of viewing religion as a form of 'knowing' he effectively marginalized the traditional cognitive-propositional reality-describing understanding of religious language. This opened up two alternative possibilities.

a) The claim that religion is a 'modification of feeling' identified transcendent experience as the basis of religious belief. The resulting experiential-expressive model of religious language argued that the primary function of religious discourse is to give expression to such experience. Adopting this model, David Hay argued that religion should be represented in the classroom as 'what it claims to be – the response of human beings to what they experience as sacred' (Hay, 1982a, p. 48). He identifies a deeply rooted suspicion of the transcendent concerns of religion, traces this back to the influence of post-Enlightenment thinkers such as Freud, Marx and Nietzsche, and calls for a counter-cultural religious education concerned to nurture pupils' innate capacity for deep spiritual experience (Hay, 1985). However, Hay's preference for a universal theology that discovers elements of truth in all religious traditions ultimately dissipates the force of his argument. His claim that the truth claims of discrete religious traditions are simply culturally relative expressions of a common universal experience of transcendence effectively bypassed the scandal of particularity (Hay, 1982b). This is because according to the experiential-expressive model the actual truth claims that are central to a cognitive-propositional understanding of religion are relatively inconsequential: hence, rather than grappling with a range of conflicting truth claims, the pupil is faced with a common religious experience that effectively binds together different traditions.

b) The claim that religion as essentially a 'doing' invites the belief that religious identity is determined by the adherent's actions, with religious language functioning merely as a pragmatic guide to behaviour. Thus, John Hull has been influential in arguing that authentic religion manifests itself not in true belief but in the adoption of non-religionist and non-tribal attitudes and actions (Hull, 1998, pp. 54ff). This effectively marginalizes the specific truth claims of different religious traditions and in doing so once again effectively bypasses the scandal of particularity.

There is, then, a consistent story to be told about the way mainstream liberal religious educators have dealt with the specific truth claims of religious traditions. Generally speaking, they are committed to enabling pupils to develop knowledge and understanding of a rich variety of religious beliefs, and accept that this involves describing the truth claims of particular religious traditions. However, such commitment operates only at a surface level: concerned about the dangers of religious particularity, convinced that religious truth claims are not open to rational evaluation, and fearful of exhibiting any hint of indoctrination, many religious educators have embraced strategies designed to avoid confronting the possibility that one or other religious or secular worldview might actually be true. The cumulative impact of these strategies has been to draw the cognitive sting from religious belief, and thus reduce learning about religion to a neutral process incapable of having any direct impact on the lives of pupils.

4.4   The ascendancy of truthfulness

How then does liberal religious education approach the issue of 'learning from' religion? A genuine and lasting strength of liberal religious education has been its insistence that religious education *must* seek to have a positive impact on the development of the whole child, even although it is no longer an option to measure such development against confessional criteria. Further, it is to its credit that, while recognizing the contribution the subject has to make to personal and social development, liberal religious education has regularly embraced a wider concern for the *spiritual* development of pupils. In doing so, it has tended to work with generic descriptions of spirituality whose primary focus is anthropological rather than theological. The following definition of spirituality, taken from a document drawn up by school inspectors, is indicative of such accounts:

> The spiritual area is concerned with the awareness a person has of those elements of existence and experience which may be defined in terms of inner feelings and beliefs; they effect the way people see themselves and throw light for them on the purpose and meaning of life itself. Often these feelings and beliefs lead people to claim to know God and glimpse the transcendence; sometimes they represent that striving and longing for perfection which characterizes human beings but always they are concerned with matters at the heart and root of existence.
>
> (DES/HMI, 1977; cf. Wright, 2000, p. 66)

Insofar as such a definition sets out to be inclusive of a range of different spiritual stances, and clearly seeks to engage with questions of ultimate meaning and purpose, it has a certain resonance with the position developed in this book. However, as we shall see, the promise of this, and other similar statements, has not been fully realized. Since I have dealt with the place of spirituality in education in some detail elsewhere, I will offer only a brief overview of the key issues here (Wright 1998a, 1999, 2000).

The crucial issue facing us is that of the relationship between spiritual experience and specific claims about the ultimate nature of reality. Liberal religious education tends to combine openness to a range of different belief systems with a relative failure to explore the connection between pupils' spiritual experiences and the actual order-of-things in any deep or systematic way. As a result, there is a tendency to view spiritual beliefs as expressions of subjective preference, rather than as objective truth claims that warrant detailed investigation. Indeed, the only sustained attempt to counter this tendency is the work of David Hay. We have already noted how he identifies a general suspicion of spirituality endemic within modern society, and makes the case for a distinctly counter-cultural approach to spiritual education concerned to provide pupils with experiential access to a domain of knowledge long since buried by the rationalistic fall-out of the Enlightenment (Hay, 1985). It is, in retrospect, unfortunate that many critics – myself included – responded negatively to his universal theology, emphasis on inner feeling, and focus on the individual, and in doing so failed to recognize his fundamental concern to rehabilitate the question of the relationship between spiritual experience and the ultimate order-of-things – that is to say, the relationship between truth and truthfulness.

Despite Hay's determination to approach spiritual education in the light of questions of objective spiritual truth, and thereby challenge the prevailing focus on subjective truthfulness, he has elected to work with interpretative categories that ultimately play into the hands of his opponents. The first such category is that of experience. In the context of spirituality, Hay tends to view language as a second-order means of expressing first-order spiritual experiences: this leads to the assessment of spiritual truth claims against the criteria of depth and intensity of feeling. The second category is that of individualism. Although Hay now talks about 'relational identity', his earlier work focused on the concept of personal 'inner space' and invited pupils to explore spirituality by turning inwards and exploring their deepest feelings (Hay, 1982b, 1998). The resulting tendency to affirm personal meaning over shared communal meaning once again had the effect of making subjective experience the basis for evaluating spiritual truth claims. The third category is that of universalism, which Hay applies both to the human capacity for spiritual experience and to his theological account of such experience: human beings have an inbuilt ability to experience the transcendent and different religious traditions express this common experience in culturally distinct, yet equally valid, ways. Such universalism does little to encourage critical debate about the relationship between individual spiritual experience and the contested truth claims about the ultimate order-of-things.

The net effect of the interpretative categories on which Hay draws falls short of his stated intentions. Rather than emancipating pupils from rationalistic suspicion of the spiritual by enabling them to experience an objective transcendent reality, Hay actually encourages them to turn inwards and embrace their deepest emotions in an uncritical and subjective manner. Consequently, the key criterion for authentic spiritual experience becomes that of the depth and intensity of pupils' inner feelings, rather than the appropriateness of the relationship between their experiences and the ultimate order-of-things. Hay is correct to identify the importance of sensitizing pupils to ultimate questions and concerns on an affective level. However, mere sensitivity is not enough: unless we go on to ask whether our deepest feelings are appropriate to the ultimate order-of-things, the practice of truthfulness will necessarily be dislocated from the pursuit of truth.

This is precisely the mistake made by some defenders of postmodern and contextual forms of religious education, insofar as they limit spiritual pedagogy to the task of enhancing pupils' capacities for deep experience and encouraging them to be true to such experience (Erricker, 2001; Erricker and Erricker, 2000; cf. Wright, 2001b). The resulting dislocation of truth from truthfulness matters on at least three counts. First, because it is possible to have deep and personally meaningful experiences that can be profoundly immoral: witness, for example, the intense spiritual experiences of those caught up in the Hitler Youth Movement. Second, because our spiritual experiences can produce or support palpably false beliefs: for example, that scientific accounts of the Big Bang are products of an anti-Christian secular conspiracy. Although selfawareness is certainly a virtue, self-awareness of oneself as a relational being – and in particular of one's place in the ultimate order-of-things – is a still greater virtue. Third, because a spiritual education limited to the cultivating of deep self-awareness constitutes an implicit confessionalism: in effect, it will induct pupils into a belief system – prevalent in much of our postmodern society – that treats individuals as the ultimate measure of their own realities and hence effectively dislocates the cultivation of truthfulness from the pursuit of truth.

Thus, contemporary liberal religious education tends to encourage pupils to learn from religion by taking responsibility for their own lives and adopting the life stances that their experience suggests best suit them. However, this insistence on truthful living does not attend to questions of truth in any deep or systematic manner; on the contrary, the criteria for truthful living tends to be that of the pupils' own preferences, rather than any considered judgement about their relationship to the ultimate order-of-things.

4.5 Political liberalism and critical religious education

Despite the dominant position comprehensive liberalism has established for itself within contemporary religious education, it has not been without its critics. In this section we will examine the work of two representative figures: Lesslie Newbigin and Trevor Cooling. Although both write from the perspective of Christian orthodoxy, it is important to recognize that neither of them is seeking a return to Christian confessionalism in multi-faith schools. Rather, their respective positions are best characterized as attempts to relocate liberal religious education within the framework of a political liberalism concerned to open up a range of different worldviews and accounts of the good life rather than indoctrinate pupils into the singular truth claims of comprehensive liberalism.

Lesslie Newbigin's paper 'Teaching Religion in a Secular Plural Society' takes the form of a critical commentary on the 1975 Birmingham *Agreed Syllabus of Religious Instruction* – one of the first, and most influential, attempts to articulate a vision of liberal religious education (City of Birmingham Education Committee, 1975). He begins by questioning its insistence that religions be studied 'objectively and for their own sake', arguing that this is inconsistent with the fact that the Syllabus adopts a range of prior assumptions that are far from neutral or objective (Newbigin, 1982, p. 99). In particular, its use of the generic term 'religion' assumes that discrete religious traditions are simply variants within a common class; such an assumption renders problematic the fact that they normally demand deep levels of commitment of their adherents (p. 98). This problem is exacerbated by the tendency to view religions as 'various manifestations of one common experience' of the divine or transcendent (p. 99). Newbigin suggests that this position is unjustifiable because the formulation of the 'essence of religion' by which all the varieties of 'religion' are brought into a single class is that of the individual thinker, and will always contain elements which are vehemently denied by other people claiming to be religious.

(p. 99)

He goes on to argue that the notion of religion as a 'stance for living' introduces a bias towards the social function of religions, as opposed to their religious function as bearers of transcendent truth.

According to Newbigin, the way the concept 'religion' is understood will always be 'governed by the prior commitment of the one who is trying to understand it' (p. 99). The Birmingham Syllabus is no exception to this rule: its attempts to view religions objectively are far from neutral since they reflect the Enlightenment's 'commitment to the methods of mathematical reasoning and experimental science' (p. 98). It follows that the framers of the Syllabus are naive in asserting that 'there can be no question of making it an aim of religious education to convert pupils to any particular religion or ideology' (pp. 100f). 'Assuming that the effect of the programme of religious education is not to be a totally vacant mind, what will in fact be communicated will be the ideology which informs this Syllabus' (p. 101).

Similarly unsustainable is the suggestion that we live in a secular society whose basic outlook is neutral and value free. In reality, we live in a plural society that 'holds together a plurality of different groups each of which has a set of shared values which is – to some extent – distinctive' (p. 102). Of course, such a diverse society needs some shared values to hold it together, for example intolerance of racism and hedonism. However, the fact that no 'democratic society can cohere without some common values which are shared and therefore – to some degree – enforced' means that schools cannot legitimately uphold the pretence of neutrality, but rather have 'a *duty* to encourage children to adopt some kinds of "stances for living" and to avoid others' (p. 103).

Turning to the role of the teacher, Newbigin notes with approval the suggestion that religious education is 'subject to the same disciplines as other areas of study' (p. 104). However, this cannot mean neutrality: science teachers do not have a non-committal approach to truth, and history teachers will invite pupils to consider and discriminate between various interpretations of the past. 'In both cases the purpose is to enable the pupils to begin to grasp for themselves what is really the case, and not just what are the various possible ways of looking at it' (p. 104). Critical thinking is never neutral between different perspectives, but is necessarily driven by a desire to distinguish between true and false viewpoints: 'Religion, like science and history, is an expression of the human attempt to understand and respond to what is really the case' (p. 105). In similar vein, Newbigin approves the suggestion that teaching should be 'directed towards developing a critical understanding of the religious and moral dimensions of human experience' (p. 104). However, the struggle for critical insight cannot operate in a vacuum because understanding necessarily *proceeds* from 'the uncritical acceptance of models which are part of the culture and experience into which the pupil is growing up' (p. 105). Since critical thinking 'is an activity in which, on the basis of one set of beliefs (A) you examine another set of beliefs (B)', it follows that it is impossible to think critically 'except on the basis of some way of understanding experience which is (for the moment) assumed' (p. 104). In the case of the Birmingham Syllabus, the possibility of critical understanding is predicated on the prior 'uncritical acceptance of a particular 'stance for living'', namely that of Western liberalism (p. 104). If for 'the framers of the Syllabus this stance is obviously simply 'what is right'', then to 'an observer from another culture it is easily recognizable as a particular stance characteristic of the present phase of Western middle class culture – a culture which has ceased to believe that the Christian faith is the truth about how things really are' (p. 105).

Newbigin draws a number of conclusions from his analysis, not least the fact that liberal religious education needs to acknowledge its given values, commitments and presuppositions. To do so will free religious educators to pursue a form of education capable of looking beyond the liberal context within which it operates, rather than simply inducting pupils into the liberal norms underlying the Syllabus. Such an education should form an essential part of the liberal curriculum 'because religion is concerned with realities . . . every human being must come to terms [with] in one way or another' (p. 106). It should teach religion not from the stance of an impartial observer, but 'in the context of a real concern for, a real passion for truth' (p. 106). In doing so, it will enable pupils to 'understand the different answers that are given in society to the ultimate questions about the meaning of human life', directing their minds 'not just to the varieties of religious experience, but to the realities with which the religions are seeking to come to terms' (pp. 106f).

Trevor Cooling's analysis of liberal religious education begins with the suggestion that it is dominated by an educational philosophy underpinned by 'the liberal ideal of rational autonomy, critical rationality, or critical openness, as it is variously called' (Cooling, 1994, p. 17). This engenders sceptical and individualistic attitudes towards religious belief. Cooling traces the presence of such scepticism in the educational sphere back to the influence of Paul Hirst, for whom 'it is fundamentally important that education develops in individuals the propensity to hold religious beliefs in a fashion appropriate to their rational status' (p. 18). Hirst's reliance on a tradition of rational thinking rooted in the Enlightenment leads him to claim that 'there are no agreed public tests whereby true and false can be distinguished in religious claims' (p. 19; quoting Hirst, 1974, p. 181). Given this set of assumptions, a sceptical attitude towards religious belief is inevitable. Cooling suggests that religious education's stress on individualism is directly linked to a commitment to rationalism. If it is 'irrational to accept contestable beliefs on someone else's authority', then a key task of religious education is to 'encourage pupils to choose for themselves' (p. 21). He accuses Michael Grimmitt of approaching 'choosing as an authenticating experience, having value in its own right, irrespective of the content of what is chosen' (p. 23). The net outcome of this combination of scepticism and individualism is to effectively remove religious belief from the sphere of public accountability and establish it as a matter of mere personal preference. Hence, liberal religious education is dominated by a philosophy 'which entails that it promotes a sceptical attitude to religious beliefs, places a high value on free, autonomous choice, and treats such choices as a purely personal matter' (p. 24).

Cooling goes on to suggest that liberal religious education's commitment to rationalism, scepticism and individualism generates various forms of theological relativism. He identifies John Hull's theology of religious pluralism, or 'universal monotheism', as being particularly influential on this count. According to Hull, religious educators should assume the equal theological validity of all the major religious traditions. The fact that they offer conflicting understandings of ultimate reality is inconsequential, since he assumes that religious doctrines have a primarily instrumental, rather than truth bearing, function. Cooling relates Hull's position to Ruben Alves' criticism of the obsession of some religious believers with questions of truth and certainty, which arises 'as a result of thinking about doctrine in terms of propositional statements about the nature of reality rather than in terms of their beneficial psychological or sociological effects' (p. 32). For Hull, a central task of religious education is to cultivate a tolerant liberal society by helping to reduce religious conflict. He claims that this objective is threatened by forms of religious tribalism that insist on the absolute truth of one or other discrete religious tradition. As Cooling observes, Hull's 'acceptance of relativism is supposed to generate a humility that is conducive to a ready acceptance of those with whom we disagree' (p. 45). In effect, the liberal principles of freedom and tolerance provide the criteria against which the veracity or, more accurately, pragmatic usefulness of religious traditions are to be assessed. For Cooling this is unacceptable, not only because 'it gives no basis for evaluating the worth of different religions, and makes choice a totally arbitrary affair', but more fundamentally because 'most believers do not see their religion in this way' (pp. 47, 49). As a result, liberal religious education ends up imposing 'a particular view of theology on the population', one entirely conducive of liberal values (p. 51).

Cooling traces the values of autonomy, objectivity and universality upon which liberal religious education is grounded back to the normative influence of Enlightenment secularism. This is seen clearly in Hirst's distinction between primitive forms of education content to transmit uncritically the 'customs and values of one generation to the next', and sophisticated forms of education 'governed by the autonomous domain of secular knowledge . . . based on objective principles that are logically more fundamental than those of a particular religious belief' (p. 51). This commitment to the values of the Enlightenment is also clearly visible in Grimmitt's claim that religious educators are essentially 'secular educators concerned with the educational value of studying religion and religions' (p. 52; quoting Grimmitt, 1987, p. 258). Similarly, Hull argues that religious education should be guided primarily by philosophy, 'an activity rooted in rationality, common to all people and, therefore, more basic than optional ways of life, such as the religious' (pp. 54f). Hull accepts that theology may have a secondary supportive role to play, but only provided 'critical enquiry and controversial examination flow directly and necessarily from the values and beliefs to which the theology is committed' (p. 54).

Cooling's response to these observations is to question the independence and universality of philosophy: it is always contextual, never independent of specific cultures and beliefs, and as such necessarily committed to a range of prior presuppositions and value judgements. It follows that thinking about education is always rooted in a specific cultural and intellectual context. When Grimmitt describes education as a process through which pupils may begin to explore what it means to be human, he presupposes an anthropological outlook rooted firmly in the Enlightenment (p. 58). This immediately rules out other possibilities, such as 'the Islamic emphasis on the importance of submitting one's life to the will of Allah', and begs the question: 'how can [a philosophy] that is contextually dependent and subject to ideological influence have an independent, universally applicable rationality?' (pp. 58 f). Indeed, Hull himself accepts that philosophy of education cannot avoid working within a particular context (p. 57). Similarly, Grimmitt implicitly concedes Cooling's point in accepting that the perspective adopted by education ought to be one 'which is consistent with the dominant ideological assumptions of the majority of pupils' (p. 59; quoting Grimmitt, 1987, p. 46).

For Cooling, the conclusion to be drawn is clear: liberal religious education adopts a specific understanding of the nature of religion and the task of religious education, one rooted in the rationalistic tradition that flows from the Enlightenment and which adopts as its primary role the cultivation of the liberal values of freedom and tolerance. In doing so, it generates a specific understanding of religion that makes individual choice the ultimate criterion for judgement, demands that belief be held in a tentative manner, insists on the relativity of contrasting religious truth claims, and stresses the instrumental function of religion (pp. 66 f). Liberal religious education's decision to evaluate religions in terms of its own pragmatic commitment to specifically liberal virtues 'has created a culture which is antagonistic to certain forms of Christian faith' and – Cooling would also contend – to other religious outlooks (p. 65). General concepts like rationality and humanization are context bound – they have to be interpreted within a particular belief system; but 'not all religions *do* accept these so-called facts *as interpreted* by liberal education theory' (p. 66). Cooling's positive response to his critique is to call for a religious education that is sensitive to religious diversity, and to insist that questions of religious truth should be engaged with in the public sphere. Although being religious may not be an inescapable part of human nature, addressing questions of ultimate concern certainly is. 'An atheist, wishing to engage in religious education, has to do theology by making some judgement on the significance of religious language, and what it means to hold a religious belief in a rational way' (p. 62). Hence the need for a sophisticated religious education concerned to open up and explore questions of truth, rather than a primitive religious education content merely to transmit liberal values and beliefs as normative.

4.6 Conclusion

In this chapter, I put forward the thesis that liberal religious educa-tion has effectively turned its back on classical religious education's commitment to the unity of the pursuit of truth and cultivation of truthfulness. Faced with the challenge of working in a plural context in which the nature of ultimate reality and the fundamental meaning of life are contested, liberal religious education allowed a division to emerge between the two. This was largely due to an implied, although nevertheless very real, shift from political liberalism to comprehensive liberalism. Once the values of freedom and tolerance became ends in themselves, it was necessary both to bypass potentially divisive questions of ultimate truth and measure the quest for truthfulness against the criteria of self-realization rather than any external standards. As a result, it no longer mattered what pupils learnt about religion, provided their understanding was likely to promote a tolerant society, and it no longer mattered what pupils learnt from religion provided the process enhanced their personal freedom. In effect, discourse about truth was submerged beneath discourse about truthfulness – and not any notion of truthfulness, but truthfulness perceived as the self-realization and self-expression of autonomous individuals.

5

Critical religious education

This chapter defends a form of critical religious education that, without losing sight of the virtues of freedom and tolerance, seeks to rehabilitate the pursuit of ultimate truth and reunite it with the cultivation of truthful living. It does so by addressing a single question: Is the claim that the pursuit of truth ought to play a central role in liberal religious education justifiable? It suggests five reasons why the question demands a positive answer. First, the National Framework for religious education in England and Wales establishes a clear mandate for the exploration of ultimate truth claims in the classroom. Second, we have a moral obligation to seek to hold true beliefs. Third, society is more likely to flourish if citizens are able to respond intelligently to questions about the ultimate meaning and purpose of life. Fourth, it has an important contribution to make to the spiritual development of pupils. Fifth, the pursuit of ultimate truth is intrinsically worthwhile.

5.1   The mandate of the National Framework

The Qualifications and Curriculum Authority (QCA) acknowledges the importance of the pursuit of truth in religious education. Its *National Curriculum Handbook for Teachers* identifies two basic educational aims: 'to provide opportunities for all pupils to learn and to achieve', and 'to promote pupil's spiritual, moral, social and cultural development and prepare all pupils for the opportunities, responsibilities and experiences of life' (DfEE/QCA, 1999, pp. 10f). The latter aim simply repeats, in slightly modified form, the substance of the aims of education set out in the 1988 *Education Reform Act* (HMSO, 1988, p. 1). The Handbook goes on to make explicit the reciprocal relationship between personal growth and learning: since the 'development of pupils, spiritually, morally, socially and culturally, plays a significant part in their ability to learn and to achieve', it follows that progress 'in both areas is essential to raising standards of attainment for all pupils' (DfEE/ QCA, 1999, p. 12). It also adds substance to the legislation by suggesting that pupils should leave school in possession of a range of personal qualities, a set of key learning skills, and an appropriate level of knowledge and understanding.

Not surprisingly, this vision of the formative task of education is located firmly in the tradition of Western liberalism: as John White points out, 'broadly speaking, the ideal pupil is an informed, caring citizen of a liberal democratic society' (White, 2004a, p. 4). We can go further, and identify four core virtues underpinning QCA's understanding of personhood: autonomy, tolerance, reason and a concern for truth (DfEE/QCA, 1999, pp. 10ff; cf. Wright, 2007b. First, personal autonomy: rooted in an inner life marked by integrity, self-esteem, self-respect and emotional well-being, such autonomy displays itself in a responsible, independent, tenacious, innovative and enterprising will to achieve. Second, tolerance of others: stemming from a willingness to respect self, family and others, such tolerance requires an awareness of social diversity and the ability to value the aspirations and achievements of others; it reveals itself in active participation in society, a concern to work for the common good, and a desire to challenge discrimination. Third, reasoned argument: flowing from a joyful and confident commitment to learning, the capacity for reasoned argument will produce enquiring minds able to think rationally, critically and creatively; it will manifest itself in informed choices, balanced consumer judgements, and an ability to manage risk and cope with change and adversity. Fourth, truth seeking: there is tacit recognition of the importance of the pursuit of truth, both in terms of the material content of the curriculum, and through the identification of a concern for truth as a key virtue alongside those of self-understanding, curiosity about the world, and the holding of reasonable beliefs.

Though QCA clearly identifies truth as an important issue, it does not go on to discuss it in any detail, and it is clearly the least significant of the four core virtues we have identified. However, in *Religious Education: The Non-Statutory National Framework* the central importance of questions of truth is self-evident (DfES/QCA, 2004). Addressing the first of the two general education aims identified by QCA – to provide all pupils with the opportunity to learn and achieve – the Framework begins by speaking generally about the place of knowledge, understanding and skills in religious education, the importance of progress and attainment, and the need to ensure that pupils find the subject stimulating, interesting and enjoyable. It then goes on to suggest that, by enhancing their capacity to think coherently and consistently, religious education will promote 'an enquiring approach in which pupils carefully consider issues of beliefs and truth', thereby enabling them 'to evaluate thoughtfully their own and other's views in a reasoned and informed manner' (p. 8). The second general aim – to promote spiritual, moral, social and cultural development in preparation for life's opportunities, responsibilities and experiences – is directly linked to the observation that 'at the heart of this national framework for religious education is a focus on ultimate questions and ethical issues' (p. 8). This focus enables pupils to 'appreciate their own and others' beliefs and cultures' and 'gain a clear understanding of the significance of religions and beliefs in the world today' (pp. 8f). Given QCA's insistence on the interdependence of these two aims, it is clear that the evaluation of issues of truth relates directly to personal development.

This interpretation is confirmed in the section of the document dealing with the importance of religious education, which begins with the assertion that religious education 'provokes challenging questions about the ultimate meaning and purpose of life, beliefs about God, the self and the nature of reality, issues of right and wrong and what it means to be human' (p. 7). Religious education should encourage pupils to 'learn from different religions, beliefs, values and traditions while exploring their own beliefs and questions of meaning', and challenge them to 'reflect on, consider, analyse, interpret and evaluate issues of truth, belief, faith and ethics and to communicate their responses' (p. 7).

QCA's reading of the 1988 legislation clearly embraces political liberalism and views the pursuit of truth as an integral part of religious education. We cannot abstract religious education from its political context, and it is significant that the government, through the National Framework, commends the importance of the pursuit of truth to the local Standing Advisory Councils for Religious Education – the bodies responsible for curriculum development in community schools – as well as to the various religious communities responsible for the subject in faith-based schools. It is also noteworthy that the Framework was prepared with the support of a steering group made up of representatives of a wide range of faith communities and professional organizations, all of whom endorsed the final document. These include representatives of the major religious traditions present in the United Kingdom, the British Humanist Association, the influential Inter-Faith Network, the Professional Council for Religious Education, and the Association of University Lecturers in Religion and Education. Hence our attempt to justify a critical approach to religious education proceeds from a general consensus across the relevant religious and professional communities that the pursuit of truth does indeed have an important place within contemporary religious education.

5.2 A moral justification

A further justification for pursuing truth in religious education is that we have a moral duty to seek to hold true beliefs because our beliefs influence the way we behave. As Richard Swinburne points out, there is a logical connection between belief and action: 'a man's beliefs carry consequences about how he will seek to bring about his purposes' (Swinburne, 1983, p. 12). Our intentional actions necessarily draw on a raft of beliefs. This is so even for our most mundane activities: we switch on a kettle in the belief that this will cause water to boil and answer the telephone because we believe somebody is trying to contact us. More profoundly, we try to respect others because we believe it is the right thing to do, and if we pray we do so because we believe God exists and will listen to us. This is not to ignore that fact that the relationship between beliefs and actions is often merely tacit, and that there are many times when – whether due to negligence, moral weakness or deliberate fault – we fail to act in accordance with our beliefs. Nevertheless, since our beliefs normally guide and influence our actions and therefore impact directly on the lives of others, it follows that we have a moral responsibility to strive to hold true beliefs.

The two attainment targets for religious education set out in the National Framework clearly reflected the moral dimension of believing (DfES/QCA, 2004, p. 34). The first target requires pupils to learn about religion: their investigation of the nature of religion will focus especially on beliefs, teachings, practices, ways of life and forms of religious expression. This process will bring them face-to-face with ultimate questions that require interpreting, analysing and explaining. The second target requires pupils to learn from religion: they will reflect on, and respond to, their own experiences in the light of their exploration of religion. This entails asking questions about personal identity, values and commitments, relationships with others, the meaning and purpose of life, and ultimate truth. By learning to interpret, evaluate and communicate their responses to such questions, pupils will begin to establish beliefs and patterns of behaviour in preparation for the opportunities and challenges that life affords. There is a reciprocal relationship between these two attainment targets. The process of learning *about* religious truth claims constitutes an integral part of the process of learning *from* such claims as pupils strive to develop an understanding of their place in the ultimate order-of-things; similarly, reflection on their own beliefs and values will enable them to engage with questions about ultimate reality and come to a better understanding of the beliefs, values and worldviews of others. One of the intended outcomes of this hermeneutical circle is clear: in order to enhance their moral development pupils ought to strive to establish, to the best of their ability, true beliefs about the ultimate nature of reality by exploring a range of different religious and secular belief systems.

There are three major criticisms of this position that we need to consider.

a) The first objection denies that holding true beliefs is a prerequisite for good actions, and claims that striving after true beliefs can even have a detrimental effect on morality. The sequence of the argument tends to run as follows: religions encourage their adherents to commit wholeheartedly to their beliefs, such deep commitment tends to breed fanaticism, and fanaticism frequently gives birth to violence (Armstrong, 2001). Moreover, this vicious cycle is most likely to be broken if we learn to hold our beliefs in a more relaxed and ambivalent manner (Rorty, 1989). This being the case, religious education ought to avoid any strenuous pursuit of truth. The underlying assumption is that by bracketing out questions of truth and thereby 'eliminating religious, political, social, and economic differences, humanity [will] finally be able to achieve unity' (McGrath, 2004, p. 173). This argument has had a significant impact on religious education. In the previous chapter, we noted the loosening of the connection between belief and action brought about by the reification of the concepts of 'learning about' and 'learning from' religion. As a result, it was assumed that pupils can develop spiritually without recourse to any specific beliefs or belief system. It was against this background that John Hull put forward his influential suggestion that, whereas strict adherence to religious doctrines tends to foster forms of 'religionism' which divide society by promoting tribalistic attitudes, forms of spirituality not overtly and aggressively concerned with religious doctrines are more likely to lead to social harmony. It follows that any connection between true beliefs and authentic morality is, at best, tenuous and, at worst, the source of significant divisions within society (Hull, 1998, pp. 54ff).

This claim is open to question. The suggestion that specific beliefs are not central to the moral outlooks of faith traditions fails to do justice to their self-understanding; on the contrary, the morality espoused by the vast majority of the world's religions flows directly from their belief systems. Thus, for example, Muslims seek to be merciful because they believe Allah to be merciful, not because they subscribe to the value system of secular liberalism. This being the case, the demand that they bracket out their beliefs and relinquish their deepest commitments in favour of an alien viewpoint imposed by Western liberals appears unlikely to promote social harmony; indeed, it is likely to be seen as a threat that requires active resistance – even, for a small but significant minority, violent resistance. The irony here is that it is not so much Islamic belief that threatens the fabric of Western society, as the liberal perceptions of its relative unimportance; or, perhaps more accurately, some Islamic responses to the hegemony of comprehensive liberalism (Gray, 2003). Further, Hull's position itself is not free from doctrinal commitment: he holds firmly to the belief that firmly held beliefs tend to undermine moral behaviour. To claim that authentic morality is grounded in the denial of cultural identity is not to identify some pre-cultural neutral space but to impose a specific cultural identity: that of the autonomous self-realizing individual brought into being by the Enlightenment. This suggests that the old slogan 'it does not matter what you believe; it is what you do that counts' is mistaken (Swinburne, 1983, p.74). What actually 'counts' is not whether or not we hold beliefs, since the holding of beliefs is unavoidable, but the nature, truth and moral content of our beliefs.

b) The second objection is that it we are not actually free to choose our beliefs. Thus, if I do not believe in God, I cannot simply make myself believe through a sheer act of will. Swinburne's response is to suggest that although we 'cannot help having the beliefs we hold at any given time, we can be held to task for not doing something about our beliefs over a period' (p. 72). Although we cannot *immediately* avoiding holding our current beliefs, there is nothing to stop us subjecting them to critical scrutiny in order to test their trustworthiness *in the longer term*. If we wish to hold rationally justifiable beliefs rather than purely arbitrary ones – and I assume that it is self-evident that this is the better option – we have no option but to investigating our beliefs in an appropriate manner: by gathering evidence, weighing-up counter-evidence, making informed judgements and so forth.

c) The third objection is that a true belief about the ultimate nature of reality is not necessarily a moral one. Imagine a world in which the ultimate reality is a despotic God who demands that his followers systematically annihilate unbelievers. In order to retain moral integrity in such a situation, we would need to respond to our true beliefs about the existence of this demonic divinity with an act of 'ontological rebellion' against what we believe to be the ultimate organizing principle of the universe (Dostoyevsky, 1958, pp. 28ff; Jones, 1976, pp. 178ff; Sutherland, 1984, pp. 1ff). If this argument is correct, there is no necessary connection between true beliefs and morality. However, in making this act of ontological rebellion, we actually affirm the belief that our sense of goodness, rather than the immoral power of God, is *itself* the ultimate moral principle in the universe. In which case, our true beliefs about the ultimate order-of-things remain profoundly moral, albeit deeply tragic: we affirm goodness as the ultimate ontological reality, and identify the despotic God as simply the most powerful – rather than ultimate – reality.

Given the fact that our beliefs impact on our actions, that it is impossible to separate actions from beliefs at any deep level, and that it is possible to take responsibility for the formation of our beliefs over a period of time, it follows that we have a moral duty to strive to hold truth beliefs.

5.3 The well-being of society

A further justification for the pursuit of truth in religious education is that it is likely to enhance the well-being of society. Ever since *Learning for Living*, the forerunner of the *British Journal of Religious Education*, ran a special edition in conjunction with the Commission for Racial Equality in the late 1960s, the role of religious education in helping promote tolerance and mutual understanding in a diverse multicultural and multi-faith society has been recognized. According to *Education for All*, the Swann Report on the education of children from ethnic minority groups, 'religious education can play a central role in preparing pupil's for life in today's multi-racial Britain [by] challenging and countering the influence of racism in our society' (Swann Report, 1985, p.496). The aspiration is repeated in the National Framework: religious education 'helps pupils to gain a clear understanding of the significance of religions and beliefs in the world' by promoting 'religious understanding, discernment and respect and challenge prejudice and stereotyping' (DfES/QCA, 2004, p. 9). This is certainly a laudable aim, which few right-minded people would wish to disagree with.

However, it raises a crucial question: Has the pursuit of truth in religious education anything positive to contribute to the liberal desire to promote social harmony? The answer is not immediately obvious. Possibly a simple *description* of the beliefs of religious communities is all that is required to achieve this end. Indeed, the rigorous *exploration* and *evaluation* of such beliefs may only serve to highlight fundamental differences between different traditions and hence run the risk of generating social tensions. My suggestion is that, on the contrary, a religious education committed to the meticulous pursuit of truth is far more likely to promote a harmonious society than one concerned merely to describe diverse truth claims.

We have already seen that a blanket tolerance is not a moral option for society, since it would require tolerance of the intolerable – racist beliefs, sexist behaviour and so forth. If social harmony is to be encouraged, pupils must learn to discriminate between situations in which tolerance is appropriate and ones that demand active intolerance. It follows that they need to learn to be attentive and discerning in their encounters with different religious and secular traditions, since judgements based on ignorance or misunderstanding are unlikely to be appropriate. Clearly, there can be no place for moral attitudes based on superficial 'religionist' attitudes: 'We are orthodox; they are infidel. We are believers; they are unbelievers. We are right; they are wrong' (Cooling, 2000, p. 76, quoting Hull, 1992, p. 70). At the same time, however, those committed to attending to the worldviews of others when making moral judgements need to avoid the danger of relying on superficial understandings filtered through the prevailing norms of Western culture. In particular, the liberal commitment to the equality of all human beings runs the risk of emphasizing similarities between religious traditions and circumnavigating fundamental differences. Ideological modes of thought, whether oriented towards differences or similarities between traditions, are unlikely to meet with universal approval, and as such threaten to leave those who think differently marginalized and disgruntled. We do well here to heed Levinas' call to acknowledge the Other as Other, and develop a profound respect for the alterity of the 'sacred space' that divides religious traditions (Wright, 2004a, pp. 48ff, 2007a). This requires pupils not merely to identify similarities and differences between different religious traditions, but more fundamentally to experience the full weight of their particular understandings of the ultimate order-of-things. In doing so, they will be demonstrating deep respect: even more so if they extend the courtesy of engaging with the possibility that an alternative worldview might actually be true. Thus, a deep attentiveness to questions of truth is necessary if pupils are to learn to choose between tolerance and intolerance is specific situations.

Further, such grappling with issues of truth will inevitably raise the question of the grounds on which to make moral decisions. Edwin Cox attacks the 1988 *Education Reform Act* for ignoring 'philosophical attempts to establish a basis for morality on rational and empirical grounds, independent of a transcendental belief system' (White, 2004b, p. 159, quoting Cox and Cairns, 1989, p. 78; cf. Wright, 2004b). This contrasts with his earlier view that 'the true motivation for moral conduct is the realization that this particular action is right in some way because it accords with the underlying purpose of creation' (White, 2004b, p.159; quoting Cox

1966, p. 59). Commenting on this shift in Cox's thinking, John White suggests that we have no grounds for assuming that there is any underlying purpose to creation; and even if we had, it does not necessarily follow that such a purpose is good rather than malevolent, especially given the fact that God's precepts, as revealed in the Bible, 'are often massively out of line with our own moral thinking' (p. 159). He goes on to draw attention to the existence of a variety of utilitarian and naturalistic moral philosophies to make clear that morality can indeed exist independently of religion.

White's argument does not establish that some form of religious belief is *not* the authentic ground of morality – merely that there are viable secular alternatives. If it is true that we have no firm grounds for belief in God, it is equally true that we have no firm grounds for affirming atheism: the simply fact is that there is currently no consensus within society about this, either amongst academics or the public at large. At the risk of oversimplification, we can say that the ground of morality is either God as the ultimate source of being, the natural order as the ultimate source of life, or human decision making by virtue of our position at the summit of the evolutionary process (Collier, 1999). While White apparently predicates his own understanding of morality on the latter of these options, others ground morality in specific religious worldviews. Thus, we cannot speak of a single morality, only a cluster of different overlapping moralities closely linked to different claims about the ultimate order-of-things.

This suggests that if pupils are to make informed moral decisions likely to enhance the well-being of society, then they must learn to be attentive to the truth claims of different religious and secular traditions within society. This is because such truth claims generate distinctive understandings of the ground, nature and substance of morality. Further, when choosing between tolerance and intolerance in any given situation, they must necessarily make their own judgements – or embrace the judgements of the communities they belong to – about the morality they espouse, and hence also about their understanding of the relationship between morality and the ultimate order-of-things. It follows that the pursuit of truth has an important role to play in the cultivation of a harmonious society: judgements about whether to respond to a moral challenge with tolerance or resistance require a broader moral framework and, in the absence of any agreement as to which of many available frameworks is the most appropriate, we must make informed choices between them. To do so requires an appropriate depth of understanding of the worldviews that support different moral visions.

But what of the fear that the exploration of mutually exclusive truth claims will serve to undermine tolerance by engineering tensions between adherents of different religious and secular traditions, thereby setting pupil against pupil and community against community? We must take this objection extremely seriously indeed, not least because of the state of race relations in Britain today. In July 2001, some of the worst riots in 20 years broke out in the northern English cities of Oldham, Bradford and Burnley. Although the rioters came from many different ethnic groups, the majority were disaffected Asian youths. The official report on the disturbances, commissioned by the former Home Secretary David Blunkett, and written by Ted Cantle, chair of the independent Community Cohesion Review Team, identified social segregation as a major contributing factor (Cantle Report, 2001). On the understanding that segregation inevitably undermines social cohesion, the Cantle Report called on politicians, community leaders and the media to promote a meaningful concept of shared citizenship. Cantle recognized that segregation is often self-imposed by minority communities, and pointed to a range of different contributory factors: economic deprivation, right-wing political extremism, the influence of the media, drug abuse, poor education, etc. He suggested that schooling has a major role to play in breaking the cycle of social segregation, and that attention should be given to citizenship education and the admission policies of both community and faith-based schools. The report recommended that at least 25 per cent of available places in faith community schools be reserved for children from alternative backgrounds.

Religious education clearly has a major role to play in nurturing a tolerant, pluralistic, multicultural and multi-faith society. The crucial issue is a pragmatic one: how best to achieve this? The Cantle Report steers a path between two extremes: on the one hand the dangers of affirming the distinctive identities of individual communities at the expense of their inclusion within society as a whole; on the other the dangers of a social assimilation that dissolves minority communal identity within a greater whole. Between the extremes of segregation and assimilation lies the option of forms of social integration that respect the distinctiveness of minority groups. I have suggested elsewhere that the British Government's policy of encouraging a mixed economy of faith-based schools alongside non-affiliated community schools constitutes a step in the right direction (Wright, 2003a). The basis of my argument is that social integration is unlikely to be successfull unless minority faith communities first feel their religious and cultural identities to be secure, and that such security involves the ability to transmit their beliefs and culture to their children.

> There is . . . good reason to think that a secure sense of shared identity constitutes a necessary pre-condition if a minority group is to engage positively with broader society. Only when a community feels secure in itself can it risk seeking to establish quality relationships with those beyond its boundaries. The examples of Judaism and Roman Catholicism come to mind here. They undoubtedly constitute the most successful of mainland Britain's religious minorities in integrating, rather than assimilating, themselves into mainstream society and contributing to the common good.
>
> (p. 149)

Our primary concern here, however, is with the exploration of religious truth in pluralistic religious education classrooms, rather than broader educational policy. What might be the consequences of *not* engaging with such questions? First, it would be profoundly patronizing of minority faith communities: 'Of course we value your culture, but not enough to have any genuine interest in your deepest beliefs, and certainly not at the level of considering the possibility that they might actually be true'. Second, it would imply the superiority of a liberal moral economy that proclaims that freedom of belief and tolerance of the beliefs of others – as opposed to, say, submission to the will of Allah – as moral absolutes. Third, it would reinforce fears amongst religious adherents about the misrepresentation of their faith, not least through a reductionism that focuses on the horizontal plane of religion-as-cultural rather than the vertical plane of religion-as-transcendent-belief. Fourth, it would do nothing to help pupils establish a formative understanding of the genuine differences that exist between groups, an understanding that is vital if mutual respect is to be anything more than skin deep. The net result of the failure to attend to questions of truth would be a form of social engineering rather than genuine education; more disconcertingly still, a form of social engineering that fails to give due respect to the self-understanding of minority faith communities. In effect, a programme of assimilation would replace a policy of integration, and as such would be likely to draw the defensive response of self-imposed segregation amongst minority pupils and hence only encourage further social division.

A flourishing plural society is one in which different groups can *both* celebrate their distinctive identities *and* engage fully in the life of society as a whole. In order to achieve this, a degree of openness and honesty is vital; this requires a willingness and ability to take both difference and commonality seriously. My contention is that the exploration of questions of religious truth, and hence the establishment of appropriate levels of religious literacy, is a basic prerequisite of such a society. Provided we conduct lessons in an appropriately sensitive manner, the exploration of religious truth promises to be a crucial tool for social integration. The genuine differences that mark our rich pluralistic society are not simply going to go away if we pretend they don't exist, nor – unless we subscribe to comprehensive liberalism – should we want them to. Sooner or later, profound, and in many cases welcome, differences within society will manifest themselves – and it is surely better to address them in a sensitive manner in a classroom context than confront them on the alcohol-fuelled streets of our inner cities on Friday nights.

5.4 Spiritual formation

Critical religious education is also justified by virtue of its contribution to spiritual formation. Our previous assumption, that a good society is by definition a harmonious one, begs many questions, since we can envisage a society in urgent need of destabilization – Nazi Germany in the 1930s, for example. Liberalism sees social harmony as a prerequisite for autonomy, and autonomy as 'a necessary condition of individuals' making for themselves what they regard as a good life' (Kekes, 1999, p. 8). This raises two crucial questions: How should pupils exercise autonomy? What constitutes 'a good life'? Political liberalism equates autonomy with the practice of wisdom: the freedom to make informed judgements about our place in the world. Comprehensive liberalism, especially in its postmodern guise, identifies freedom simply with the unconstrained pursuit of personal desire. Both responses are procedural: they point to the *process* through which human beings might flourish, rather than to the *substance* of such flourishing. Comprehensive liberals, as we have already noted, respond by equating process with substance: to act freely *is* to live the good life. Political liberals, although they raise questions about the good life, studiously avoid offering any concrete answers, beyond that of insisting of the value of approaching such questions intelligently.

Comprehensive liberal accounts of the spiritual quest tend to reject the notion that human flourishing has anything to do with questions of truth. If the exercise of autonomy is an intrinsic good, and there are no external criteria with which to assess spiritual development, then we are free to establish our own preferred understanding of human flourishing. In a postmodern context, in which personal preference is equated with desire, we are free to create the spiritual visions that satisfy us, without reference to any external authority. However, it is not clear that seeking to satisfy our desires is an adequate basis for human flourishing. Given both the degree of evil in the world and the fallibility of human nature, many of our immediate desires may be deeply harmful, both to ourselves and to those around us – we cannot, for example, promote a society that encourages paedophiles to fulfil their deepest wishes. Further, despite its professed disinterest in questions of truth, comprehensive liberalism actually offers a clear picture of the nature of reality, as experienced by human beings, and of the kind of spiritual quest appropriate to that reality: if individuals are free to create meaning in a manner that satisfies their desires, then self-determination constitutes the ultimate spiritual truth.

Political liberalism's approach to the spiritual quest, which recognizes the need to temper desire with reason, has far more to offer. An informed respect for reason and its limitations constitutes a more reliable guide to the spiritual quest than raw desire. This turn to reason suggests a need to establish a true understanding of our place in the ultimate order-of-things, and implies that, as relational beings, we cannot fully engage with spiritual issues merely by exploring our private 'inner space'. As I have argued elsewhere, our spiritual lives are determined by the nature of our relationships with ourselves, with other people, with communities and institutions, with the natural world and with the reality – or non-reality – of a transcendent realm (Wright, 1998a, p. 88).

In *Star Trek the Motion Picture*, V'ger – a probe designed to travel through space and gather information about the universe – returns to its home planet in order to fulfil its mission by discharging the knowledge it has amassed. During its travels it has evolved into a sentient life form, and consequently seeks not merely to download its knowledge, but to speak face-to-face with its creator. She – since V'ger has long ceased to be an 'it' –wants to learn the meaning and purpose of her existence. According to one available version of the script – which differs slightly from the actual soundtrack – Spock muses about the dilemma facing V'ger: 'Each of us, at some time in our lives, turns to someone, a father, a brother, a God, and asks "Why am I here? What was I meant to be?"' Kirk, in a moment of rare lucidity, rephrases Spock's questions: 'Is this all that I am? Is there nothing more?' (Star Trek, 2005).

Such questions are fundamental to the human condition, and pupils should learn to engage intelligently with them. They are questions not merely about inner feelings, but more fundamentally about our place in the ultimate order-of-things. The National Framework suggests religious education should contribute to spiritual development by raising 'key questions of meaning and truth such as the origins of the universe, life after death, good and evil, beliefs about God and values such as justice, honesty and truth' (DfES/QCA, 2004, p. 14). Despite strenuous attempts in some sections of society to avoid such questions, religious education has a clear mandate to address them directly. Indeed, not to do so would have a detrimental effect, leaving pupils vulnerable to a range of severely restricted accounts of human flourishing – not least, accounts glorifying the economic forces of consumer capitalism and seeking to make us slaves of the advertizing industry. Although it may not be appropriate to advocate particular *answers* to such questions, teachers ought to affirm their inherent importance, offer a range of possible responses, and provide guidance on ways of exploring them.

What, then, of objections to this position?

a) One potential objection to the spiritual value of the pursuit of truth is that it threatens human freedom. Such a view has roots in the claim that confessional religious education's concern for truth is ultimately indoctrinatory. However – aside from the dubious nature of this claim – the pursuit of truth advocated here is immune to the charge because it seeks to engage critically with a diverse range of possible truths. However, the objection may run deeper, invoking both Foucault's claim that the very notion of objective truth is inherently repressive, and the claim of progressive child-centred educators that any impartation of knowledge is necessarily restrictive.

As we have already seen, political liberalism understands freedom as simultaneously freedom *from* coercive social and psychological forces and freedom *for* truthful relationships. This opens up a vision of education as empowerment for responsible and accountable citizenship. This contrasts sharply with comprehensive liberalism's reification of the notion of freedom *from* all forms of coercion into a moral absolute. Thus, Rousseau's twin doctrines of natural goodness and social corruption led him to advocate a negative education through which the child could develop naturally, isolated from all external influences. Rousseau's argument reflects Descartes' individualistic anthropology, with its suggestion that we discover our true selves through inner-contemplation and self-reflection. Drawing on this romantic tradition, progressive educators tend to regard any impartation of knowledge as indoctrinatory, while postmodern advocates of progressivism tend to equate knowledge with power, and consequently view any pursuit of truth as a threat to freedom. Such child-centred pedagogy is prevalent in contextual approaches to religious education that focus 'on the concrete and the particular, and less on the abstract and general . . . on religious life and less on religious doctrine' (Leganger-Krogstad, 2001, p. 55). Although contextual religious education is a complex phenomenon, there are certainly those amongst its adherents who seek to enable pupils to create their own spiritual meanings (Heimbrock, Scheilke and Schreiner, 2001; cf. Wright, 2003b). As such, they affirm the 'constructive responsibility' of pupils and 'the role of the subject as his/her owner of the formation process' (Heimbrock, Scheilke and Schreiner, 2001, p. 9). This implies we should assess spiritual development against the benchmark of the unique perspective of the individual pupil, and that any pursuit of truth threatens freedom by opening up the possibility of identifying some alternative external benchmark, such as the will of God or the doctrines of a particular religious community.

However, this negative notion of freedom is illusory: even if it were possible to achieve, the net result would be merely an induction into, and captivation within, a specific ideological claim – namely, that we encounter our true selves *only* by withdrawing from all external relationships and exploring our unique personal 'inner space'. In reality, we are relational creatures and consequently genuine autonomy lies in our ability to establish appropriate relationships with the outside world. This requires *both* emancipation from those repressive forces that distort our relationship with reality, *and* the ability to cultivate appropriate associations. Since we cannot possible escape the range of power structures that surround us, we must seek to establish appropriate responses to them. It is not a matter of avoiding authority, but of responding to authority in an appropriate manner: I choose to accept the authority of my doctor and car mechanic, but do not do so blindly – if I have reasonable cause to doubt their expertise, then I am free to seek a second opinion. I exercise my freedom not by ignoring authority, but by making reasoned judgements between authorities. If religious education bypasses the pursuit of truth, it will effectively deny pupils the freedom to make informed judgements between different authorities, and hence between religious and secular truth claims.

b) A second potential objection to the spiritual value of the pursuit of truth is that it is inherently intolerant. In addressing this objection, we return to a set of issues already touched on in this chapter. As we have observed, tolerance is an underdeveloped concept: there are many evils in society that are unworthy of tolerance, and some that require active intolerance. Comprehensive liberalism tends to generate a weak notion of tolerance, which seeks merely to affirm similarities and dissipate differences between potentially conflicting strands of society. This preference for sameness and similarity tends to support forms of Orientalism and Occidentalism: the former seeks to familiarize the 'Other' be exalting it as exotic and alluring, while the latter seeks to emasculate the 'Familiar' of its threatening features (Said, 1978, 1993). Thus – with apologies for the stereotype – certain white liberals appear as quick to celebrate and 'orientalize' the enthusiasm of black Pentecostal gospel choirs, as they are to despise and 'occidentalize' the zeal of white guitar-strumming evangelical Christians. Whether we make the unfamiliar familiar, or seek to rid the familiar of that which disconcerts us, the result is the same: an economy of sameness that can be profoundly patronizing. The pursuit of truth presents a direct threat to this weak notion of tolerance: affirmations of truth run hand-in-hand with presumptions of falsehood and hence inevitably highlight differences between individuals and groups.

I do not intend to question the basic value of tolerance here; however, the concept certainly requires qualification – we cannot invoke it to appease evil or cultivate a naive economy of sameness. Genuine tolerance demands forbearance: the humble and honest determination to live alongside those whose beliefs are incompatible with our own. When we gaze into the face of the 'Other', we have a mutual duty to maintain eye contact and acknowledge the differences between us, rather than look away and hide behind the pretence of similarity (Wright, 2004a, pp. 48ff, 2007a). Tolerance requires us to acknowledge our own beliefs and engage as respectfully as possible with the beliefs of others: finding points of accommodation where possible, but never hesitating to identify tensions, and even irreconcilable differences, when they arise. Failure to embrace the 'dignity of difference' in this way opens the door to hypocrisy, insincerity and paternalism (Sacks, 2003). The demand of the 'Other' is clear: 'don't patronize me, don't turn a blind eye to my deepest beliefs, just recognize me for whom I am'. As the people of South Africa discovered following the collapse of apartheid, there can be no peace without justice, no tolerance without honesty, no reconciliation without truth.

c) A third potential objection to the spiritual value of the pursuit of truth is that it is intrusive and fails to respect the privacy of pupils; a concern reflected in the fact that school inspectors in England and Wales can only assess the *provision* schools make for pupils' spiritual development, rather than their *actual* spiritual development. It is clearly inappropriate for teachers to invade pupils' 'inner space'. However, our spiritual identity does not reside exclusively in that place: insofar as we are relational creatures, there are certain spiritual issues that can properly be attended to in the public sphere. It is certainly true that our beliefs may be the result of intense soul searching in the light of key events in our private lives; however, it is equally true that it is possible to engage deeply with questions of ultimate truth without the need for intimate confession. Indeed, it is a sign of spiritual health that pupils are able to identify, articulate, celebrate and defend their core beliefs. A common criticism of religious education is its failure to engage with the crucial issues that give the lives of pupils meaning and purpose: if we are serious about supporting the development of the whole child, then we must find ways of doing so. The objection highlights the need for sensitive classroom teaching, rather than warrants the exclusion of questions of truth from the curriculum.

5.5 The intrinsic value of the pursuit of truth

The final argument for the justification of the pursuit of truth in religious education is that it constitutes an end in itself: the holding of true beliefs about our place in the ultimate order-of-things is intrinsically valuable, and as such requires no further validation. Of course, there may be occasions when believing a 'white lie' might *possibly* be a good thing: for example, hiding the true nature of a terminal illness from a sick child. Nevertheless, under normal circumstances the holding of true beliefs is intrinsically worthwhile, regardless of any other positive outcomes that might accrue. More broadly, it is inherently worthwhile to live a life in harmony with the ultimate order-of-things by holding true beliefs and attempting to live truthful lives in the light of them: thus, if God does not exist then is intrinsically good to be an atheist.

Is this claim justified? Is there not a danger of slipping into an infinitely regressive argument, in which every attempt to justify the intrinsic value of the pursuit of truth immediately requires further justification? This need not be the case. Many of our most valued beliefs are tacit ones to which we hold fast despite being unable to explain precisely why they are so important to us. Thus, we might acknowledge that genocide is intrinsically evil, but still struggle to provide an *absolute* explanation as to why *precisely* this is the case. As Wittgenstein once observed, eventually our deliberations hit bedrock and we have to say 'This is simply what we believe' (Wittgenstein, 1968, p. 85). This implies that whenever we assert the intrinsic value of something, then the truth of our claim ought to be immediately self-evident to us. The problem, however, is that the claim that the pursuit of truth constitutes an end in itself is, for some people at least, far from being patently obvious. However, if we cannot look for definitive proof in resolving this dilemma, we can at least seek for informed and balanced judgement. My suggestion will be that, despite reservations in some quarters, the intrinsic value of the pursuit of truth is *sufficiently* self-evident to justify its place within the religious education curriculum.

Before proceeding to the core of our argument, it will be helpful to pause and reflect on the notion of intrinsic value in the light of Gadamer's discussion of the role of art in our understanding of the world (Gadamer, 1979, pp. 91ff). He points out how, under the influence of Kant and Schiller, modern aesthetics came to see art in terms of the subjective states of mind of the artist and those enjoying the work of art. According to this view, when viewing a painting, we focus attention on our emotional responses and, through them, on the possibility of an empathetic engagement with the subjective emotions of the artist. Gadamer seeks to challenge this romantic approach to art by rehabilitating the 'the mode of being of the work of art itself' rather than focusing on responses to it (p. 91). Art, according to Gadamer, exists as an end in itself, not merely as a vehicle for the artist's self-expression or our sensual delight. If Picasso's *Les Demoiselles d'Avignon* has extrinsic value for many reasons – economic, social, psychological, political, cultural, and so forth – it is most fundamentally intrinsically valuable *in itself*. This is not simply to proclaim the message of 'art for art's sake', since the intrinsic worth of the painting lies precisely in its ability to challenge our ordinary horizons of understanding by opening out new horizons of meaning, new ways of looking at the world, new avenues towards truth. However, and this is the crucial point, these potential new horizons are embedded in the painting itself, and could not be available to us apart from its ontological reality.

Gadamer illustrates the intrinsic transformative value of art through the concept of 'play'. There are many extrinsic reasons why I might take part in a sporting event: to please the spectators, to keep fit, to obtain financial gain, to bolster my ego by scoring the winning goal, etc. On the one hand play is clearly not serious since 'the player himself knows that play is only play'; yet, on the other hand, it is 'only seriousness in playing [that] makes the play wholly play' (p. 91f). The person 'who does not take the play seriously' while all the other participants are doing so 'is a spoilsport' (p. 92). This is why we must play the game seriously by losing ourselves in it and accepting 'the primacy of play over the consciousness of the player' (p. 94). In such circumstances 'the real subject of the game . . . is not the player, but instead the game itself', and consequently the game becomes an intrinsic end in itself, something that is uniquely worthwhile and as such requires no further justification or explanation (pp. 95f). As in sport, so in the ordinary course of life; we encounter objects, people and beliefs, and engage in actions and events, within which we 'lose ourselves', and which become for us at the time intrinsically valuable and worthwhile.

Kant invites us to 'suppose there were something the *existence of which in itself* has an absolute worth, something which is *an end in itself*' (Kant, 1998, p. 36). What might this 'something' be? For Kant such absolute worth exists in the sphere of morality, specifically in the categorical imperative to treat people as possessing intrinsic worth, never as simply means to other ends (p. 38). There are, however, many other candidates: the sphere of nature, through contemplation of the intrinsic wonder of the natural world; the sphere of aesthetics, through experience of the intrinsic beauty of art, music and literature; the sphere of love, through the intrinsic value of the reciprocal gaze of lover and beloved; the sphere of religion, through the intrinsic worth of worshippng God or encountering transcendence. If both play and artistic creativity are basic human activities, then what holds them to together is a primal response to the world we find ourselves cast into – a primal response to the moral, natural, aesthetic, personal and spiritual order-of-things. If these are all intrinsically worthwhile activities that flow from the brute fact of our existence, then *absolute* worth lies in seeking to engage with, and respond to, the *ultimate* order-of-things.

John White has questioned my affirmation of 'the intrinsic value of an informed and critical engagement with the truth claims of religious and secular world views' (White, 2005, p. 22, commenting on Wright, 2004b, pp. 170f; cf. also White, 2004b; Wright, 2005). Although he accepts a certain value in encouraging children 'to reflect on religious and secular claims about the nature of reality', he views this merely as a path to the greater – and for him, intrinsically worthwhile – end of promoting the formation of pupils as autonomous beings. White's chief criticism is that I merely state my preferred position, 'without giving any more backing for it' (White, 2005, p. 22). He points out that many different activities constitute ends in themselves: 'For you these may include listening to Mozart and running marathons; for me, eating out and entomology' (p. 22). White here assumes the default position that we are free to choose for ourselves that which we consider to be of intrinsic worth, and argues that – this being the case – I have not shown why the pursuit of ultimate truth 'should be an end in itself for (virtually) *all schoolchildren*'(p. 22).

However, it is possible to reverse White's argument: he has no more shown why the pursuit of autonomy and specifically the freedom to designate *for ourselves* that which is of ultimate value constitutes an end in itself, than I have offered grounds for my claim that the pursuit of truth is intrinsically valuable. We have both hit the bedrock of our respective positions. However, there is a basic difference between us: White is concerned to proceed on the basis of a default position rooted in secular humanism's advocacy of autonomy is the greatest good: my concern, however, is to recognize that there are many different, and potentially viable, positions – including that defended by White himself – that warrant exploration in the classroom. Hence, where White seeks to impose a premature closure on the question of ultimate truth rooted in his commitment to secular humanism, I wish to empower pupils to grapple with a range of different responses to this question. In a plural society, the option of pursuing questions of truth seems to me to be more valid than that of imposing a single contested solution. White is actually advocating a form of secular confession-alism which, given its close structural parallels with traditional forms of Christian confessionalism, is singularly unsuited to the needs of a modern liberal society.

This criticism of White assumes that education should be concerned, at least in part, with questions of truth for their own sake. For White this is highly questionable:

> Good reasons have to be given why the pursuit of truth (in its different forms) for its own sake should be a key aim of education – as distinct from, for instance, equipping children to lead flourishing lives or become responsible citizens.
>
> (p. 22)

My response to this is challenge is two-fold. First, a negative comment: if I have an obligation to justify my position, White is under a similar obligation to give reasons why the pursuit of truth should *not* be a key aim of education. His response to this challenge is to claim that, following the demise of the 'transcendental' arguments of Peters and Hirst – which sought to ground education in the pursuit of objective 'forms' of knowledge generated by distinctive linguistic traditions – there are no viable foundations upon which to base a knowledge-driven curriculum. The implication is that learning in fields such as morality, aesthetics and religion cannot claim to be a pursuit of truth, merely an exchange of opinion. We will examine this charge in greater depth later in this book. For the present, it is sufficient to note that developments in epistemology since the work of Hirst and Peters, particularly those associated with the philosophy of critical realism, have shown the pursuit of moral, aesthetic and theological knowledge to be entirely valid intellectual exercises (Collier, 1999; Collier, 2003; Archer, Collier and Porpora, 2004). Interestingly, although Hirst himself recognized such developments, and in his later work sought to develop a new non-transcendental and non-foundationalist approach to the pursuit of truth in education, White takes the position that 'no arguments for it which are more reliable have since come my way' (White, 2005, p. 23).

Second, a positive comment: there are good reasons why the pursuit of truth for its own sake should be a key aim in education. We have already seen that both the secular and faith communities, in putting their names to the National Framework for Religious Education, treated the value of the pursuit of truth as self-evident. Further, the recognition that education and truth are necessary partners is deeply rooted in both the classical humanistic and religious traditions of Western education. Knowledge of ourselves, and of our place in the universe, has consistently been seen as a vitally important dimension of a rounded education, not merely for any potential pragmatic capital or cultural utility, but simply because it has been seen to be important in itself. As Swinburne points out:

> Governments and other benefactors give billions of pounds to men to investigate the structure of the atom, the distribution of the galaxies, the history of science and of culture, and the geological history of the Earth; and they do not give solely because they suppose that such knowledge has technological value.
>
> (Swinburne, 1983, p. 76)

If an activity is of intrinsic worth, then, by definition, it cannot be justified by any other criteria than its own intrinsic value. The fact that the pursuit of truth has always been central to human nature, to the progress of culture, and to the history of education is sufficient warrant for recognizing its intrinsic value.

> Knowledge is valuable in itself, and especially knowledge of things which concern the nature, origin and purpose of our particular human community; and the nature, origin and purpose of the Universe itself . . . [and] what more central piece of knowledge could there be about the origin, nature and purpose of man and the Universe, than whether they depend for their being on a God who made them, or whether the Universe and all that is in it, and the laws of their operation, just are, dependent upon nothing?
>
> (pp. 76, 80)

5.6   Conclusion

I have argued that there are good reasons for embracing a critical religious education that seeks to pursue questions of truth and cultivate truthful attitudes and behaviour in the context of a plural society organized around the principles of political liberalism. The current legislation for religious education gives a clear mandate for critical religious education, and there are good moral, social and spiritual reasons why this mandate should be followed. In addition, many human beings hold it to be self-evident that pursuing questions about our place in the ultimate order-of-things is a supremely worthwhile activity.

Part III
A Heuristic Framework

6

Ontology: the ultimate order of things

Part III will map the contours of a heuristic conceptual framework for critical religious education designed to foster the pursuit of truth and cultivate truthful living. Such a framework will need to meet a number of criteria. First, it must be *focused*, capable of clearly identifying and articulating the key issues. Second, it must be *inclusive*, capable of guiding the work of the vast majority of religious educators regardless of any faith commitments or educational philosophies. Third, it must be *open*, capable of doing justice to a broad range of religious and secular truth claims, including those of non-realists. Fourth, it must be *flexible*, capable of responding to new thinking and practices. Fifth, it must be *permissive*, capable of entertaining conversations with those who find themselves unable to embrace it wholeheartedly. The framework will be multidimensional, designed to open up four complementary perspectives on the issue of religious truth: ontological, semantic, hermeneutic, and epistemological. Each raises a distinctive set of questions. The *ontological* perspective addresses questions about the ultimate nature of reality. The *semantic* perspective addresses questions about the way we use language to describe ultimate reality. The *hermeneutic* perspective addresses questions about the process of understanding different truth claims. The *epistemological* perspective addresses questions about our ability to judge between conflicting truth claims.

The present chapter focuses on the first of these perspectives: the ontology of the ultimate order-of-things. Since our access to ultimate reality is mediated, we must look for appropriate authorities for our knowledge. The reality of epistemic relativism means that such authorities are contested, and hence we must employ judgemental rationality to weigh-up their respective merits. Given the historical identity of religious education, I take it to be entirely proper that the subject focus primarily on *religious* accounts of ultimate reality; however, in order to put these into proper perspective it is necessary to explore non-religious accounts as well. I will propose three foci designed to help guide the exploration of religious truth claims. First, a focus on *transcendent realism*: religions make realistic claims about the existence of some form of ultimate reality transcending the immanent reality of our time-and-space-bound universe. Second, a focus on *discrete religious traditions*: the primary bearers of such claims are distinct religious traditions, rather than generic accounts of religion generated in the academy or the spiritual experiences of individuals. Third, a focus on *salvific communities*: the world's religions present their distinctive belief systems in the context of communities orientated towards salvation and/or enlightenment.

6.1 Transcendent realism

We begin with the claim that most religions offer realistic accounts of transcendent reality. The vast majority of religious traditions embrace a realistic understanding of truth: 'being religious' is not simply a way of looking at the world, rather it entails making a substantial 'claim about the nature of all reality' (Markham, 1998, p. 16; Moore, 2003; Patterson, 1999). If reality exists independently of our ability to know it, then a religious proposition is true 'if and only if the state of affairs that it expresses (describes) is real' (Bhaskar, 1977, p. 249). Peter Byrne defines 'minimal theistic realism' as 'any interpretation of theism which holds that the governing intent of core theistic concepts is (or ought to be) to refer to a reality which is epistemically independent of human beings, ontologically distinct from them and transcendent' (Byrne, 2003, p. 16). This is a helpful definition, provided we extend it to include non-theistic religious traditions and recognize that it is possible to hold such beliefs without utilizing the language of the Western philosophical tradition.

The precise scope and nature of the ultimate order-of-things is, of course, a matter of dispute. It might be that reality is simply the sum total of the objects, events and forces in the natural world; religions dispute this, claiming that the natural world is contingent or illusory and looking beyond it to some transcendent reality. Back in 1975, the Birmingham *Agreed Syllabus of Religious Instruction* courted controversy by including Humanism and Communism alongside discrete religious traditions as life stances worthy of consideration in the classroom (City of Birmingham Education Committee, 1975). *Living Together*, the accompanying teachers' manual, was clear that these secular life stances are not religions, but rather *alternatives* to religion (City of Birmingham District Council Education Committee, 1975). What then distinguishes a distinctively *religious* life stance from a secular one? Ninian Smart's six-fold typology differentiates between 'historical' (ritualistic, experiential and social) and 'parahistorical' (doctrinal, mythological and ethical) dimensions of religion (Smart, 1968). Since the life stances of religious communities are inseparable from their belief systems, 'to omit the parahistorical would be to seriously distort the nature of religion' (Hull, 1984, p. 95). If religious and secular worldviews both offer particular stances for living, what distinguishes them is the substance of their respective belief systems: where secular life stances offer accounts of reality rooted in the natural world, religious life stances offer accounts rooted in some transcendent order.

The Birmingham Syllabus offered an understanding of religion that continues to be an appropriate starting point for religious education. Mircea Eliade's identification of the essence of religion, rooted as it is in a contrast between the transcendent/sacred and immanent / profane, supports this position (Eliade, 1987). Religion, he argues, is oriented towards some ultimate being or reality that transcends the natural world bounded by time and space. The spatial metaphor of transcendence identifies a realm over and above that of nature and ordinary human experience, and invokes a fundamental distinction between supranatural (religious) and natural (secular) accounts of reality. (It is important to note, as will become clear later, that the appeal to Eliade in this context does *not* imply acceptance of his notion of the 'essence' of religion.)

The traditional term for this transcendent realm is 'supernatural'. However, the debasement of the term following the emergence of the natural sciences, and it subsequent association with superstition, magic and the occult, invalidates its use in the present cultural context. Hence, my employment of the less value-laden term 'supranatural' to describe that reality which, according to most religious traditions, transcends the natural order. Other metaphors, in addition to transcendental ones, could potentially prove valuable in this context. In the 1960s, John Robinson, following Paul Tillich, famously argued that the spatial metaphor of 'depth' might prove more valuable for Christians seeking to understand God than the more traditional metaphors of 'height', 'distance' and 'separation' (Robinson, 1963; Tillich, 1951, pp. 163ff). The image of God as the 'depth of being' and 'ground of life' avoids the associations of supernaturalism with magic and transcendence with crude images of a 'god up in the sky'. Since 'we are familiar today with depth psychology, and with the idea that ultimate truth is deep or profound', it follows that 'this simple substitution can make much religious language suddenly appear more relevant' (Robinson, 1963, p. 45). Whatever our choice of metaphor, it is the ontological reality to which religious language refers that is of central importance here.

Pantheism, in identifying the sacred with nature, apparently undermines the suggestion that religions make transcendent truth claims. This is an important issue, especially given the inclusion of the Hindu tradition and the New Age Movement in many syllabuses. It is a characteristic belief of the New Age that 'all life – all existence – is the manifestation of Spirit, of the Unknowable, of that supreme consciousness known by many different names in many different cultures' (Heelas, 1996, p. 225). However, this is closer to panentheism, according to which the natural world is not identical to the divine, but rather 'constitutes an expression of a higher, more comprehensive divine nature' (p. 226). Even if we concede the existence of a thoroughgoing pantheistic equation of nature and divinity, this does not undermine our basic thesis that the religions are *in the main* concerned with a supranatural reality. Supranatural belief as sufficiently normative of religion in general to constitute an appropriate heuristic vantage point from which we can go on to address and contrast pantheistic, naturalistic and non-realistic alternatives.

What then of potential objections to the proposition that religions make supranatural truth claims? We will consider naturalist and non-realist accounts that accept that religions make such claims but deny their truth, and reductionist accounts which hold that religions do not actually make such claims.

We begin with naturalistic and anti-realistic claims that such accounts of reality are mistaken. Naturalistic interpretations of religion are represented by a tradition flowing from Nietzsche that includes luminaries such as Marx and Feuerbach and Freud (Kung, 1980). According to this tradition, religious adherents are mistaken in believing in a transcendent reality, and it is possible to explain the emergence and persistence of such beliefs on purely naturalistic grounds – for instance, as the product of psychological projection. Whether we accept this critique of religious belief is immaterial here; what *is* significant is that naturalistic critiques of religion assume the realistic nature of religious belief and as such confirm the basic supranatural orientation of religion. Anti-realistic accounts of religion constitute a distinctively postmodern interpretative tradition. According to Don Cupitt, whatever the function of religious language might be, it certainly cannot be that of engaging with ultimate reality (Wright, 2004a, pp. 82ff). He insists that the correspondence theory of truth is a 'poor tool to use for assessing religious beliefs', that 'much of religious language and ritual is expressive rather than descriptive in its force', and that 'theological realism is therefore a crude mistake' (Cupitt, 1980, p. 11). Consequently, theologians should abandon any notion that the role of religious language is to engage with ultimate reality and instead learn to use the term 'God' as 'a unifying symbol that eloquently personifies and represents to us everything that spirituality requires of us' (p. 9). The crucial issue here is the fact that a staunchly anti-realist theologian such as Cupitt takes for granted the basic realistic orientation of traditional religious belief systems, and sees this as something in urgent need of deconstruction. The very fact that Cupitt views theological realism as intellectually, morally, aesthetically and spiritually untenable, and seeks to replace it with a thoroughgoing anti-realistic theology, simply serves to underline the inherently realistic orientation of the vast majority of religious traditions. The aspirational 'ought' of anti-realistic a/theology, unimaginable apart from the pragmatic outlook of postmodernity, simply confirms the 'is' of traditional religious realism.

Turning then to reductionist interpretations, which deny religions actually extend realistic truth claims: what are we to make of the suggestion that generally speaking religious communities have no interest in proffering accounts of transcendent reality? A recent discussion of contextual religious education claimed that, 'except in special practices such as science', human beings 'do not strive for the final truth about the world' but instead 'are content with satisfying meanings . . . that enable them to act in a satisfying manner in a given situation' (Heimbrock, Scheilke and Schreiner, 2001, p. 28). Such claims do not offer secondary interpretations of religious practice designed to highlight their non-realistic status despite their realistic intentions, but rather primary empirical descriptions of the actual self-understanding of religious believers. The suggestion is not that religious adherents ought to abandon their realistic beliefs, but that *it is a mistake to assume that they actually hold such beliefs.* How justifiable is this claim that mainstream adherents of the Buddhist, Christian, Hindu, Jewish, Muslim and Sikh traditions are aware that their beliefs are simply pious fictions, functioning instrumentally to enable them to live flourishing lives yet bearing no relationship to any actual state of affairs in the real world? There are four prima facie reasons for rejecting this position.

a) The presence of non-realistic believers in a community is not in itself sufficient warrant for claiming religious beliefs are basically non-realistic. There will always be religious adherents whose beliefs are at odds with those of their religious communities. Take, for example, the many so-called 'nominal' members of the Church of England who apparently utilize the ceremonies of the established church to celebrate key rites of passage without demonstrating any deep-rooted interest in transcendent truth claims embodied in Anglican doctrine. It is palpably clear that such behaviour does not warrant the conclusion that the Church of England does not make realistic truth claims. Rather, in utilizing Christianity for what – on the surface at least – appears to be merely cultural purposes, such Anglicans embrace a *reductive* understanding of Christianity that falls short of the collective self-understanding of mainstream members of the Church of England, as evidenced in the historical continuity of its preaching, teaching, liturgy and creedal statements. The fact that some Anglicans occasionally express reservations about the potential *misuse* of their church buildings and liturgy for cultural rather than religious purposes supports the suggestion that the appropriate default position from which to begin to explore Anglicanism is that of its realistic theological commitments. Further, the fact that Anglican defenders of non-realism, such as Don Cupitt, accept that their theological position constitutes a radical departure from the historical norm helps confirm this argument (Cupitt, 1980; cf. Cowdell, 1988). Indeed, one struggles to discover a single sustained and developed example of Anglican non-realistic theology prior to the 1960s: historically speaking, Anglicanism has always been, and remains today, a fundamentally realistic faith tradition. Objectors might argue that this assumes mainstream orthodox Anglican Christians have a monopoly on the authentic interpretation of Christianity. However, the issue before us is not that of the truth or otherwise of orthodox and non-realistic interpretations of Anglicanism. Rather, our concern is to identify the most appropriate starting point from which to frame a curriculum designed to enable students to establish a critical understanding of, in this instance, Anglicanism. My suggestion is that this point of departure ought to be that of the realistic truth claims embedded in the historical continuity of the Anglican tradition, with the cultural reductionism of nominal Anglicans, together with the radicalism of non-realist theologians, viewed as departures, whether valid or invalid, from that norm. That is to say, our understanding of religious belief should proceed from the mainstream collective intentionality of the community as a whole.

b) The suggestion that we should not take religious truth claims at face value is dependent upon a distinctively Western post-Enlightenment agenda. A significant number of modern philosophers draw a distinction between the domains of fact and value, contrasting objective fact with subjective moral, aesthetic and spiritual values. The assumption that religious truth claims are unverifiable according to strict empirical procedures led to the belief that they are best treated as emotive expressions rather than factual statements (Ayer, 1971). This received support from Christian apologists who sought to circumnavigate a potential clash between religion and science by representing theological statements as expressions of inner spiritual experience rather than realistic descriptions of reality (Schleiermacher, 1976). In a parallel move, some postmodern philosophers developed a functional understanding of religious language, arguing that its primary role is to enable religious adherents to live flourishing lives rather than depict reality (Kee, 1985). A classic example of this rejection of the realistic role of religious language is found in the work of D. Z. Phillips. He claims that we cannot assess religious language against scientific criteria and judge it in terms of its ability to account for reality. This is because the discourses of science and religion employ different language games and as such are radically incommensurate. The role of religious language is not to state realistic truth, but to enable believers to explore questions of spiritual meaning that emerge in the context of prayer and worship. Since religious adherents encounter the 'reality' of God through praise, thanksgiving, confession and intercession rather than philosophical reflection, it follows that 'coming to God is not coming to see that an object one thought did not exist does in fact exist' (Phillips, 1976, p. 181). Phillips' assumption, that the language games of scientific description of the natural order and theological description of the transcendent realm are both incommensurable with the language game of spiritual expression, is directly dependent on both the modernist distinction between fact and value and the postmodernist contrast between realistic and pragmatic truth. Historically speaking, the contrast between the realistic-descriptive and spiritual-functional role of religious language is spurious: in most religious traditions there is a direct and necessary link between beliefs about the nature of ultimate reality and the spiritual search for salvation or enlightenment. One of the key motives behind Philips' work is a concern to uphold the integrity of religious language, a task that he believes requires religions to avoid entanglement in an inevitably losing battle with the natural sciences. This desire to affirm the authenticity of religious language is reflected in his rejection of any suggestion that 'religious beliefs are the product of elementary mistakes due to a primitive mentality, emotional stress, or social pressure' (p. ix). The result is a thorough-going relativism: if religious language games are only valid to the extent that they enable religious adherents to live truthful lives – rather than by virtue of the accuracy of their descriptions of reality – it follows that they have the potential to be equally effective, and hence equally valid. The deep source of this thoroughgoing relativism can be traced back to forms of comprehensive liberalism that, in the name of tolerance, reject any attempt to identify one cultural tradition as more valid or truthful than any other.

c) There is an overwhelming lack of historical evidence for religious adherents treating the stories they tell and the creeds they recite as merely pragmatically useful fictions, and distinguishing between such fictions and misplaced realistic accounts of the order-of-things. Indeed, for them to do so would require a remarkable degree of sophistication: in particular, it would require a relatively detailed knowledge of the post-Enlightenment distinction between the non-realistic genre of narrative fiction and the realistic genre of scientific proposition. Pre-modern religious believers did not enter into sustained discussions about the non-realistic nature of their beliefs, nor did they attempt to refute those who made the categorical mistake of assuming a realistic understanding of religion. There is, on the contrary, much discussion about the realistic truths of different religious traditions, especially – although not exclusively – within the various Western monotheistic traditions. It is not too much of an exaggeration to claim that we can only discover genuinely sustained and developed discussions of religious non-realism amongst Western academic theologians cognisant with modern and postmodern philosophical thought forms. Further, the assumption of the existence of a self-consciously non-realistic pragmatism amongst religious adherents is incapable of explaining the phenomenon of deeply rooted commitment, and in particular the willingness of many to purse their supposedly pious fictions to the point of martyrdom. Whatever the social, cultural and psychological factors that help create religiously motivated suicide bombers, it is extremely unlikely that their belief that the reward for their actions will be immediate entry into paradise is held in anything other than a thoroughly realistic manner.

d) The notion that ordinary religious adherents embrace functional forms of spirituality which academic theologians have inappropriately transformed into realistic truth claims is unsustainable. Bertrand Russell once recollected how Ludwig Wittgenstein used to come to his apartment in the middle of the night, pace the floor, and announce that he was contemplating suicide. On one such evening 'after an hour or two of dead silence, I said to him "Wittgenstein, are you thinking about logic or about your sins?", "Both", he said, and reverted to silence' (Hudson, 1975, p. 10). The impact of Russell's anecdote lies in the apparently awkward juxtaposition of Wittgenstein's intellectual and existential interests. As such, it simultaneously illustrates and challenges the common assumption that academic scholarship is dislocated from the lifeworlds of ordinary people – an assumption closely linked to reductionist assertions of the non-realistic status of religious belief. The suggestion is that where ordinary theology uses story, metaphor and narrative in its struggle for spiritual authenticity, academic theology uses reified propositional language in its search for theological truth – and never the twain shall meet. It is certainly difficult to deny that the history of Western Christianity has seen periods in which the intricacies of scholastic theology, in both its Catholic and Protestant forms, has become so disconnected from the lifeworlds of ordinary Christians as to appear largely irrelevant to them (Astley, 2002; Kavanagh, 1984). Despite this, the Christian tradition stresses the unity of the struggle for spiritual authenticity and the pursuit of truth, as expressed in 'the ancient rubric *Lex orandi, lex credendi*: The law of prayer is the law of faith, or more freely translated, What we pray as a church is what we believe as a community' (Martos, 2001, p. 123). It follows that authentic theology is 'always set in some context, rooted in some life experience or issue' (Astley, 2002, p. 3). 'What Christians believe affects the manner in which they pray and worship; the manner in which Christians pray and worship affects what they believe' (McGrath, 1994, p. 191). As Colin Gunton points out, Calvin's explicitly propositional theology, which sought 'to integrate the knowledge of God and of ourselves', approached theology as 'saving and existentially relevant knowledge . . . [that] had to be given cognitive form if it was to be worthy of belief' (Gunton, 1995, p. 9). Such an intimate relationship between academic and ordinary theology is visible in the fact that creedal propositions, despite being the subject of intense intellectual scrutiny, find their true home in the context of the liturgy.

These considerations suggest that the notion that the vast majority of ordinary religious adherents have no interest in realistic truth is groundless. We are surely justified in demanding extremely good reasons for *not* assuming that when believers pray to God they believe themselves to be in communication with an objective reality rather than engaged in some subtle form of psychological projection. Hence, the common sense option is to begin the exploration of religion by taking religious beliefs at face value: the burden of proof lies on those who wish to refute their basic realistic orientation.

6.2 Discrete religious traditions

We turn then to our second claim, that the primary bearers of transcendent truth claims are (relatively) discrete religious traditions –

Buddhism, Christianity, Hinduism, Islam, Judaism, Sikhism, etc. Whether religious education should centre on the generic notion of religion, on discrete religious traditions, or on the spiritual lives of individuals is a deeply controversial issue. Although most religious educators recognize the need for some level of dialogue between all three, there is no agreement as to which of them offers the most appropriate default position against which to compare and contrast the others. I will argue that it is indeed discrete religious traditions that ought to constitute the starting point for the exploration of transcendent truth, and thus provide the context for the subsequent exploration of religion as a universal category and of personal spirituality. This position is supported by the legal requirement that religious education should 'reflect the fact that religious traditions in Great Britain are in the main Christian whilst taking account of the teaching and practices of the other principles religions represented in Great Britain' (Wright, 1993, p. 21; cf. HMSO, 1988). Further, although the National Framework identifies important universal questions about the meaning and purpose of life, and provides opportunities for personal reflection and spiritual development, its core focus is clearly on 'Christianity, other principle religions, other religious traditions and other world views' (DfES/QCA, 2004, p. 7). I will present discrete religions not as essential entities, but as substantial yet dynamic, malleable and emergent realities whose identities develop – at least in part – in response to other religious and secular spiritualities and traditions. Challenges to the priority of discrete religious traditions tend to operate on two distinct levels: at the macro-level, some seek to amalgamate discrete traditions into a greater whole – the generic category of religion; at the micro-level, others seek to break them down into their constituent parts – the spiritual lives of individuals. Here we will concentrate on the challenge to our proposal offered by defenders of generic readings of religion, reserving discussion of individual spiritualities for the following section.

Whether we view religions as relatively discrete entities or as manifestations of the single entity 'religion' has links with the theological debate between exclusivism and inclusivism. One approach to Christianity 'finds salvation only in Christ and little, if any, value elsewhere'; another 'recognises the salvific richness of other faiths but then views this richness as a result of Christ's redemptive work and as having to be fulfilled in Christ' (Hick and

Knitter, 1987, p. viii; cf. D'Costa, 1990, pp. viiif). Ontologically speaking, both these approaches represent forms of theological exclusivism: despite offering different accounts of the scope of salvation, each assumes the basic truth of the Christian account of reality. In contrast, theological inclusivism constitutes 'a move away from the insistence on the superiority or finality of Christ and Christianity towards a recognition of the *independent* validity of other ways' (Hick and Knitter, 1987, p. viii, my emphasis). Ontologically, this means that no religious tradition can claim exclusive access to knowledge of ultimate reality; at the same time, the fact that they offer equally valid paths to salvation indicates that each must have at least *some* connection with reality. Hence, for theological inclusivists it is to the generic category of religion, rather than any one discrete religious tradition, that acts as the primary bearer of knowledge of the ultimate order-of-things.

John Hick's theology is a paradigmatic example of theological inclusivism. He argues that it is 'illuminating to see the different [religious] traditions, movements and ideologies . . . as forming a complex continuum of resemblances and differences analogous to those found within a family' (Hick, 1989, p. 4). He draws a comparison with the Copernican revolution in astronomy, which saw 'a shift from the dogma that the earth is the centre of the revolving universe to the realisation that it is the sun that is at the centre, with all the planets, including our own earth, moving around it' (Hick, 1977, p. 130f). By analogy,

> the needed Copernican revolution in theology involves an equally radical transformation in our conception of the universe of faiths and the place of our own religion in it. It involves a shift from the dogma that Christianity is at the centre to the realization that it is *God* who is at the centre, and that all the religions of mankind, including our own, serve and revolve around him.
>
> (p. 131)

This suggests that all religions have their roots in a common experience of transcendence, which is then 'differently conceived, experienced and responded to from within the different cultural ways of being human' (Hick, 1989, p. 14). Monotheistic religion may represent ultimate reality as 'deity' (Yahweh, the heavenly Father, Allah, Vishnu, Shiva, etc.), non-theistic traditions that same reality as the 'absolute' (the Tao, the Dharmakaya, Brahman,

Sunyata, etc.). Different religious expressions constitute 'different phenomenal awareness of the same noumenal reality and evoke parallel salvific transformations of human life' (p. 15).

In sharp contrast, Karl Barth's theology is a paradigmatic example of theological exclusivism. He sought to distinguish divine revelation from all religions – including the Christian religion (Barth, 1956, pp. 280ff). The fact that God's revelation meets humanity in Christianity means that, despite sharing many common features, it is not simply one amongst many religions, a particular manifestation of common human religiosity 'rooted in the general structure of the spiritual life of man' (Torrance, 2002, pp. 57f; cf. Barth, 1956, p. 299). Barth views revelation as the *Aufhebung* of religion: that is to say, revelation is simultaneously the 'abolition' and the 'lifting up' of religion (Bromiley, 1979, p. 29). Revelation abolishes religion insofar as it is a form of idolatry driven by 'man's attempts to justify and to sanctify himself before a capricious and arbitrary picture of God' (Barth, 1956, p. 280). Revelation lifts up religion insofar as 'the outpouring of the Holy Spirit' constitutes the 'reconciling presence of God in the world of human religion' (p. 280). The church is a form of idolatry insofar as it is simply a human endeavour, but is 'the locus of true religion, so far as through grace it lives by grace' (p. 280). Ultimately, for Barth, transcendent ontological truth is revealed exclusively to the Christian community, which struggles to witness to it in an all-too-human manner.

The theological debate between exclusivists and inclusivists raises a crucial ontological question: do discrete religious traditions offer complementary or incompatible accounts of the ultimate nature of reality? Christians believe Jesus of Nazareth was God incarnate, Muslims that he was a prophet of Allah: if these beliefs are mutually exclusive, discrete religious traditions constitute the primary bearers of transcendent truth claims; if they are reconcilable, we must look instead to the generic category of religion. One influential strand of liberal religious education tends to prioritize generic religion over discrete religious traditions, seeking inter-faith support for a 'common policy for religious and moral education' grounded in universal 'questions about the nature of man and the conditions of human existence' (Smith, 1969, pp. 17, 41). Smart's influential six-fold typology – doctrine, myth, ethic, ritual, experience, institution and symbol – helped establish the perception that religions enjoy a common phenomenological configuration (Smart,

1978). Such phenomenological description also led to the identification of religion as a *sui generis* phenomenon rooted in 'a distinct
form of experience with its own essence and structure' (Surin,
1980, p. 99; cf. Marvell, 1976). Hay placed this in a theological
context, defining religion as the response of human beings to their
experience of the sacred (Hay, 1985, p. 142). Hull offered a
robust defence of generic religion on moral grounds: stressing the
thematic links between religions, questioning the socially divisive
'religionism' of those who sought to retain the purity of discrete
religious traditions, and defending his position against charges of
promoting a relativistic 'mish-mash' (Hull, 1998). Reflecting on
this generic approach, Smart recognizes that the 'danger of separate
[religious] histories is that each may fail to see certain aspects of
the dynamics which can be gleaned from cross-cultural comparison'; at the same time however, he also identifies the 'danger of
the comparative study of religion is that it may crassly bulldoze the
particularities of the traditions' (Smart, 1995, p. 183). It is clearly
important to establish an appropriate hermeneutical balance here.
My suggestion is that there are cogent reasons for religious educators treating the truth-bearing claims of discrete religious traditions
as primary, and approaching generic accounts as secondary interpretations.

a) Theological critiques of generic approaches to religious education argue that the self-understanding of most discrete religious
traditions is significantly at variance with the generic claims of
academic commentators. Thus, for Hardy, the reification of religion
and its interpretation within a neo-Kantian framework ignores the
particular truth claims of all the major world religions (Hardy,
1975, 1976, 1982). Religious education should present religious
traditions 'in a fashion which accords with their nature . . . [and]
each religious tradition is, according to its nature, the vehicle for
truth' (Hardy, 1982, p. 110). He recognizes that this raises a
problem, since the 'presentation of a tradition as "absolutely true"
prejudges other religions, or non-religious views, as false or defec-
tive' (p. 112). However, the appropriate response is 'not to prejudge
the question of which is true by asserting that all are alike', since
this is untrue for the vast majority of traditions (p. 112). Rather,
each tradition should be presented in a way which acknowledges
their exclusive truth claims as well as the contested nature of such

claims. In similar vein, Cooling traces the roots of generic religion in religious education back to a theology of 'radical Christian liberalism' that seeks to establish the parameters of educationally acceptable religious belief. Such belief must be rational, tolerant, committed to freedom of choice, suspicious of absolute commitment, and antagonistic towards religious nurture (Cooling, 1994, p. 1). Advocates of this position deny that religious language is reality describing, and insist instead that 'neither secular nor religious metaphors are necessarily right or wrong, they are simply vehicles we use to articulate experience' (p. 93; quoting Hammond, et al., 1990, p. 125). Cooling's 'major criticism of this approach is that it violates the pluralist principle, namely that secular schools should not impose a particular form of religion on their students' (p. 1). It is not 'fair in its treatment of the religions because it discriminates in favour of *radical theology*, and against *more traditional forms of religious commitment*' (p. 1).

b) Philosophical critiques of generic approaches to religious education argue that it is impossible to identify any core essence or structure of religion. Robert Jackson has been at the forefront of such arguments, suggesting that there are no grounds for treating religion as a generic category with an essence. While acknowledging the value of exploring commonalities between religious traditions, he warns of the dangers of overgeneralization and misrepresentation that flow from 'phenomenology's tendency to take religious data out of its original context in place, time, society and culture' (Jackson, 1997, p. 22). It is, he suggests, philosophically questionable whether specific hermeneutical methods can actually reveal the existence of universal essences. He appeals to Wittgenstein's later philosophy of language, which insists that linguistic meaning flows from the language games and forms of life of particular communities, rather than through the referencing of ideal types and abstract structures. Although the 'emphasis on the importance of context in understanding other ways of life does not imply that there is no commonality in human nature or experience', we should nevertheless be cautious about 'looking for a variety of universal essences embedded in the consciousness of people' (p. 23).

c) Further, the notion of religion as a *sui generis* entity possessing a distinct essence is the product of a specific philosophical tradition

(Wright, 2008). Classical Western philosophy was committed to the search for secure knowledge. Thus Plato, rejecting Heraclitus' claim that the order-of-things is in a constant state of flux, sought to ground knowledge in eternal and unchanging Platonic Forms. In similar vein, Aristotle argued that objects have both essential and accidental properties: it essential that a chair has a seat, but entirely accidental if it possesses four legs and is made of wood. The combination of Plato's ontology of the Forms and Aristotle's metaphysical essentialism brings us to the heart of philosophical idealism, which sets out to offer clear descriptions of those essential and unchanging realities existing above and beyond the everyday world of fleeting appearances. According to idealism, to identify the essence of religion is to identify some timeless reality transcending the contingent manifestations of religion encountered in the immanent ebb and flow of human culture. Thus Hegel, in the *Phenomenology of Spirit*, argues that distinctive religious cultures are bound together in an underlying essence (*Wesen*) or unity of Spirit (*Geist*): his 'ultimate objective was that of discerning unity behind diversity, of reaching an understanding of the one essence of religion behind its many manifestations' (Sharpe, 1986, p. 221). This, together with the Kantian distinction between the contingent world of phenomena and the transcendent world of the numinous, provided the basic metaphysical framework for religious essentialism. It was Saussaye who first represented the phenomenology of religion as an 'attempt to investigate the essence and meaning of religious phenomena' (King, 1995, p. 51). According to Husserl, the twin phenomenological tasks of *epoche* (the suspension of prejudice and presupposition) and *eidetic vision* (the intuitive grasping to the essence of phenomena) enables the observer to penetrate beneath surface appearances and enter into an understanding of the essential core of religion. Under the influence of Husserl, the phenomenology of religion became 'bound up greatly with the search for essences' (Smart, 1995, p.182; cf. Van der Leeuw, 1992; Otto, 1931; Eliade, 1987). Without the presence of this idealistic tradition within Western philosophy it appears unlikely that the interpretation of religions as culturally specific variants on a common religious experience would have developed in the way it did.

d) Many advocates of generic universal theology accept they are campaigning for a departure from the established norm. Hick, for example, acknowledges that the self-understanding of religious adherents is normally rooted in discrete religious traditions (Hick, 1977). Hence his vision of a universal theology is self-consciously aspirational: in terms of the implications of his theology, he is arguing for what he thinks *ought* to be the case rather than describing actual reality. Thus, although the majority of religious traditions offer exclusive truth claims, it would be more appropriate if they were to adopt his own theological perspective. It is clear from this that theological universalism offers one of a number of possible secondary interpretation of the primary self-understandings of various discrete religious traditions. This position is strengthened by the observation that universal theology is largely a product of the modern Western academy: there is little evidence that it has had any significant impact on the shared understanding, liturgical practices, or creedal statements of any specific religious tradition. Just as no society speaks Esperanto as a matter of course, so no religious tradition actually practices Hick's universal religion – at least not in any sustained, sophisticated and theologically astute manner. This suggests that we have no warrant for treating generic religion as the default position from which to explore questions of ultimate truth; on the contrary, we have good reason to begin with the self-understanding of discrete religious communities.

e) The moral argument that a focus on discrete religious traditions encourages forms of religionism that engender tribalistic attitudes and threaten the stability of society is largely spurious. In this particular instance, it is illegitimate to extract an 'is' from an 'ought': to argue that particular truth claims ought to be rejected because they tend to undermine social harmony is not the same as claiming that discrete religious traditions do not make such claims. There would be a strong case for accepting theological universalism as the basis for religious education in the context of an education system structured around comprehensive liberalism. Such an education would constitute an explicit form of confessionalism, concerned to induct pupils into the normative beliefs and values of a closed liberal system. This would require nurturing them in the belief that exclusive truth claims are a potential barrier to the well-being of society, and that consequently they should treat all religious traditions as equally true – despite the fact that this goes against the grain of the self-understanding of the vast majority of religious traditions. Our concern here, however, is to help develop a form of critical religious education rooted in an understanding of political liberalism as an open interim ethic. In such a context, pupils are required to engage with a diverse range of contrasting and conflicting interpretations of religion in an informed and reflective manner. This means being open about the fact that 'the history of religion is a story of conflict and dissent, often bloody, as well as of striving for peace and reconciliation' (Yates, 1988, p. 143; cf. Wright, 1993, pp. 89–92). It also means being honest about different responses to this situation, as these emerge from both the liberal tradition and the traditions of discrete religious communities. Rather than pre-package one particular representation of the problem of religious violence, together with one specific solution to this problem, a critical religious education will require students to engage with a number of variant readings and draw their own informed conclusions. This, in the long term at least, constitutes the best means of helping establish and preserve social harmony: first, because the proposed strategy appears likely to help develop a society appropriately informed about the issue; second, because imposing a closed liberal interpretation on the problem appears likely to alienate those individuals and communities whose core values and commitments are not liberal (Wright, 2003a).

There is certainly a case for encouraging pupils to explore religion as a generic category in the classroom. However, there is no case for presenting generic religion and universal theology as normative; rather, the starting point for the exploration of religious truth ought to be the primary bearers of transcendent truth claims – relatively discrete religious traditions.

6.3 Salvific communities

We turn then to our third claim, that the world's religions offer their adherents not only comprehensive belief systems but also holistic community-based life stances. Religions combine a commitment to truth with a deep concern for truthful living, and religious adherents seek to make sense of her life by striving to live in harmony with ultimate reality. As Byrne points out, religious people perceive that 'the apparent order of the world around them is not a moral order; it is indifferent to the achievement of human happiness and the realisation of human goodness; it presents itself as blind and indifferent to justice' (Byrne, 2003, p. 17). Faced with the prevalence of suffering and meaninglessness in the world, religious believers seek enlightenment or salvation through their developing relationship with that transcendent reality which is ultimately real. Religions offer their followers a 'theodicy': a picture of the true order-of-things that challenges the apparent emptiness of the world, illuminates the lifeworlds of religious adherents, and guides them to live 'in proper relationship to, in harmony with, that which is most real' (p. 18). Hence, being religious entails both embracing claims about the nature of reality and adopting an all-embracing worldview that touches every aspect of life (Markham, 1998, pp. 7ff).

Central to this understanding of the holistic nature of religions is the recognition that religious life stances are for the most part inseparable from religious belief systems. In the religious sphere, there is normally an organic relationship between truth and truthfulness: in traditional Christian terminology, orthodoxy is inseparable from orthopraxis. This does not mean that all religions adopt distinctive creedal statements similar to those found in the Christian tradition, or that it is possible to reduce religious belief to the mere intellectual acceptance of creedal formulas. Such views lead all too easily to the mistaken assumption that the pursuit of religious truth is necessarily an obscure academic exercise. For many believers, the process of living out their faith is certainly of far greater importance than the nuances of technical doctrinal formulae; nevertheless, their spiritual lives remain bound up with a set of beliefs and assumptions about the nature of reality. Hence, our holistic understanding of religion assumes that religious life stances include at least a minimal level of 'belief expressed in one or other form of reasonable discourse' (Houlden, 2002, p.6).

To dislocate religious belief from religious practice runs the risk of reducing religion to the level of mere pragmatism. According to William James, pragmatism is simply 'the expedient in the way of our thinking' (James, 1978, p. 106). This suggests that religious ideas function not as tools for engaging with the way things actually are in the world, but rather as instruments that 'become true just in so far as they help us to get into satisfactory relation with other parts of our experience' (p. 34). Hence, James' claim that 'if the hypothesis of God works satisfactorily in the widest sense of the word, it is true' (p. 143). Such pragmatism is exemplified in Cupitt's suggestion that religious beliefs are valuable insofar as they help us to live autonomous lives, but distinctly unhelpful if we mistakenly assume that they refer to an objective God 'out there' who demands our absolute obedience (Cupitt, 1980). Of course, on one level, religious adherents do indeed embrace their religious beliefs because they 'work' by enabling them to live richer and more fulfilled lives. Nevertheless, for most believers they are effective precisely because they offer true accounts of the real world, not mere pious fictions. This suggests that the pragmatic reading of religion is reductionist: it claims to understand the faith of religious believers better than they understand it themselves. Where most ordinary religious adherents ground their faith in an understanding of the way things actually are in the world, the pragmatist claims that such faith is of value merely because it happens to 'work' for a particular individual or group. Since the vast majority of the world's religious traditions do not espouse pragmatism in this sense, a holistic understanding of religion, which affirms an intimate connection between religious life stances and religious beliefs, constitutes a more appropriate starting point for religious education than a fragmented one that assumes discontinuity between the two.

Robert Jackson's commitment to a contextual approach to religious education, focused on the immediate lifeworlds of pupils and concerned to help them negotiate their emergent sense of personal identity, clearly resonates with our own concern for the holistic development of pupils. However, like many contextual religious educators he tends to view religions as the artificial constructions of academics, devoid of any substantial identity, and constitutive only of loose groupings of individuals. This represents a significant challenge to the position defended here: if religious communities do not possess substantial collective identities they can no longer offer relatively stable, coherent and distinctive truth claims; instead, they will be reduced to the level of providing no more than a habitus in which individuals seek the pragmatic cultivation of truthful spiritual lives. If, in the previous section we considered the dissolution of discrete religious traditions into a greater generic whole, we here we must address the deconstruction of such traditions into their atomistic parts (Wright, 2008).

Jackson justifies his contention that the representation of religions 'as discrete belief systems should be abandoned in favour of a much looser portrayal of religious traditions and groupings' on two main grounds (Jackson, 2001, p. 35). First, he claims that the notion of religions as stable, static and schematic systems of belief is a construct of the European Enlightenment (Jackson, 1997, pp. 49ff). We can deal with this issue fairly briefly. It is certainly true that modernity produced overly rigid and essentialized accounts of religion. However, there is a danger of an overreaction that denies the substantial reality of discrete religious traditions: such a move simply replaces a modern economy of construction with a post-modern economy of deconstruction. Thus, for example, the fact that the term 'Hinduism' was invented by Western scholars should certainly cause us to be suspicious of accounts of that tradition that presented is a tightly structured tradition akin to, say, Roman Catholicism; at the same time, however, the term was coined in response to a substantial sociocultural reality, and we should beware of losing sight of that reality by surrounding our descriptions of Hinduism with an endless series of qualifications. Second, Jackson draws attention to ethnographic evidence of significant levels of disparity between the perspectives of ordinary religious adherents and normative representations provided by faith community 'gatekeepers' and academics (Jackson and Nesbitt, 1993). This raises the fundamental issue of how to account for the relationship between the parts and whole of any given tradition, an issue that warrants detailed consideration.

Jackson's understanding of the identity of religious traditions is a variant of that proposed by Wilfred Cantwell Smith, who rejects the terms 'religion' and 'religions' as 'confusing, unnecessary, and distorting' (Smith, 1991, p. 50; cf. Jackson 1997, pp. 60ff). According to Smith, religions are nothing more than a loose amalgam of 'faith plus tradition': faith is 'an inner religious experience or involvement of a particular person . . . [with] the transcendent, putative or real'; while tradition is the cumulative 'mass of overt objective data that constitute the historical deposit . . . of the past religious life of the community . . . temples, scriptures, theological systems, dance patterns, legal and other social institutions, conventions, moral codes, myths and so on' (Smith 1991, pp. 156f). Ultimately, Smith denies religious traditions any substantive form or structure, treating them merely as the arbitrary sum of the spiritual experiences of individuals. Following Smith, Jackson rejects the notion of religions as 'bounded and uncontestable systems' and limits knowledge of them to 'the various constructions . . . made by different insiders and outsiders' (Jackson, 1997, p. 64). Consequently, he rejects representations of religions that threaten to 'entrap insiders within schematic formulations of key beliefs and concepts' (p. 69). It follows that the representation of particular religions as diverse and constantly changing entities should function only as a heuristic tool designed to illuminate the lifeworlds of religious adherents. Further, recognition of 'the internal diversity of religious traditions' creates space for 'more personal accounts [of religion] which link individual experience to social experience' (p. 69). Jackson argues that the interpretation of religious lifeworlds should have a three-fold focus: on individuals; relevant groups to which they belong; and the wider religious tradition (pp. 65f). However, his concern 'not to identify individuals with the key concepts and practices of a 'constructed' religion', and to avoid 'locking individual persons into stereotypical group identities', tilts the hermeneutical circle in favour of the lifeworlds of individual religious adherents (p. 66). It is these lifeworlds, rather than discrete religions, that according to Jackson, should provide the starting point for religious education: faith, that is to say, is distinguishable from, and takes precedence over, tradition.

Jackson has criticised me for failing to give due attention to 'contested representations within traditions', trimming off 'the fuzzy edges of real life', and interpreting 'the personal syntheses and multiple allegiances revealed by ethnographic study . . . as deviations from doctrinally pristine religious narratives' (Jackson 2004, pp. 81f). He speculates that either I am 'using conceptual overviews of religions as a rough framework, a tool to help children to see the relationship between their own "dialects" and other related viewpoints', or I am striving to maintain an essentialized and reified understanding of discrete religions (p. 83). As I have observed elsewhere, such use of binary opposites – subject v. object, sacred v. secular, central v. marginal, essential v. nominal, etc. – tends to 'encourage superficial arguments based on simplistic either/or choices and constrain the way we think by inviting us to privilege one side of the equation and marginalise the other' (Wright 2004a, p. 33). Representations of discrete religious tradition, I suggest, do not need to choose between the extremes of essential description and arbitrary construction; rather, they possess substantial, although not essential, identities in their own right.

Such dualistic thinking reflects the long-standing philosophical dispute between idealism and nominalism. Whereas, as we saw earlier, idealism is concerned to describe the underlying essence of things, nominalism denies the existence of universal essences and views reality as nothing more than the sum total of its constituent parts. Thus, William of Ockham insisted that, since everything that exists is a particular object or thing, any reference to universals is merely a linguistic convention through which we construct pictures of reality; that is to say, any connection between the atomistic parts of reality exists only nominally – 'in name only' (Gilson, 1955, pp. 489ff). Consequently, there is no underlying essence of the concept 'chair', only individual chairs; no underlying essence of the concept 'Christianity', only particular manifestations of individual spiritualities. It follows that talk of a religion cannot refer to its timeless essences that we *discover*, merely to contingent patterns of human behaviour that we *construct* as meaningful wholes.

There is a danger here of allowing the conflict between idealism and nominalism to set the parameters of the debate, and consequently of imposing an unnecessary either/or choice between essential and nominal accounts of religion on religious educators. Critical realism opens up the possibility of developing descriptions of natural, social and cultural realities without resorting to either of these extremes (Sayer, 2000). Thus, for example, the laws of nature as described by scientists do not enjoy some eternal, transcendental or essential status: they are the products of fallible human beings, and as such are necessarily contingent and subject to revision. However, this is no warrant for dismissing them as mere arbitrary constructions, since they clearly offer relatively accurate representations, however provisional, of the natural world. Hence, critical realism maintains *both* that we can identify form, structure and order within many dimensions of reality (natural, psychological, social, moral, aesthetic, religious, etc.) *and* that, given the contingent nature of human rationality, it is not necessary to posit these as unchanging essences. The choice between contextual parts and essential wholes is a false one.

On one level, Jackson is quite correct: our representations of discrete religious traditions are human constructions. The crucial issue, however, is the extent to which such constructions accord with reality. If Jackson is correct, then our knowledge of religions is limited to the sum total of particular instances of individual religiosity. This hints at a pre-critical understanding of the scientific process. In biology, for example, it is not sufficient simply to create taxonomies of life on our planet: the scientific task is to develop theoretical insights into the structures and forces that bind the natural order together in a meaningful way. Thus, for Darwin the accumulated data of biology 'pointed to the existence of processes which had not yet been observed, and might even be unobservable, which could only be described theoretically in terms of "natural selection" (McGrath, 2003, pp. 15f). Theorizing is the 'attempt to identify universal *a posteriori* patterns in local situations. . . . [while ensuring] that the particularities of the observed situation are not displaced or superseded by the universal patterns they are held to disclose' (p. 9). In the terminology of critical realism, we need to penetrate beyond the domains of the experiential and actual to engage with the domain of the real, thereby identifying the forces and structures that make reality what it is: description needs to give way to explanation, edifying conversation to critical judgement (Bhaskar, 1977, p. 56).

John Searle has drawn attention to the phenomenon of 'collective intentionality': the fact that human beings engage together in cooperative behaviour (Searle, 1996, pp. 23ff). Thus, a jazz band is not simply a collection of individuals 'doing their own thing', but a community of musicians engaged in a common task. Such collective intentionality is a primary or basic phenomenon, one irreducible to the sum of individual intentionalities: despite appearances, the formula 'you intend + I intend = we intend' does not add up. This is because collective intentionality is dependent upon a shared agreement to act together: 'we intend, *therefore* you intend + I intend'. The collective intentionality of American citizens to treat certain pieces of paper as twenty-dollar bills, or of Roman Catholics to treat baptism as the means of entry into the Christian community, constitute social facts that cannot be altered by any *individual* act of will. Further, social facts are frequently rule driven. Regulative rules organize antecedently existing activities: thus, the regulative law that we drive on the left in the UK organizes the antecedent activity of driving in a particular way. Constitutive rules, on the other hand, do more than merely regulate; rather, they *create the very possibility* of certain activities. Thus, the rules of chess do not merely regulate an antecedently existing activity, since without such rules it would be impossible ever to play chess. 'It is not the case that there were a lot of people pushing bits of wood around on boards, and in order to prevent them from bumping into each other all the time and creating traffic jams, we had to regulate the activity' (pp. 27f). My suggestion is that the identity of discrete religious traditions is grounded in the collective intentionality of the tradition as a whole, which is ontologically prior to the intentionality of individual adherents. Further, such collective intentionality often reflects constitutive agreements, whether implicit or explicit, which guide the beliefs and actions of adherents.

Gavin Flood defines religions as '*value-laden narratives and behaviours that bind people in their objectivities, to each other, and to non-empirical claims and beings*' (Flood 1999, p. 47). Religious identity is a binding category: there are objective constraints in the narratives and rituals of religions that preclude representations from descending into 'more or less arbitrary abstractions from a range of beliefs, emotions and behaviours selected by our interest' (p. 47). Thus, for example, 'while it might not be possible to arrive at a watertight definition of Hinduism, this does not mean that the term is empty' (Flood, 1996, p. 7). Hindu identity lies not in any essential attributes, but in prototypical forms of belief and practice. This notion of 'prototypical properties' is derived from George Lakoff, who maintains that 'categories do not have rigid boundaries, but rather there are degrees of category membership; some members of a category are more prototypical than others' (p. 7; cf. Lakoff, 1987). Thus the 'beliefs and practices of a high-caste devotee of the Hindu god Visnu living in Tamilnadu is south India, fall clearly within the category of "Hindu" and are prototypical of that category' (p. 7). On the other hand, the

> beliefs and practices of a Radhasaomi devotee in the Punjab, who worships a God without attributes, who does not accept the Veda as revelation and even rejects many Hindu teachings, are not prototypically Hindu, yet are still within the sphere, and category, of Hinduism.
>
> (p. 7)

A photograph of, say, Gordon Brown offers a substantial representation of the British Prime Minister: it is a mistake to assume that it constitutes either *the* definitive representation or nothing more than a random series of ink dots on the page. Similarly, a description of a religion can offer a substantial depiction of its prototypical beliefs and practices as they reflect the collective intentionality of its adherents: it is a mistake to assume that it constitutes either *the* essentially definitive representation or nothing more than an arbitrary construction. Contra Jackson, the existence of Anglican children who believe in reincarnation does nothing whatsoever to undermine the fact that reincarnation has never been a prototypical Christian belief (Jackson, 2004, p. 83). This does not mean that such children cease to be members of the Anglican Communion; they are simply Anglicans who, for whatever reason, hold heterodox beliefs. This is but one small example of the many fuzzy edges that surround all religious traditions, one that certainly exists as a social reality but which does not impinge on the Christian belief system as a whole. Christianity did not begin as a loosely knit spiritual community that later decided the basis of membership should be the belief that the God reveals himself in a new and exclusive way in the person of Jesus of Nazareth. Rather the community arose as a direct result of that belief: in Searle's terminology, the earliest Christian kerygma was not regulative of the early church, but constitutive of it. It follows that the later articulation of the doctrine of incarnation was not merely an arbitrary construction, but rather an attempt to articulate the core prototypical beliefs of Christianity. This suggests that it is indeed possible to represent discrete religious communities as substantial social facts rather than as essentialized entities or arbitrary social constructions. This keeps open the option of the search for truthful living taking place in the light of the truth claims proclaimed by and through the collective intentionality of discrete religious traditions.

6.4   Conclusion

In this chapter I began to map the contours of a heuristic framework designed to aid the pursuit of truth and truthfulness in religious education. Focusing on ontological questions of ultimate truth, I asked where we might look to discover the primary religious bearers of such truth claims, since these ought to constitute the default position from which to explore questions of truth and truthfulness in religious education. I then identified three key foci:

first, communities that make specifically *transcendent* truth claims; second, discrete religious traditions rather than generic accounts of religion; third, salvific communities offering holistic worldviews orientated around the unity of belief and practice, rather than the atomistic spiritual experiences of individuals.

7

Semantics: the language of life

I have argued that religious education should proceed on the assumption that the primary bearers of transcendent truth claims are the world's major religious traditions, whose adherents seek salvation or enlightenment by engaging, through activities such as prayer, worship and meditation, with ultimate reality. This chapter explores the nature and function of religious language in the belief that it provides the best means of accessing transcendent truth claims and understanding communal practices oriented towards truthful living. I will assume throughout that the linguistic systems of discrete religious traditions are open and accessible to non-adherents. Although the 'outsider' can never obtain the same level of sympathetic insight into a tradition as the 'insider', a certain level of mutual understanding is clearly possible. If this were not the case, inter-faith dialogue would cease, university departments of Theology and Religious Studies close, and teachers of religious education become redundant. In affirming a basic commensurability between belief systems, I am not to suggest that communication between them is an easy matter; there is a constant danger of missing the subtlety and nuance of religious expression, and even of seriously misrepresent a tradition. Nevertheless, a partial and hesitant search for understanding is eminently preferable to resigning ourselves to the complete breakdown of communication. The chapter begins by considering how religious creeds and propositions describe reality, goes on to consider their place in the speech acts and language games of religious communities, and then identifies metaphor and narrative as key components of religious worldviews.

7.1   Creeds and propositions

At its most basic, religious language proffers propositional statements that seek to depict the ultimate order-of-things. This reflects

Ludwig Wittgenstein's early 'picture theory' of language, inspired in part by the use of toy cars in a courtroom to provide jurors with a model of a road traffic accident (Wittgenstein, 1974). According to the Wittgenstein of the *Tractatus Logico-Philosophicus*, reality consists of the sum total of facts in the world; we picture these facts in our minds and express them in the form of cognitive propositions; such propositions are true insofar as they accurately depict states of affairs in the world; by refining and expanding them, it is theoretically possible to describe the whole of reality, the sum of true statements corresponding to the totality of the actual order-of-things. A classic example of religious proposition is the Nicene Creed, which affirms the objective reality of 'God, the Father, the Almighty,' of 'Jesus Christ, the only Son of God', and of 'the Holy Spirit, the Lord, the giver of life' (Kelly, 1950, pp.205ff). The minimal function of such creedal formulations is to make realistic truth claims: 'There is no getting around the fact that people who express their religious convictions are in so doing referring to a specific – usually divine and divinely instituted – reality and intend to assert something as true of it' (Pannenberg, 1976, p. 327).

Given the affinity between Wittgenstein's early philosophy and logical positivism, this affirmation of the cognitive status of religious propositions needs to be carefully distinguished from empiricism. In Chapter 2, we noted Roy Bhaskar's identification of the domains of the empirical, actual and real (Bhaskar, 1977). Empiricism limits propositional language to the task of naming objects in the domain of the empirical, as they present themselves through our immediate sense experience (Hume, 2000). This is problematic for religious believers, few of whom claim any direct sense experience of God. However, our knowledge can penetrate beyond the empirical to the actual and real: thus, we know that water consists of hydrogen and oxygen without being able to taste either. Hence, cognitive propositions seek to describe a dynamic and complex world that cannot be reduced to its surface appearance but rather contains deep structures and forces that organize reality in a meaningful way.

At the same time, it is impossible to ignore the peculiarity of religious propositions when measured against normative assumptions regarding propositional language in the natural and human sciences. Some of the propositions in the Nicene Creed make factual assertions that would be at home in standard historical discourse ('crucified under Pontius Pilate'). Nevertheless, the

Creed as a whole clearly deviates from Wittgenstein's twin assertions that 'the world is all that is the case' and 'what we cannot
speak about we must pass over in silence' (Wittgenstein, 1974,
pp. 5, 74). Specifically, it identifies a divine reality that is quite
obviously *not* one of the facts in the world as Wittgenstein
understands it ('God, the Father, the Almighty'), and does so by
utilizing metaphorical ('seated at the right hand of the Father') and
mythological ('came down from heaven . . . ascended into heaven')
language. Although the use of metaphor has parallels in scientific
language, the resort to mythology does not. It appears, then, that
theological propositions are both similar to and distinct from the
propositional language utilized by the natural and human sciences.
This raises issues that we will explore later in the chapter. However,
before proceeding further, we must pause to consider two objections to the claim that one of the primary functions of religious
language is to offer cognitive descriptions of transcendent reality.

a) The first objection suggests that the creedal nature of Christianity
is atypical of the other world religions. Judaism is certainly not a
creedal religion in the manner of Christianity, and the closest
Hebrew Scripture comes to a creed is the Shema: 'Hear, O Israel:
The LORD is our God, the LORD alone. You shall love the LORD
your God with all your heart, and with all your soul, and with all
your might' (Deuteronomy 6: 4f). Nevertheless, Judaism is clearly
committed to a set of fundamental beliefs about the existence and
nature of God, his relation to the world, his covenant with his
chosen people, his gift of the Torah, and the implications of this
for the ethics and worship of the community. Judaism, that is to
say, owns a clear set of realistic beliefs that help constitute Jewish
identity: any sharp distinction between orthodoxy and orthopraxis
here is untenable. Indeed, the modern distinction between religious
and secular Jews assumes a distinction between those who seek to
organize their lives in response to the truth claims of Judaism and
those who merely participate in Jewish culture. Although the
community expresses its beliefs in a variety of different ways, it
is clearly possible to restate them in propositional form. Thus
the Jewish encounter with Islam in the medieval period led to
attempts to affirm Jewish identity by articulating its core beliefs in
creedal form, as exemplified in the *Confession of Faith* of Moses
ben Maimonides (Kung, 1992, p. 158). In similar fashion, the

orthopraxis of Islam flows from a set of realistic propositions. The *shahadah* offers a minimalist creed: 'I bear witness that there is no God but Allah . . . I bear witness that Muhammad is the Messenger of Allah'; the *usul al-din* supplements this basic statement of faith by identifying, alongside the five pillars of ritual performance, the five fundamentals of Islamic belief: Allah and his attributes, his prophets, angels, scriptures, judgment day, divine omnipotence, and predestination (Hamidullah, 1979, pp. 44ff).

Turning eastward, the Buddhist teaching of the four noble truths articulates a distinctive understanding of the ultimate order-of-things: key foundational concepts, such as *samsara* and *karma*, express the quest for *nirvana*, the definitive cessation of suffering, which for the Buddhist constitutes the spiritual goal and ultimate reality towards which life should be oriented. Of course, the realism of Buddhism stands apart from the realism of the Western monotheistic religions, especially in its very different assessment of the lasting significance of the natural world. Nevertheless, to reduce the Buddhist worldview to the status of an embryonic form of some psychologically oriented therapeutic technique is to deny the historical integrity of Buddhism, specifically – to borrow the language of Western philosophy – its core metaphysical and onto-logical assumptions. We cannot, without spiritual and intellectual violence, demythologize Buddhism and force it into the procrustean bed of a secular worldview in which the realm of fact is dislocated from the realm of value, and orthopraxis disengaged from ortho-doxy. Gavin D'Costa has shown how similar dangers surround Western interpretations of Hinduism: although 'Hindu philosophy covers a wide spectrum, and includes atheism, materialism, theism, pantheism, and monism', these all form part of the *Vedanta*, the end of the *Vedas* or collection of revealed scripture (D'Costa, 2000, p. 54). Whatever the diversity of Hinduism, however much the various Hindu worldviews differ from Western conceptions of reality, the conceptual world of *atman, karma* and *maya*, as encountered in the various Hindu scriptures, sets out to achieve far more than provide fictional support for a Hindu lifestyle. One of the chief functions of the rich cluster of Hindu language systems is clearly to refer to the ultimate transcendent order-of-things.

The fact that many of the world's religious traditions do not have creedal affirmations at the centre of their worship, and are as concerned with spirituality and praxis as they are with belief and doctrine, does not warrant the conclusion that they have no interest in questions of realistic truth. Whether the language is explicit or implicit, whether articulated through creedal formulas or less direct methods of communication, the major world religions are fundamentally concerned to engage with ultimate reality. As Wolfhart Pannenberg points out:

> Even forms of religious language which have no direct propositional character, such as the language of prayer and the performative formulas which accompany liturgical acts, presuppose, in the linguistic expressions they use, other statements which contain assertions about divine and divinely instituted realities.
>
> (Pannenberg, 1976, pp. 327f)

b) The second objection, which carries more weight than the first, suggests that it is impossible to reduce the complexity of religious language to a simplistic propositional model. Religious propositions are rooted in a wider religious discourse, and there is an intricate relationship between propositional language and the lifeworlds of ordinary religious adherents. This suggests that although we have good cause to hold fast to the propositional nature of much religious language it would nevertheless be wise to seek a richer understanding of its nature and function. This brings us back to Wittgenstein, whose later philosophy developed a multifaceted, understanding of language. Although never denying the capacity of language to describe reality, he rejected his earlier view that the propositional model offers an appropriate 'picture of the essence of human language' (Wittgenstein, 1968, p. 2). Instead, he argued that 'language can be seen as an ancient city: a maze of little streets and squares, of old and new houses, and of houses with additions from various periods' (p. 8; directly challenging Descartes, 1970, pp. 15ff). According to Wittgenstein, the clue to understanding this richer picture lies in the ways in which language is actually used, an issue that forms the topic of the next section.

7.2   Religious speech acts

Religious language both offers propositional descriptions of reality, and also enjoys an intimate relationship with the everyday lives of religious adherents. This raises the question of the relationship between propositional knowledge and the 'language of life'. Speech-act theory offers a way of understanding how religious language can function to support religious lifeworlds without losing touch with the core truth claims of religious traditions. In the early 1950s, philosophical interest in propositional language gave way to a concern for the way in which language functions in practice – an issue previously assumed to be the preserve of psychological investigation. In particular, philosophers focused on the role of speakers of ordinary language and their actual use of language in the context of everyday life (Strawson, 1952; Wittgenstein, 1968). According to Wittgenstein, we learn to use language through interpersonal communication rather than by listing and labelling objects in the world. Since we have no god-like perspective on reality, our language is necessarily rooted in specific cultural contexts, and consequently our statements become those of pilgrims embarked on a journey towards truth. Wittgenstein employed the phrase 'language-game' 'to bring into prominence the fact that the *speaking* of language is part of an activity, or a form of life' (Wittgenstein, 1968, p. 11). We use language to give orders, describe objects, report events, speculate, make up a stories, play-act, guess riddles, tell jokes, solve problems, translate one language into another, ask, thank, curse, greet, pray, etc. (pp. 11f).

In *How to Do Things with Words*, John Austin developed a systematic description of the way in which language functions in everyday life (Austin, 1976). Believing that philosophical jargon frequently obscures meaning, he examined the role of non-philosophical language as it engages with fundamental philosophical questions, as well as the way in which non-philosophers use philosophical terms such as 'meaning', 'truth' and 'reality'. Questioning the fundamental assumptions of logical positivism, and rejecting the traditional distinction between thought and action, he argued that language is capable of doing far more than simply describe the world. Thus, the sentence 'I bequeath my watch to my brother', when spoken in the context of the reading of a will, functions not as a 'constative utterance' providing a true description of reality, but as a 'performative utterance' bringing about a material change in the actual order-of-things. As the will is enacted, so the watch that was previously owned by the bequeather actually *becomes* the property of the brother to whom it is bequeathed (p. 5). Significantly, the sentence 'I promise to be at the meeting' functions as *both* a performative *and* a constative statement: I have both made a promise (performative utterance) and described a potential state of affairs in the world (constative utterance). Austin goes on to draw a distinction between 'locutionary', 'illocutionary' and 'perlocutionary' acts. A locutionary speech act derives meaning from the reference it makes to things in the world; an illocutionary speech act derives meaning from the intentionality of the speaker: betting, promising, praying, asserting, proclaiming; a perlocutionary speech act derives meaning from the effect it has on others – persuading, infuriating, challenging – regardless of whether the effect is intended by the speaker or not. A single statement can involve all three of these speech acts: if I were to publish the sentence 'Hanki, my daughter Elizabeth's cat, is fat' in this book, I might simultaneously identify an actual state of affairs in the world (locutionary speech), intend to poke fun at my daughter (illocutionary speech), and draw the response of playful anger (perlocutionary speech).

For some philosophers, this recognition of the interpersonal nature of language casts doubt on its referential function. Peter Winch criticizes Edward Evans-Pritchard's suggestion that, given the insights of meteorological science, we are justified in viewing the Azande belief that magic can influence the weather as mistaken (Winch, 1964; Evans-Pritchard, 1976). He argues instead that the social sciences should not adopt the realistic assumptions of the natural sciences, but rather seek to be hermeneutically sensitive to so-called 'primitive' cultures (Winch, 1990). Winch interprets Wittgenstein's notion of 'language games' and 'forms of life' as a reference to closed communities whose understanding of reality is incommensurable with alternative worldviews. This suggests a thoroughgoing relativism, in which science and magic inhabit different worlds and indulge in different language games: one seeking to describe the world, the other striving to cultivate a particular form of life. The implication is that the Azande engage in speech acts that are not concerned to offer propositional descriptions of reality. Stanley Fish adopts a similar anti-realistic stance, advocating a socio-pragmatic hermeneutic in which interpretative communities *construct* meaning (Fish, 1980, 1999). Here, the true meaning of a text is not inherent in the text itself, in the intentionality of the author, or in any connection with external reality; rather, it is located in the self-understanding of the interpretative communities as they read and interpret it (Wright, 2004a, pp. 23ff). According to his radical reader-response theory, the 'reader's response is not *to* the meaning; it *is* the meaning' (Fish, 1980, p. 3). Thus, a text will have as many meanings and truths as there are communities that read and interpret it; the authenticity of any given interpretation is reliant on the authority of the particular reading community. It follows that any knowledge of a realistic world 'out there' is always relative to the interpreting community. Like Winch before him, Fish moves from the observation that language functions as a means of interpersonal communication to the conclusion that truth is necessarily relative to the interpretative community rather than to the actual state of affairs in the world. The passage from propositional statements to speech acts is, according to this view, a journey from realism to non-realism.

Two comments are apposite here. The first is that Winch misreads Wittgenstein's notion of 'forms of life' and 'language games'. Rather than operating on the meta-level of discrete worldviews, Wittgenstein's examples always focus on the micro-level of one-to-one linguistic interactions: reporting, speculating, joking, telling stories, etc. His concern is to defend the universality of language: communication is possible only because we can recognize common micro-level language usage across different cultures. If a lion were to speak, we would not be able to understand it, since lions do not partake in the language games and forms of life that are common to human beings (Wittgenstein, 1968, p. 223). On the other hand, when the Azande speak, we are able to understand them because we recognize similarities between their language games and our own. The common range of human emotions, experiences, hopes and aspirations, expressed in shared language games and forms of life, effectively bridges any potential gulf between the rational Western philosopher and the Azande. We might struggle to tell whether a lion is grieving, but we quickly recognize human grief whether – according to cultural context – it manifests itself as raw emotion or studied stoicism. Because our speech acts are necessarily interpersonal, it follows that the communication of meaning is always a public affair and any notion of a private language fundamentally incoherent (pp. 88ff). Contra Winch, Wittgenstein's notion of forms of life and language games opens up, rather than denies, the possibility of cross-cultural understanding. This casts doubt on the claim that only Western scientists strive to engage with the real world, and that primitive forms of magic are not – in part at least – genuine, although mistaken, attempts to manipulate the natural order. The second comment concerns Fish's assumption that, by locating language in the everyday ebb and flow of interpersonal communication, we must inevitably embrace a thoroughgoing relativism. There is no reason why the culture-bound nature of our language should make it impossible to make informed judgements between conflicting truth claims. Fish appears to assume that, once one abandons the Cartesian criteria of absolute certainty as the basis for knowledge of the world, the only viable alternative is a thoroughgoing relativism. Anthony Thiselton welcomes Fish's '*emphasis on the historical contingency of the life-world as against a purely formal system*' (Thiselton, 1992, p. 539). However, in refusing to consider any position between the extremes of pure objectivity and absolute relativism, he effectively abandons the 'quest for any principle that would *relate* the life-world to a broader system' (p. 539). As a result, his reader-response theory bypasses the search for meaning and truth, and as such '*ultimately betrays the function which hermeneutics arose to perform*' (p. 539).

We can conclude that recognition of the complex and multi-faceted nature of interpersonal communication does nothing to undermine the claim that one of the primary cross-cultural functions of language is to describe reality. On the contrary, speech act theory recognizes the intimate relationship between locutionary statements ('God exists'), illocutionary statements ('I wish to persuade you that God exists'), and perlocutionary statements ('I have been convinced that God exists'). As Thiselton observes, this 'sheds light on the logical fallacy reflected in the overworn dualism . . . between on the one hand, description, objectification, report, and proposition, and on the other hand, address, promise, understanding and self-involvement' (p. 294). Religious texts 'frequently *address the reader as warnings, commands, invitations, judgements, promises or pledges of love*', yet at the same time 'these speech-acts also embody a propositional content' (p. 294). Thus, for example, Saint Paul is explicit about the necessary relationship between Christian faith and the propositional truth claims of the early church: 'If Christ has not been raised, then our proclamation has been in vain and your faith has been in vain' (1 Corinthians 15: 14). The illocutionary skill of the preacher is mere empty rhetoric, and the perlocutionary impact of preaching profoundly meaningless, unless the locutionary *content* of the proclamation actually converges with ultimate reality.

I began this section by asking how propositional language might relate to the ordinary lifeworlds of religious adherents and, as the discussion progressed, moved toward two conclusions. First, that speech-act theory offers a rich framework for understanding the range of communication that takes places within religious communities. Second, that speech-act theory, far from opening the door to a relativistic exclusion of propositional truth claims, actually enables us to locate propositional language within the ordinary everyday communications of religious adherents.

7.3 Metaphor and religious cognition

Metaphor, 'the application of a name or descriptive term or phrase to an object or action to which it is imaginatively but not literally applicable', is a common feature of religious language (Thompson, 1995, q.v. 'metaphor'). Metaphorical language includes a range of figures of speech or tropes. It can be metonymic, using the name of an attribute of an object to act as a substituted for the object itself: 'crown' for 'king', 'turf' for 'racecourse'. It can be synecdochic, taking a part as representative of the whole: 'there were many new faces at the meeting'. It can also be similetic, comparing one thing of another: 'the Word of God is a two-edged sword'. This raises a crucial question: can the imaginative, as opposed to literal, application of language have any cognitive role in describing reality?

The standard philosophical account of tropic language, which dominated Western literature from the time of Aristotle down to the Romantic era, viewed metaphor as mere rhetorical decoration, lending vividness, colour and emotional impact to speech, but lacking any cognitive value. On this reading, it is quite possible to substitute literal language for figurative language without altering the fundamental sense of a statement. Indeed, in the seventeenth and eighteenth centuries rational philosophers claimed that metaphor only serves to obscure meaning. According to John Locke, since figurative speech is designed simply to give pleasure it threatens to obscure clear ideas, and as such has no place in philosophical discourse:

> But yet, if we would speak of Things as they are, we must allow, that all the Art of Rhetorick, besides Order and Clearness, all the artificial

and figurative application of Words Eloquence hath invented, are for nothing else but to insinuate wrong *Ideas*, move the passions, and thereby mislead the Judgement.

(Locke, 1975, p. 508)

Nicholas Wolterstorff notes the irony of Locke's position: 'the persuasive power of Locke's writing depends heavily on his extraordinary gift for metaphor: "the white tablet of the mind", "the state of nature", "the candle of the Lord"' (Wolterstorff, 1996, p. 157). Retaining this sharp division between literal and metaphorical discourse, Rorty reverses traditional priorities by insisting on our freedom to create our own imaginary metaphorical worlds. This, he suggests, constitutes 'the final victory of poetry in its ancient quarrel with philosophy – the final victory of metaphors of self-creation over metaphors of discovery' (Rorty, 1989, p. 40; cf. Collier, 1994, p. 99). From a modernist perspective, metaphor threatens to shroud clear understanding in empty rhetoric; from a postmodern perspective, metaphor is itself threatened by crass literalism and base fact. Either way, the tradition running from Aristotle through Locke to Rorty assumes a gulf between literal and metaphorical language, and insists that metaphor has no cognitive value.

The rise of Romanticism in the late eighteenth and early nineteenth centuries challenged this separation between literal and metaphorical statements and suggested the latter makes a significant contribution to our understanding of reality. Putting the self-conscious constructions of poets to one side, it is clear that the tacit use of metaphor infuses every aspect of our ordinary lives (Lakoff and Johnson, 1980). We habitually use metaphor to refer to abstract entities not immediately accessible to our sense-experience. For example, we employ spatial metaphors to refer to the mind: 'I have it *in* mind to go shopping', 'the idea was *in the back* of my mind', 'it *comes to* mind that'. Since it is difficult to imagine how else we might refer to the mind, it is tempting to conclude that figurative language plays a *necessary* role in everyday communication.

Scientific discourse is similarly replete with metaphor: Big Bang, black hole, electro-magnetic field, gravitational pull. Indeed, 'metaphorical reasoning is at the very core of what scientists do when they design experiments, make discoveries, formulate theories and models, and describe their results to others' (Brown, 2003,

p. 14). In scientific discourse 'simple, fundamental concepts, such as time, quantity, and energy, are understood in terms of directly emergent, embodied experience (e.g. time as a linear dimension extending backward and forward from the present; energy as a surface)' (p. 160). We conceptualize microscopic entities in terms of our experience of familiar macroscopic objects: thus, we imagine an electron as a 'particle' or 'wave'. In conceptualizing complex systems, scientists draw on metaphors from the domain of social experience: in biology, a cell can function as a 'factory', and 'chaperone' proteins assist other proteins in folding (pp. 146ff). Hence, science understands the natural world 'largely in terms of metaphorical concepts, based on embodied understandings of how nature works' (p. 11).

It is possible to go further still and suggest that metaphor enables us to understand the world in ways that would otherwise be impossible. Roy Bhaskar, following Isaiah Berlin, invites us to contrast the following accounts of Germany under Nazi rule: (a) 'the country was depopulated', (b) 'millions of people died', (c) 'millions of people were killed', (d) 'millions of people were massacred' (Bhaskar, 1998, p. 59). He points out that, although all four of these literal, non-figurative, statements are true, all but account (d) 'generate the wrong perlocutionary force', because talk of depopulation, death and even killing bypasses the reality that the deaths 'were part of a single organized campaign of brutal killing' (p. 59). Hence (d) 'is not only the most evaluative, but is also the best (that is the most precise and accurate) description of what actually happened' (p. 59). Bhaskar's discussion alerts us to the fact that is it possible to describe precisely the same reality in different ways, and with different levels of truthfulness. With this in mind, consider Ulrich Simon's observation, with reference to Auschwitz, that the 'grapes have been trodden, the red juice flows, the harvest of a moral evaluation cannot be kept at bay' (Simon, 1978, p.64). The introduction of this image does not merely supplement the literal statements presented by Bhaskar: it invites us to engage with the situation in a manner that would be impossible without the use of the chosen metaphor.

This suggests that metaphor offers a unique and irreducible means of understanding reality. We encounter metaphor in its most develop state in poetry, and the great poets offer us not mere entertainment, but rather a depth of insight in the human condition that would not otherwise be available to us. As Hans-Georg Gadamer points out, 'it is the prejudice of a theory of logic that is alien to language if the metaphorical use of a word is regarded as not its real sense' (Gadamer, 1979, p. 389). According to Paul Ricoeur, poetic language has an irreducible power of disclosure and surplus of meaning that generates the possibility of deep understandings of reality (Ricoeur, 1977; cf. Stiver, 2001, p. 110). Although metaphor undoubtedly has enormous illocutionary and perlocutionary force in the way it enables us to *respond* to the world, it also has an irreducible locutionary function in *revealing* the nature of reality to us. This suggests, in turn, that religious metaphor plays a necessary cognitive role in the pursuit of ultimate truth: it is able to cross the border between the seen and unseen, known and unknown, immanent and transcendent, and as such possesses the ontological power to transform our understanding of the world (McFague, 1982). According to Ricoeur, religious metaphor is able to 'eclipse the objective, manipulative world' of brute fact and 'make way for the revelation of a new dimension of reality and truth' (Ricoeur 1976, p. 68; cf. Ward, 1996, p. 19). This recovery of the cognitive function of metaphor frees religious language from the reductionist strategies of empiricism, thereby enabling the believer to take talk of God, 'bound as it is within a wheel of images', as 'reality depicting' while still 'acknowledging its inadequacy as a description' (Soskice, 1985, p. 141).

7.4 Narrative and story

Without narrative and story, our speech acts would be little more than an arbitrary flow of atomistic expressions and performances (Loughlin, 1996, p. 139). Unless we are mad or drunk, we do not normally perform random acts and articulate haphazard ideas and subsequently try to understand them; on the contrary, our speech and actions flow from the stories we share with our fellow human beings, stories that give our lives meaning and purpose (Wright, N. T., 1992, p. 38). Thus, the Christian creeds are not merely a set of abstract theological propositions; rather, they derive their meaning from the overarching story they tell of God's creative, salvific and regenerative engagement with his creation, a story that frames the lives of Christians and reveals to them the meaning and purpose of existence. The role of narrative is substantial rather than merely stylistic: it is not simply that 'Christian convictions are best conveyed in story, rather than in proposition and maxim'; rather, the stories we live by constitute a *basic mode of human existence,* without which it would be impossible to live life in any deep or purposeful way (Loughlin, 1996, p. 64). Ricoeur argues that life itself embodies a basic drive towards narrative: human action is intentional and purposeful, occurs in the context of shared symbolic systems of meaning, and as such constitutes an 'activity and a passion in search of a narrative' (Ricoeur, 1991, p. 29). Drawing on Aristotle, he argues this basic drive leads us to tell stories that order and fuse the complexity of life: we do not view events as arbitrary occurrences, but rather make sense of them through narratives that bind character, event and situation into meaningful patterns. Such stories are located in time and, as such, enable us to understand history not merely as a random succession of events, but as a passage from a significant past towards an anticipated future. Stephen Crites goes further, proposing a 'narrativist phenomenology' that identifies a basic narrative structure at the heart of human consciousness and suggests that recollection and anticipation govern our sense of self even before we begin to tell stories (Crites, 1989, pp. 65ff).

According to Alasdair MacIntyre, our sense of personal identity is rooted in our life stories. He offers the illustration of a husband working in his garden: he may be gardening, preparing for winter, or pleasing his wife by taking exercise. All three descriptions may well be equally correct, but they have different functions: the first addresses the question of his primary intention at the time, the second places his endeavours in an annual cycle of domestic activity, the third situates his actions in the narrative history of his marriage and hence his life as a whole. If we are to establish a deep understanding of human action, we need to place isolated events in their broader historical patterns and sequences. More fundamentally, we all need to address the question of our place in the ultimate order-of-things – for the religious believer this involves understanding time-bound events in the light of eternity, for the secular believer this entails interpreting such events in the context of the natural order. 'Narrative history of a certain kind turns out to be the basic and essential genre for the characterization of human actions . . . we render the actions of others intelligible in this way because action itself has a basically historical character' (MacIntyre, 1985, pp. 208, 211f). MacIntyre recognizes that there is significant opposition to such a holistic approach to personal identity, and suggests two basic reasons for this (pp. 204f). The first is social: a tendency to partition life into various segments, each of which has its own accepted norms and modes of behaviour: work v. leisure, private v. public, corporate v. personal, etc. The second is philosophical: a tendency to analyse human action in atomistic terms, assuming that complex actions can be reduced a series of simply actions. This net result is the creation of a distinction between persons in themselves and their adopted roles, actions and personas. These are, for MacIntyre, inadequate reasons for rejecting narrative identity. First, because my personal identity cuts across the various social roles I perform: I am the person I am *because* I am a teacher, not *despite the fact* that I am a teacher. Second, because holistic actions take priority over atomistic ones, it is not possible to understand fully the simple actions of planning lessons, setting tasks and marking assignments apart from the complex act of being a teacher.

Interest in narrative identity amongst biblical theologians has lead to growing dissatisfaction with the tendency of modern historical criticism to dig beneath the surface narrative of the Bible in the quest for some underlying historical substrata. As Robert Alter points out, such approaches to biblical interpretation utilize 'a variety of analytical tools intended to uncover the original meanings of biblical words, the life situations in which specific texts were used, the sundry sources from which longer texts were assembled' (Alter, 1981, p. 13). Reacting against such reductive readings of the biblical text, which tend to assume a naturalistic worldview and bracket out transcendent explanations, Alter draws on the tools of literary criticism to recover a sense of biblical narrative as a whole:

> The religious vision of the Bible is given depth and subtlety precisely by being conveyed through the most sophisticated resources of prose fiction . . . The biblical tale, through the most rigorous economy of means, leads us again and again to ponder complexities of motive and ambiguities of character because these are essential aspects of its vision of man, created by God, enjoying or suffering all the consequences of human freedom . . . Almost the whole range of biblical narrative . . . embodies the basic perception that man must live before God, in the transforming medium of time, incessantly and perplexingly in relation with others.

(p. 22)

Karl Barth was one of the first modern theologians to attempt to read the Bible as an overarching narrative telling the story of God's reconciliatory dealings with his fallen creation. Building on his work, Hans Frei argued that what he terms the 'eclipse of biblical narrative' led to the deconstruction of the Christian story and its reformulation within the framework of secular naturalism: this effectively transformed the story of God's interaction with his creation into a story of the human generation of ancient texts. Consequently, biblical interpretation became 'a matter of fitting the biblical story into another world with another story rather than incorporating that world into the biblical story' (Frei, 1974, p. 130). Frei sought to counter this process by reading the Bible as a realistic narrative telling the story of God's dealings with humanity. He argued that this requires a hermeneutical circle that interprets the whole in terms of its parts, and the parts in terms of the whole. The 'whole' being the entire salvation history that begins with creation and ends with the final consummation of all things, and the central 'part' being the life of Jesus of Nazareth, whose identity as the Word of God incarnate as a human being within creation provides the interpretative key to the whole story.

The work of a number of theologians complements Frei's narrative reading of the Bible. Bernard Child's canonical approach to biblical interpretation seeks to read the biblical canon not as a loose bundle of separate literary texts, but holistically as the singular sacred narrative of the Christian Church (Childs, 1992). George Lindbeck sees the Christian narrative as providing 'communally authoritative rules of discourse, attitude, and action' that structure and organize the life of the Christian community, and within which the Christian lives and breathes (Lindbeck, 1984, p. 18). Stanley Hauerwas has developed a narrative approach to Christian ethics grounded in the development of virtue and character: 'The task of Christian ethics . . . is not to establish universal moral principles but to call Christians to preserve a community that tells the stories that make Christian virtues possible' (Placher, 1998, p. 349). As such, the church seeks to offer 'a political alternative' by witnessing to 'the kind of social life possible for those that have been formed by the story of Christ' (Hauerwas, 1981, p. 12).

For some theologians, narrative theology implies a rejection of propositional theology and hence of religious truth claims – a response closely linked to the modern equation of 'narrative' with 'fiction'. Thus, Colin Gunton views Lindbeck's critique of 'the cognitive-propositional conception of theology' as a direct 'attack on the notion of revealed religion' (Gunton, 1995, p. 7). Gunton is guilty of setting up a false either/or here: the creedal proposition that God was incarnate in the person of Jesus of Nazareth simply contracts and explicates the narrative theology presented in the four Gospels. As such, Christian creeds can be read simultaneously as narrative summaries of the Gospel story and propositional statements. Indeed, Lindbeck himself is clear that narrative theology need not entail a rejection of propositional theology: 'There is nothing in the cultural-linguistic approach that requires the rejection (or the acceptance) of the epistemological realism and correspondence theory of truth which, according to most of the theological tradition, is implicit in the conviction of believers' (Lindbeck, 1984, pp. 68f).

The claim that biblical narratives make realistic truth claims does not imply the factual or historical content of all biblical stories: the parables of Jesus, for example, together with the story of Jonah, and indeed many other biblical narratives, are clearly fiction. The fact that the truth of Christianity rests on the veracity of factual assertions, above all concerning the actuality of the incarnation and resurrection, does not preclude fictional narrative from illustrating, illuminating, and making a substantial and irreducible contribution to the Christian story as a whole. As Loughlin puts it, we can 'understand how the bible stories might be both history and poetry, remembrance and possibility, testaments of both past and future: faithful fictions' (Loughlin, 1996, p. 153). For the Christian, since the bedrock of reality is the Trinitarian God rather than the natural order-of-things, the criteria of truth is that of the appropriate relationship of any given narrative to divine reality rather than to naturalistically conceived historic events. Thus, both historical description and literary fiction can function to reveal theological truth. As Eric Auerbach notes, whereas a work of fiction constitutes an entertainment that intends 'merely to make us forget our own reality for a few hours', the biblical narrative 'seeks to overcome our reality':

> we are to fit our own life into its world, feel ourselves to be elements in its structure of universal history . . . Everything else that happens in

the world can be conceived as an element in this sequence; into it everything that is known about the world . . . must be fitted as an ingredient of the divine plan.

(Auerbach, 2003, pp. 15f)

Although our discussion has focused on developments within Christian theology, its potential application is far wider. My contention is that a narrative approach to ultimate truth is of relevance to all religious and secular traditions. There is enormous pedagogical value in approaching the worldviews of the religions and their secular counterparts in narrative terms. The Christian story tells of the Trinitarian God who creates the universe out of nothing, and responds to the reality of the fall of this creation through the redemptive incarnation of the Son and regenerative activity of the Spirit to bring about the final consummation and perfection of creation. A common secular story tells of the beginning of the universe in the Big Bang, the evolution of life culminating in the emergence of humanity, and the subsequent development of civilization and of attempts of humanity to live reasonably, responsibly, and justly in harmony with one another. Buddhism tells the story of human beings entrapped in the cycle of karma, of the Buddha as one of a series of enlightened beings, and of a path of deliverance from the universal experience of suffering, through which the attainment of nirvana – the cessation of desire and absorption of the self into the infinite – becomes a possibility. Approaching religious and traditions in terms of their overarching stories, and contrasting one with another, provides genuine insight into their respective truth claims. Indeed, it could be argued that contemporary religious education tends to focus on particular parts of a religious tradition at the expense of a coherent vision of the tradition as a whole.

One final observation: we need to recognize that we are talking about a series of religious and secular *meta-narratives*, and in doing so are pushing against the grain of a postmodern philosophy that seeks to deconstruct all such worldviews. Three brief comments are apposite here. The first is that religious education cannot afford to allow itself to be the slave of current intellectual fashion: the world's religions predate postmodernity by many centuries, and the status of postmodernity itself is currently the subject of sustained philosophical criticism in Western academies. Second, despite postmodern claims, meta-narratives are actually impossible to avoid; as I have argued elsewhere, postmodernity is itself a meta-narrative – one that, paradoxically, proclaims the end of all meta-narratives (Wright, 2004a). Third, the notion that meta-narratives are simply authoritarian stories that, if accepted, lead to the premature closure of responsible thought and action is untenable: properly understood, meta-narratives have the potential to emancipate our thinking by opening our minds to different ways of understanding reality.

7.5 Religious and secular worldviews

Narratives are not freestanding entities: they are rooted and embedded in the lifeworlds of communities and as such constitute one aspect of the basic worldviews through which we live out our lives. The following discussion returns to the work of Tom Wright that we considered briefly in Chapter 3. According to Wright, worldviews 'form the grid through which humans, both individually and in social groupings, perceive all of reality' (Wright, N. T., 1992, p. 32). The term 'embraces all deep-level human perceptions of reality', and as such is profoundly theological – using the term in its broadest sense to indicate all conversation that is concerned to examine, whether affirmatively or negatively, the transcendent nature of reality – since wherever 'we find the ultimate concerns of human beings, we find worldviews' (p. 122f). Although narrative constitutes a key element of all worldviews, they also include three other significant dimensions: basic questions, cultural symbols, and ways of being in the world (praxis). Since worldviews normally function on an implicit level, Wright cautions against overstressing the metaphor of sight: we should not take worldview to imply a primary process of stepping back and adopting some spectator-like perspective on reality, although it is in principle possible to step back from a worldview and reflect on it in such a manner (p. 123).

Wright is keenly aware of various deconstructive and reductive criticisms of the notion of worldview, and hence places his discussion in the context of a critically realistic epistemology. His understanding of worldviews should not to be taken as implying infallible knowledge of objective reality: as we shall see, worldviews are always provisional and subject to revision. However, the alternative to such epistemic certainty is not thoroughgoing scepticism. Steering a path between these two epistemological extremes, Wright maps out an understanding of

> the process of 'knowing' that acknowledges the *reality of the thing known, as something other than the knower* (hence 'realism'), while also fully acknowledging that the only access we have to this reality lies along the spiralling path of *appropriate dialogue or conversation between the knower and the thing known* (hence 'critical').

> (p. 35)

For the critical realist, initial observation of the world must be challenged by critical reflection on both the matter under observation and the process of observation, and only knowledge that can survive this challenge may claim to speak truly of reality. Since such dialogue constitutes an ongoing process, knowledge is always provisional. A crucial dimension of critical realism for Wright is that it deals not with atomistic packets of isolated sense data, from which we construct objects and events, but directly with the objects and events themselves. As such, it 'sees knowledge of particulars as taking place within the larger framework of the story or worldview which forms the basis of the observer's way of being in relation to the world' (p. 37). We do not discover knowledge by constructing an edifice from the building blocks of empirical data; rather 'knowledge takes place, within this model, when people *find things that fit* with the particular story or (more likely) stories to which they are accustomed to give allegiance' (p. 37). These methodological considerations are vital if we are to grasp the significance of worldviews for our understanding of reality. Negatively, critical realism enables us to avoid the traps of either reducing reality to merely the sum total of atomistic facts, or embracing a thoroughgoing scepticism about our ability to know anything of the actual order-of-things. Positively, by enabling us to identify different worldviews and reflect on our own, critical realism makes it possible to discern meaning, purpose and intention by asking crucial questions about truth.

Having established the epistemological and hermeneutical basis of Wright's argument, we can now go on to consider the four basic factors that, he suggests, come together to form distinctive worldviews: narrative and story, basic questions, cultural symbols, and praxis or ways of being in the world.

a) Worldviews provide *narratives or stories* through which human beings view reality. Indeed, a basic mode of human life 'can be seen as grounded in and constituted by the implicit or explicit stories which human beings tell themselves and one another' (p. 38). Stories are not merely illustrations or rhetorical adornments that function as a 'poor person's substitute for the "real thing"' (p. 38). All worldviews contain an irreducible narrative element that forms part of the implicit bedrock within which individuals and communities live out their lives. Although this implicit bedrock can – both in principle and at times in practice – emerge into explicit consciousness, for many it remains buried in the ebb and flow of ordinary life. It follows that the story or stories 'which characterize the worldview itself are thus located, on the map of human knowing, at a more fundamental level than explicitly formulated beliefs, including theological beliefs' (p. 38). If such foundational narratives are most obviously discernable in the myths of so-called 'primitive' cultures, modern examples are not hard to come by. The use of narrative is a significant feature of modern political debate: accounts of 'how things were in the Depression are used to fuel sympathy for the oppressed working class; stories of terrorism are used to justify present right-wing regimes' (pp. 38f). Such stories provide vital frameworks through which we experience the world and, as such, can be both instruments of ideological repression and emancipatory tools with which to challenge inadequate worldviews and unjust practices.

b) Worldviews address the *basic questions* that determine human existence. Drawing on a structural analysis of narrative, Wright identifies four such questions as crucial. Who are we? Where are we? What is wrong? What is the solution? All cultures cherish deep-rooted beliefs that provide answers to these questions, and although they are often merely implied in communal narratives they can, in principle, be made explicit both by 'insiders' and 'outsiders'. 'All cultures (that is to say) have a sense of identity, of environment, of a problem with the way the world is, and of a way forward – a redemptive eschatology to be more precise – which will, or may, lead out of that problem' (p. 123). We should not read this identification of a set of basic questions common to all humanity as an imperialistic attempt to force all cultures and traditions into a common straitjacket. On the contrary, the fact that different communities respond differently to these questions emphasizes their distinctive and distinguishing features, and us such offers the possibility of doing justice to the alterity and otherness of contrasting and conflicting worldviews.

c) Worldviews provide *cultural symbols* that help secure communal identity. Such symbols, which take the form of a rich variety of artefacts and events, reflect both the core narratives of a community and its key responses to basic questions. As the boundary markers through which 'insiders' and 'outsiders' are identified, such symbols function 'as the acted and visible reminders of a worldview that normally remains too deep for casual speech' (p. 124). Forming the core grid through which the world is encountered, they determine how reality is perceived on a daily basis, and 'what will, and what will not, be intelligible or assimilable within a particular culture' (p. 124). 'All cultures produce and maintain such symbols', and 'they can often be identified when challenging them produces anger or fear' (p. 124). We noted earlier Wright's example of a military victory parade through the street of Manhattan as symbolic of the American way of life: in the light of the anger and fear engendered by the subsequent terrorist attacks on the World Trade Centre, his words now appear prophetic.

Recognition of the universality of such symbol structures enables us to appreciate cultural differences better. This is seen clearly in Wright's comparison of the symbols of national identity in the United States of America today, and those of Jewish identity at the time of the destruction of the Temple in Jerusalem in 70 CE:

> In first-century Palestine, celebrating the Passover functioned similarly, with Jerusalem and the Temple taking the place of Manhattan, and the Passover sacrifice and meal taking the place of the victory parade. The buildings, instead of speaking of economic / ethnic goals, spoke of religious / ethnic ones; instead of the celebration speaking of triumph achieved over the forces of darkness, it spoke of vindication yet to come.
>
> (p. 123)

d) Worldviews provide a *praxis*, or *way of being in the world*. This follows directly from the last of Wright's basic questions: What is the solution? The response to this question implies some form of eschatology or future hope that inevitably requires some form of action. Indeed, Wright contends that the best way to understand a worldview is to observe how groups behave.

The choice of life aim – to make money, to raise a family, to pursue a vocation, to change society or the world in a particular way, to live in harmony with the created order, to develop one's own inner world, to be loyal to received traditions – reflects the worldview held.

(p. 124)

Recognizing that human intentionality and action is often neither clear nor consistent, Wright argues that this does not invalidate the place of action as a dimension of a worldview, rather it 'merely shows that the issue is complicated, and that the answer to the third question ("what is wrong?") should certainly include human muddledness' (p. 124).

Wright concludes that worldviews 'are thus the basic stuff of human existence, the lens through which the world is seen, the blueprint for how one should live in it, and above all the sense of identity and place which enables human beings to be what they are' (p. 124). If we choose to ignore worldviews, whether in the religious traditions we are studying or in the assumptions that we bring to such study, then our understanding will inevitably be impoverished.

7.6   Conclusion

If discrete religious traditions are the primary bearers of transcendent truth claims, then the best way of exploring such claims is by attending to the language employed by religious believers. I argued that the vast majority of religious traditions, whether explicitly or implicitly, make propositional claims about the ultimate nature of reality. However, to properly understand them, we have to attend to the role such propositions play in the broader life of religious communities. In particular, the way in which their speech acts serve to guide their efforts to live truthful lives in harmony with ultimate reality. I then noted that religious language is frequently metaphorical in nature, and defended the cognitive potential of metaphor as a means of engaging with reality. Such metaphors are not free-standing: they form part of the stories and narratives – more properly, the meta-narratives – through which religious believers make sense of their lives. Such meta-narratives form part of the worldviews of both religious and secular faith traditions. Hence, to fully appreciate the truth claims of discrete religious traditions we must attend to their worldviews.

8

Hermeneutics: understanding reality

We turn to the hermeneutical issue of the process of religious understanding. If discrete religious traditions are the primary bearers of transcendent truth claims, and such claims are most clearly visible in the cognitive propositions and worldviews presented by these traditions, then we must enable pupils to engage with them in a manner that engenders appropriate levels of critical insight and discernment. I begin by unpacking the basic contours of contemporary philosophical hermeneutics, go on to suggest that liberal religious education's hermeneutical presuppositions do relatively little to encourage critical thinking, and then offer my own reading of the potential contribution of contemporary hermeneutics to the pursuit of truth in religious education.

8.1 Philosophical hermeneutics

The 'realization that human expressions contain a meaningful component, which has to be recognized as such by a subject and transposed into his own system of values and meanings, has given rise to the "problem of hermeneutics"' (Bleicher, 1980, p. 1). In our plural world, it is impossible to avoid the tension between our own meanings and those of texts and traditions that present themselves to us as alien and difficult to decipher, hence the centrality of hermeneutics in contemporary thought. Modern hermeneutics has its roots in the Renaissance, which combined a renewed interest in the classical world with a growing historical awareness of the vast differences between ancient and modern culture. The Reformation further spurred its development, as the Protestant reformers struggled to make sense of the corpus of biblical and patristic literature newly stripped of centuries of Catholic veneer. The human-centred, naturalistic Enlightenment found itself struggling to find meaning in traditional God-centred, supranatural worldviews. Add to that the dramatic developments in both transport and communication, which effectively relocated occidental cultural in a broader global village populated by a plethora of previously unknown cultures, and the rise of modern hermeneutics appears, in retrospect, to have been inevitable (cf. Bleicher, 1980; Mueller-Vollmer, 1986; Palmer, 1969). Initially, the hermeneutics of the Enlightenment focused almost exclusively on the interpretation of written texts, quickly establishing itself as a general theory of the rules and methods of philological exegesis. As such, it supported a rich tradition of detailed textual exegesis that enjoyed its initial flowering in the work of Renaissance humanists, of whom the figure of Desiderius Erasmus was pre-eminent (Rummel, 2004).

Freidrich Schleiermacher recast the emergent tradition of modern hermeneutics within a romantic framework, seeking to go beyond philology by attending to the realm of personal experience (Schleiermacher, 1977). In doing so, he accepted the romantic reaction to the rationalism of the Enlightenment as it sought to rehabilitate the dimensions of aesthetic, moral and spiritual sensibility deemed to lie at the heart of authentic human existence. As a romantic theologian, Schleiermacher had a particular interest in biblical interpretation, which he approached in the light of his general understanding of religion. He argued that religion is a response to spiritual experience, which he understood as 'the consciousness of being absolutely dependent on, or, which is the same thing, of being in relation to God' (Schleiermacher, 1976, p. 12; 1958). Religious language offers expressions of such experience, rather than direct descriptions of divine reality: 'Christian doctrines are accounts of the Christian religious affections set forth in speech' (Schleiermacher, 1976, p. 76). The key function of language is to give outward expression to inner experience. Schleiermacher identified two hermeneutical phases in the interpretation of a text: the grammatical and the psychological. The former is concerned with the actual language of the text, while the latter seeks to engage with the experiences of the author lying behind the text. To understand a text, it is necessary to penetrate beyond its outer linguistic form into its inner experiential core.

> Just as every act of speaking is related to both the totality of the language and the totality of the speaker's thoughts, so understanding a speech

always involves two moments: to understand what is said in the context of the language with its possibilities, and to understand it as a fact in the thinking of the speaker.

(Schleiermacher, 1977, p. 97)

Understanding is impossible unless we first undertake the necessary grammatical groundwork: using the tools of philology to establish an accurate text; translate it correctly; identify its form and structure; and locate it in its historical and cultural context. However, words are mere dry bones unless fleshed out and brought to life through an appreciation of the human experience that lies behind them. Hence, the primary task of the reader is to establish a 'feel' for the subject matter of the text and thereby enter empathetically, in an act of imagination, into the psychological reality of the mind responsible for its creation. For Schleiermacher 'understanding as an art is the reexperiencing of the mental processes of the text's author' (Palmer, 1969, p. 86). This enables the interpreter to look beyond language towards the dynamic spiritual realities that underlie the text and to which the text refers to. The act of understanding is 'the act of a living, feeling, intuitive human being' and us such necessarily extends far beyond mere linguistic comprehension (p. 85).

Wilhelm Dilthey extended the scope of hermeneutics beyond textual interpretation to the human sciences – the *Geisteswissenschaften* – whose 'realm extends from the style of life and the forms of social intercourse to the system of purposes which society has created for itself and to custom, law, state, religion, art, science and philosophy' (Mueller-Vollmer, 1986, 155). In doing so, he sought to make Schleiermacher's romantic hermeneutics the basis of a comprehensive methodology for the emerging human sciences, whose task is to approach history and culture as expressions of lived experience.

The tradition of romantic hermeneutics culminated in the phenomenology of Edmund Husserl (Husserl, 1976). When attempting to understand the various phenomena that present themselves to us, it is necessary to penetrate beyond their surface appearances to reveal their hidden essences. Husserl grounds his hermeneutics in the twin principles of 'epoche' and 'eidetic vision'. The process of epoche, from the Greek 'abstention' or 'suspension of judgement', seeks to bracket out the presuppositions of the observer and thereby establish a neutral attitude towards the object of investigation. At the heart of all cultural phenomena stands the irreducible intentionality of the human participants, an intentionality that the observer must not explain away in the light of her prejudices and presuppositions. The establishment of a neutral vantage point makes possible the emergence of eidetic vision, which is concerned to identify essences within or behind phenomena. Husserl here draws on the Greek term *eidos*, in its Platonic sense of 'universal essence': 'such essences express the "whatness" of things, the necessary and invariant features of phenomena that allow us to recognize phenomena as phenomena of a certain kind' (Allen, 1987, p. 275). Thus, in observing the phenomenon of religion, the interpreter must first bracket out any presuppositions regarding the truth and value of religion, and then seek to allow the phenomenon to manifest itself to her. As a result, she comes to understand that at the heart of all distinctively religious phenomena is the intentionality of the participants, which is directed towards the realm of the transcendent, sacred or divine. This is why, strictly speaking, Ninian Smarts influential six-fold typology of religion is not genuinely phenomenological: the doctrinal, mythical, ethical, ritual, experiential and social dimensions that he identifies as being central to religion are also present in other non-religious traditions, such as Humanism and Marxism. What these secular traditions lack, but which religious traditions embrace, is a fundamental intentionality orientated towards the realm of the supranatural or transcendent.

Hans-Georg Gadamer's *Truth and Method*, first published in 1960, constitutes a watershed in the history of modern hermeneutics (Gadamer, 1979; Warnke, 1987; Weinsheimer, 1985). Where romantic hermeneutics had primarily been concerned with establishing methods and procedures for the process of understanding, Gadamer took the view 'that hermeneutics has nothing to do with the creation or validation of specific methodologies' (Mueller-Vollmer, 1986, p. x). His own view was that hermeneutics should adopt a broader philosophical perspective and concern itself with fundamental ontological questions concerning the nature, ground and possibility of understanding. 'I am not proposing a method, but I am describing what is the case' (Gadamer, 1979, p. 465). In effect, Gadamer brought about a seismic shift in the hermeneutical tradition: no longer concerned merely with explicating an interpretative methodology, hermeneutics took on the task of offering a phenomenological description and philosophical analysis of the nature of understanding itself.

Recognizing that Husserl's desire to bracket out the presuppositions of the interpreter has its roots in the Enlightenment's vision of objective value-free knowledge, Gadamer insisted that understanding is necessarily rooted in presupposition and prejudice. He argued that the subjectivity of the interpreter is unavoidable, and that, far from threatening understanding, our presuppositions form an integral part of the learning process. Hence he was concerned to rehabilitate *Die Vorurteile* – prejudice, prejudgement, presupposition – as a necessary dimension of the hermeneutical process. As we have already had occasion to note, the fact that, 'long before we understand ourselves through the process of self-examination, we understand ourselves in a self-evident way in the family, society and state in which we live', means that 'the prejudices of the individual, far more than his judgements, constitute the historical reality of his being' (p. 245). Since we necessarily understand the world from within the traditions we inhabit, it follows that 'there is no unconditional antithesis between tradition and reason' (p. 250). Hence the ironic observation that the Enlightenment's rejection of prejudice itself constitutes a particular prejudice rooted in a specific historical tradition: 'the fundamental prejudice of the Enlightenment is the prejudice against prejudice itself, which deprives tradition of its power' (p. 239). Once we recognize that we always carry a set of presuppositions with us, we can come to understand the process of understanding as a dialogue between our horizon of meaning and the horizon of meaning of that which we are seeking to understand. Gadamer here develops the notion of the hermeneutical circle, shifting its focus from an interest in the relationship between the whole and the parts of a text to a concern for the circular relationship between text and interpreter. The fact that these two horizons of meaning are frequently at odds with one another provides the hermeneutical process with its basic drive: the 'recognition that all understanding inevitably involves some prejudices gives the hermeneutical problem its real thrust' (p. 239).

Gadamer suggests that a 'person who is trying to understand a text is always performing an act of projection' (p. 237). Interpreters come to the text with a set of presuppositions which they then projected onto the text in anticipation that they will be proved correct. As such, they

> 'jump the gun', as it were, because they anticipate a meaning for the whole before arriving at it. What the interpreter projects in advance is what he understands already – that is, before the beginning. He tries out a meaning already familiar to him and proposes it as a possibility. This projected meaning is his own possibility in that he has projected it; it is part of the world he already knows his way around, and is something he can and does understand.
>
> (Weinsheimer, 1985, p. 109)

If we allow our prejudices to dominate the text, then it is likely, unless there is already agreement between the two, that our understanding of it will be inadequate, distorted, or simply wrong. Hence, the projection of presuppositions is only the first stage in an ongoing dialectical process: if we are genuinely open to the text, we will recognize any tensions that exist between its claims and our presuppositions, and consequently seek some form of resolution. Gadamer's vision is one of a process of ongoing dialogue in which text and interpreter continually push each other towards deeper understanding. It is of course possible to start entirely on the wrong foot and project a meaning that is inappropriate to the text. If the interpreter holds her initial projection firmly and is not open to the possibility of its revision following her encounter with the text, misunderstanding is likely. If, on the other hand, the interpreter has the openness and sensitivity to realize that her interpretation has misunderstood what the text is saying, she will attempt a new projection in the light of the lessons learnt as a result of her initial encounter, and thus the possibility of true understanding will remain open. 'In this process our prejudices will have to either prove adequate to the subject-matter or have to be modified, and it is in this trial and error approach that the truth claim of the text can come to the fore' (Bleicher, 1980, p. 111).

For Gadamer, this dialogue between horizons of meaning is fundamentally concerned with questions of truth, an issue effectively bracketed out by romantic hermeneutics. This is because to 'understand what a person says is . . . to agree about the object, not to get inside another person and relive his experiences' (Gadamer, 1979, p. 345). No amount of empathetic engagement with a text can answer the question as to whether what it has to say is actually true. Romantic interpretations of the bible and classical literature became 'completely detached from all dogmatic interest' (p. 173). 'Neither the saving truth of scripture nor the canonical exemplariness of the classics was to influence a procedure that was able to grasp every text as an expression of life and ignore the truth of what was said' (p. 173). In sharp contrast, the model of hermeneutics as a conversation between different horizons of meaning opens up the possibility of a text revealing something new, of its challenging our acknowledged interpretative framework. 'A person trying to understand a text is prepared for it to tell him something . . . [which] is why a hermeneutically trained mind must, from the start, be sensitive to the text's quality of newness' (p. 239). Such sensitivity will enable the text 'to assert its own truth against one's own fore-meanings' (p. 239).

This opens up the possibility of a transformative hermeneutic in which the interpreter learns directly from the text. Such learning will inevitably alter her horizon of meaning: 'to reach an understanding with one's partner in a dialogue is not merely a matter of total self expression and the successful assertion of ones own point of view, but a transformation into a communion, in which we do not remain what we are' (p. 341). For Gadamer

> the interpretative situation is no longer that of a questioner and an object, with the questioner having to construct 'methods' to bring the object within his grasp; on the contrary, the questioner suddenly finds himself the being who is interrogated by the 'subject matter'.
>
> (Palmer, 1969, p. 165)

Gadamer's work has drawn two very different sets of responses. The first, that of postmodern hermeneutical theory, challenges the very possibility of a transformative hermeneutic oriented towards the pursuit of truth. Since I have dealt with postmodernity in some depth elsewhere, our reflections here will be brief (Wright, 2001b, 2004a). Postmodern hermeneutical theory has a twin focus: the deconstruction of false claims to knowledge, and the affirmation of the contingency and relativity of all understanding (Eco, 1981; Fish, 1980; Noble, 1994, 1995). Negatively, it encourages recognition of, and emancipation from, the belief that the discovery or disclosure of authentic knowledge is possible. Positively, it seeks to maximize and celebrate the diversity of possible interpretations of a text. Reader-response theories 'call attention to the active role of communities of readers in constructing what counts for them as 'what the text means" (Thiselton, 1992, p. 15). Since such constructs are relative to specific communities, there can be as many meanings of a text as there are reading communities: indeed more, since a community can choose to read the text in different ways at different times. Exegesis becomes eisegesis – not the reading *out* of the original meaning of the text, but the reading *in* of the preferences of the reading community – as interpreters embrace the ongoing postmodern cycle of creating, deconstructing and recreating arbitrary worldviews. Although religious language may have some utility in offering raw material for the postmodern game of arbitrary reality creation, its truth does not extend beyond its pragmatic value for those with religious inclinations who choose to engage with it (Cupitt, 1991; Hart, 1991; Taylor, M. C., 1982, 1984).

The second response to Gadamer's work is that of critical hermeneutics, closely linked to Jurgen Habermas and Frankfurt school of critical theory (Habermas, 1989, 1991). Habermas' fundamental interest is a moral one, rooted in his recognition of the spiritual fragmentation of modernity. He identifies one of the primary causes of this fragmentation in a form of instrumental reasoning, associated with the technological fruits of positivistic science, which differentiates fact from value and identifies practical efficiency as *the* basic criteria for success. The result is a spiritually impoverished society that stakes its well-being on its ability to manipulate the natural world. For Habermas, it is not possible to secure protection against the excesses of instrumental reason through either the romantic turn to experience or the postmodern deconstruction of scientific realism. Both the romantic and the postmodernist react against the excesses of Enlightenment rationalism by attempting to bypass reason rather than transform it. The hope for spiritual rejuvenation lies within language itself, since it is the 'structural limits and possibilities of language [that] define the scope of possible understanding' (Ingram, 1987, p. 116). Hence, Habermas seeks to recover the original emancipatory promise of the Enlightenment by transforming our understanding of the nature and scope of language.

Gadamer and Habermas share a number of common concerns. First, both reject romantic and postmodern hermeneutics as embodying an innate conservatism and lack of critical edge. Second, both recognize the complexity and cognitive potential of language, and consequently reject any ostensive model of language that reduces it to the functions of providing surface descriptions of the natural world, and bringing to expression inner states of consciousness. Third, both recognize the two horizons of the inter-preter and the text, and affirm the possibility of a transformative reading of a text.

Habermas' critique of Gadamer focuses on what he sees as his inherent idealism, which leads ultimately to a lack of critical rigour (McCarthy, 1978, pp. 187–193). He contends that Gadamer's notion of the fusion of horizons implies a neo-Hegelian consensus theory of truth, in which both horizons of meaning merge into some middle-ground compromise. This fails to take account of the pos-sibility that one or other horizon of meaning might be irredeemably mistaken: in which case the fusion of mutual understanding needs to give way to the rejection of one horizon by the other. Under-standing must 'reflect the possibility of ideological distortion within the tradition's self-formulation' (Warnke, 1987, pp. 140f). Habermas links the potentially ideological nature of the text to the fact that language is communal in nature and always functions within a social context. As such, it is impossible to abstract language from the various power structures operating within society. Reason can function instrumentally in the service of such power structures, in the process imposing ideological representations that lead to the loss of freedom and distortion of truth. Habermas analyses this through a distinction between lifeworlds and systems (Habermas, 1989, pp. 113ff). As we noted earlier, 'lifeworld' refers to the given, pre-reflective horizon of meaning through which members of society live out their everyday lives: the assumptions, values and expectations that they take granted and which do not require analysis or justification. Modernity has engendered a series of political, technological, economic and educational systems, often in the form of state agencies, which alienate the lifeworlds of particular communities. The spiritual crisis of modernity stems from the fact that the ideological authority of these systems imposes itself on our lifeworlds in a process of colonization. The concern of these systems is instrumental, seeking to regulate the lifeworld for ideological and political purposes. In effect, the 'system integrates diverse activities in accordance with the adaptive goals of economic and political survival by regulating the unintended consequences of strategic action through market or bureaucratic mechanisms that constrain the scope of voluntary decision' (Ingram, 1987, p. 115).

The rationality utilized by such systems tends to be instrumental in nature, operating with the intention of achieving a specific end. Habermas identifies a number of forms such instrumental communication adopts. In *teleological communication,* the speaker seeks to influence others 'in order to bring opponents to . . . grasp beliefs and intentions that are in the speaker's own interest' (Habermas, 1991, p. 95). The process of *normative communication* 'presupposes language as a medium that transmits cultural values and carries a consensus that is merely reproduced with each additional act of understanding' (p. 95). The language of *dramaturgical communication* serves as a means of self-expression or self-presentation in which 'language is assimilated to stylistic and aesthetic forms of expression' (p. 95). In each case, the act of communication restricts individual freedom and distorts truth, either by persuading people to think and act in a certain way, by imposing a set of norms on them, or by imposing a relativistic ideology that insists that all self-expression is necessarily correct.

Habermas draws his proposed solution to this dilemma from the critical theory of the Frankfurt School, which looked for emancipation from distorted communication in the form of linguistic exchanges capable of identifying and bringing to public consciousness the various sources of ideological repression (Wiggershaus, 1995). Habermas' own version of critical theory transcended the original Marxist orientation of the Frankfurt School. His theory of 'communicative action' sought to defend a form of rationality that transcends the limitations of instrumental reason by introducing a critical dimension to the very heart of interpersonal discourse. Communicative action accepts that truth claims are always contestable and recognizes the dangers of ideological distortion. Its fundamental concern is that communication be orientated towards the pursuit of truth.

> Only the communicative model of action presupposes language as a medium of uncurtailed communication whereby speakers and hearers, out of the context of their preinterpreted lifeworld, refer simultaneously to things in the objective, social and subjective worlds in order to negotiate common definitions of the situation.
>
> (Habermas, 1991, p. 95)

Such 'common definitions' are not compromises for the sake of harmony, but judgements about truth.

Habermas is committed to a notion of contingent rationality. Ideally, all partners in the educational context will enter it with an initial commitment to the truth, as they understand it within their own given traditions. All will be committed to the public establishment of truth, and recognize that others understand reality in ways that may converge, contrast or conflict with their own. Hence, public education becomes a medium concerned to enhance and develop the quality of conversations about the true nature of reality. Its aim is mutual understanding through shared discourse, rather than premature agreement around a false consensus or the imposition of the views of one group upon another. Although such understanding can be genuinely transformative in Gadamer's sense, it is no longer dependent on an idealized fusion of horizons: ongoing conversation between horizons is committed to the pursuit of truth rather than any premature shared agreement. If the long-term goal remains that of establishing such agreement, the limitations of human knowledge mean that the short term goal must be that of forms of mutual understanding that recognize areas of fundamental disagreement and retain a commitment to continue to search for truth.

8.2   The hermeneutics of liberal religious education

This rich hermeneutical tradition has influenced contemporary religious education on an implicit level: many of the themes and issues that it raises, and the various responses it suggests, are clearly visible – albeit often in fragmented form – in the literature. However, there has been relatively little attempt to think through the hermeneutics of religious education in a systematic manner (Wright, 1997, 1998b). There is no space to attempt such a task here, and our discussion must necessarily limit itself to a consideration of the ways in which contemporary religious education has assimilated fragments of the hermeneutical tradition, together with – in the next section – an outline sketch of a hermeneutical framework for critical religious education. In undertaking the former task, I will focus on four main trajectories within contemporary religious education: implicit, phenomenological, spiritual and contextual.

a) Hermeneutics first emerged as an issue in contemporary religious education during the era of *implicit religious education* in the 1960s (Loukes, 1961, 1965). Retaining a commitment to Christian confessionalism, implicit educators held fast to a clear conception of the horizon of meaning of religion itself, albeit one limited to the truth claims of Christianity. The key hermeneutical issue was that of the perceived gulf between the ordinary lifeworld of pupils and the worldview of Christianity. As we have already seen, the basic reason for this gulf was the emergence of an increasingly secular and plural society, in which Christianity play only a limited role in the lifeworlds of many pupils. Loukes' response to this situation was to employ a neo-romantic hermeneutic that sought to start from the lifeworlds of pupils, to encourage them to articulate their core experiences and questions about the meaning of their lives and, from there, to build a bridge to the experiences of Christians and the answers that Christianity provides to such questions. However, Loukes failed to recognize that the fragmented relationship between the lifeworlds of pupils and the system of Christianity had plunged the latter into a crisis of legitimacy, and that attempts to encourage pupils to embrace an increasingly alien system of thought in a non-critical and frequently paternalistic manner simply reinforced perceptions of religious education's engagement in a tacit process of indoctrination. While implicit religious education, in the form advocated by Loukes, succeeded in taking the horizons of meaning of pupils and Christianity seriously, its lack of any critical perspective meant that religious education was attempting, in effect, to colonize the former with the latter.

The reading of the hermeneutical challenge facing implicit religious education developed by Goldman involved a subtle change of emphasis (Goldman, 1964). Adopting an experiential-expressive model of religion, which viewed religious language as the external expression of inner spiritual experience, he argued that the reason for the gulf between pupils' horizons and the horizon of Christianity was the result of inadequate teaching grounded on a misunderstanding about how pupils think. Claiming that pupils move from concrete to abstract modes of thought, he suggested that religious educators introduce pupils to Christian teaching prematurely, thereby instilling in them the habit of thinking concretely about Christian truth claims. Once they move to the stage of abstract thought, such concrete thinking leads to the confusion of religion with forms of magic; that is to say, literalistic thinking about Christian beliefs leads directly to a conflict with modern science and hence to the rejection of Christianity as outmoded superstition. If Christianity is to be understood as an expression of profound spiritual experience, pupils must understand Christian teaching in abstract rather than concrete terms. In order for this to happen, religious education must avoid presenting explicit accounts of Christianity while pupils still think in concrete terms. Hence the initial task of religious education was to nurture the capacity of pupils for deep spiritual experience. Once this is firmly in place, and pupils are old enough to think in abstract terms, then explicit accounts of Christianity can be presented to them in a manner that enables them to look beyond the external expressions of Christianity into its experiential heart. Goldman's experiential-expressive model of religion effectively sidelined Christian truth claims: if Christianity makes primary reference not to the ultimate order-of-things, but to the deep experiences of believers, then the question as to whether such experiences accord with reality remains unanswered. Further, the horizon of meaning of pupils is limited to their capacity for spiritual feeling and empathy, and little attention is given to their specific beliefs and worldviews. In addition, the engagement between the horizons of meaning of pupil and Christianity is an uncritical one. Like Loukes, Goldman's primary aim was to establish an experiential bridge between the two, in the belief that once-established critical questions about the truth of Christianity need not be asked, since its truth would be apparent once pupils cross the bridge provided by their teachers.

Both Loukes and Goldman adopted, albeit by default, versions of Schleiermacher's romantic hermeneutic. According to implicit religious education, the emergence of a gulf between pupil and Christianity is rooted in the failure of pupils to properly understand Christianity. Since they have only a limited depth of spiritual insight, they cannot engage with the spiritual insights of Christianity unless the teacher first facilitates changes in their horizons of meaning. In all of this, implicit educators assumed the basic truth of Christianity: hence, implicit religious education constituted a form of neo-confessionalism that sought to colonize pupils into a Christian worldview in an uncritical manner.

b) Forms of *phenomenological religious education* sought to take pluralism seriously by structuring the curriculum around the horizons of meaning of a range of religious and secular traditions (Sharpe, 1975). At the outset, it was concerned to hold fast to the transcendent truth claims of the religions, identifying the phenomenological essence of religion as the intentionality of religious adherents, as this was directed towards the realm of the sacred, divine or transcendent. The major problem with the phenomenological treatment of the horizon of religion was its tendency to treat discrete religious traditions as variations of the generic phenomenon of religion itself. This meant that the distinctive truth claims of particular religious traditions was subsumed into the broader generic truth claim of the existence of some form of transcendent reality, to which different traditions offer culture-bound, and hence relativistic, responses. The horizon of the pupils fared even worse. The phenomenological version of romantic hermeneutics required pupils to bracket out their presuppositions and engage empathetically with the transcendent vision of religion. The combined failure to take the truth claims of discrete religions seriously, together with the lack of interest in the actual beliefs and worldviews of pupils, meant the any critical engagement with these two horizons of meaning was exceedingly difficult, if not impossible, to sustain. The fact that the primary medium of understanding was that of non-linguistic experience only served to exacerbate this situation. Although teachers encouraged pupils to describe religious phenomena, such description was necessarily superficial. It was assumed that secondary expressions of religious culture derived from primary spiritual experiences. Hence, in line with standard romantic hermeneutics, religious understanding was expected to pass beyond secondary expressions and establish empathy with religious adherents in order to relive at first hand their spiritual experiences. This left little space for pupils to engage directly with questions of ultimate truth. The best one could expect to achieve was to produce spiritually sensitive pupils attuned to a generic experience of transcendence. Critical questions as to whether such experience accords with the actual order-of-things, and whether all such experience possesses equal veracity, were bracketed out of the agenda of phenomenological religious education.

c) The turn to *spiritual religious education* was inspired, at least in part, by the increasingly reductive nature of phenomenological approaches. As we have seen, David Hay called for a radically counter-cultural approach to religious education (Hay, 1982a, 1982b, 1985). Insisting that there is good empirical evidence to see the capacity for spiritual experience of transcendence as part of our biological make-up, he insisted that the subject should challenge the secularizing tendency of modernity; in particular its deeply rooted and fundamentally misplaced suspicion of the spiritual. Although it is refreshing to encounter such a vigorous intent to place the pursuit of spiritual truth centre stage in religious education, Hay's agenda ultimately suffers from his dependence on a romantic hermeneutic. In terms of the horizon of religion, his focus on the universality of our capacity for spiritual experience combined an experiential-expressive model of religion that down-played the role of cognitive truth claims and a universal theology that saw discrete religious traditions as culturally bound, and hence relativistic, expressions of a universal experience of tran-scendence. In terms of the horizon of pupils, Hay was concerned to develop a child-centred pedagogy that took their experiences seriously. However, his stress on the primacy of experience over linguistic expression, coupled with a thoroughgoing individualism, invited pupils to contemplate their private spiritual inner space at the expense of any concern for their relationship with others, with the natural world, and with the ultimate order of things. Although Hay later replaced his individual focus with a stress on relational spirituality, his romantic adherence to the primacy of prelinguistic experience remained firmly in place (Hay, 1998). The net effect of Hay's reading of the twin horizons of religion and pupil was to undermine the possibility of a critical engagement between the two. Hay's pedagogy – remarkably similar in form to that of implicit religious education – assumed that pupils failed to understand religion because their capacity for any depth of spiritual experience had been eroded by the forces of secularism. Hence the primary task of religious education was to reignite their latent capacity for spiritual experience. Once this had been achieved, pupils would be able to appreciate the experiential heart of religious traditions. However, this left little room for assessing the veracity of such experience. Since the empirical evidence Hay presents shows only the universality of our capacity for self-transcendence, it remains

196 Critical Religious Education and Multiculturalism

an open question as to whether such self-transcendence requires a specifically religious interpretation, and if so, in terms of which particular religion. This theological ambiguity is only resolved in favour of Hay's universal theology through a process of uncritical confessionalism. Once again, the implied use of a romantic hermeneutic failed to engender a critical engagement between our two horizons of meaning.

As a result, Hay's theological realism quickly gave way to forms of spiritual anti-realism (Erricker and Erricker, 2000; Erricker, 2001). According to this tradition, whether our experience of transcendence are a response to nature, or to some transcendent realm is immaterial. What matters is that pupils have the capacity for self-transcendence: that they are able to break free from the shackles of the dominant culture(s) they find themselves trapped within in order to create their own autonomous spiritual lives. Hence, it invokes a postmodern reader-response hermeneutic. This concern for autonomy was closely associated with a concern that pupils tolerate the spiritual experience of others. Hence postmodern forms of spiritual education came to see the twin virtues of freedom and tolerance as ends in themselves: it does not matter what pupils believed, so long as they were free to pursue their preferences in an atmosphere of mutual tolerance. This position marks the complete collapse of critical thinking in religious education, and the ultimate triumph of comprehensive liberalism over political liberalism.

d) The approach of *contextual religious education* is more ambiguous: one strand of this tradition points towards a genuinely critical hermeneutic, while another merely reinforces the poverty of a romantic-based hermeneutic. One of its great strengths is its concern to ground the study of religion in the immediate life-worlds of pupils. Unlike forms of spiritual education, contextual approaches are generally concerned to move beyond abstract experience, encourage pupils to attend to the language they use to describe their core beliefs, and locate these beliefs in the context of their personal and social relationships. At the same time, it is also concerned to take the horizon of religions seriously, and engage – albeit to a limited extent – with the lifeworlds of discrete religious traditions. Further, it has a far richer conception of the nature of the engagement between the horizons of pupil and religion. Thus, for example, work in continental Europe concerned with 'theologizing' with pupils specifically encourages them to engage with, and respond to, selected religious texts (Kraft, 2004). Generally speaking, this points towards a far richer hermeneutic, one with enormous potential for critical religious education.

However, despite displaying such potential, much contextual religious education – although by no means all – carries with it a range of hermeneutical assumptions that threaten to undermine the critical process of engaging with ultimate truth claims. First, it tends to play down the substantial identity of discrete religious traditions and, in doing so, undermines their status as bearers of ultimate truth claims. Such traditions, it is claimed, are basically artificial academic constructions that contain no substantial identity and, as such, should be broken down to their constituent parts. Second, if discrete religions can no longer be seen as primary bearers of ultimate truth claims, then that role can only be played by individual believers; consequently, we should attend to their individual perceptions of reality. Third, the implied use of reader-response theory suggests that perceptions of reality are relative to the individual, that therefore religious traditions can only be judged on the basis of their pragmatic value, and that ultimately it is the freedom and responsibility of individuals to create their own preferred worldviews.

These two very different readings of the hermeneutical strategies of contextual religious education suggests that this emergent approach to religious education stands at a crossroads, with the possibility of turning in either a critical or non-critical direction. This issue is exemplified in the work of Robert Jackson. He argues the case for interpretative or hermeneutical methods in religious education, and suggests that one basic aim of religious education should be to 'develop an understanding of the grammar – the language and wider symbolic patterns – of religions and the interpretative skills necessary to gain that understanding' (Jackson, 1977, p. 129). He insists that the subject needs to be critically aware of its presuppositions, especially the way in which it represents religion in the classroom, since 'particular received views of cultures, or views constructed by those with power and influence, can have a major impact on the ways in which religious traditions are perceived and evaluated' (p. 129). This requires the introduction of a critical edge to classroom teaching and learning, in which 'the debates about the nature of religions and cultures become *part* of religious education' (p. 129). Further, he claims that 'the critical element can also open up questions of truth and meaning for anyone participating in religious education' (p. 129). In all this, Jackson is fundamentally concerned to respect the horizons of meaning of pupils: they 'are themselves from a range of religious and non-religious backgrounds, and bring their own knowledge and experience, their questions, observations and their own critical edge to the classroom' (p. 130).

Jackson's hermeneutical position resonates with the concerns of critical religious education, and parallels in many respects the hermeneutical framework set out in the next section of this chapter. However, Jackson's use of the notion of 'edification' to draw together his hermeneutical reflections raises a number of concerns. Jackson portrays the engagement between the horizon of pupil and religion in ethnographic terms: it is a process of 'grasping another's way of life', one 'inseparable in practice from that of pondering on the issues and questions raised by it' (p. 130). Jackson draws on Rorty to describe such pondering as a potentially transformative process of edification: 'to be edified, in this sense, is to be taken out of one's own self', since in ' "unpacking" another worldview one can, in a sense, become a new person' (pp. 130f). The crucial issue here is precisely what such 'unpacking' involves, and Jackson's answer is ambiguous. On the one hand, his commitment to the importance of truth suggests a critical engagement with questions about ultimate reality of the kind favoured here. On the other, his claim that discrete religious traditions are mere academic creations would appear to rule them out as bearers of truth, and he pays relatively little attention to philosophical and theological debates about truth, preferring instead to ground his discussion in a sociological framework notorious for its preference for forms of naturalism and relativism. Further, and perhaps most significantly, in discussing the process of contemplating different worldviews he insists that 'such reflective activity is personal to the student' (p. 130). This suggests that there can be no external criteria for assessing the results of such contemplation, beyond that of the utility of the process for the individual student. This being the case, Jackson's notion of 'edification' – like that of Rorty, upon which it draws – actually constitutes a pragmatic move within an ultimately relativistic vision of the world rather than the basis for a rigorous pursuit of truth.

Thus, liberal religious education has tended to assume romantic and postmodern hermeneutical outlooks, although the emergence of contextual religious education reflects, in some instances, a new interest in critical hermeneutics. It is illuminating to consider modern religious education in the light of Habermas' hermeneutical analysis. Here the subject functions within a public education system that is increasingly differentiated from the lifeworlds of adherents of most religious and non-religious traditions. In the main, effective ownership of religious education has passed from the religious communities to the state and, as such, it reflects the state's agenda of instrumental rationality: if the state requires social stability through the recovery or development of public systems of value, then religious education justifies its place within the public education system by providing just that. Thus the neo-confessionalism of the 1960s operated with a *teleological rationality* in which children were taught to grasp the truth of Christianity in order to rehabilitate a previously dominant value system. Phenomenological religious education in the 1970s and 1980s adopted a *normative rationality* concerned to pass on the liberal values of freedom and tolerance in a multi-faith context. The contemporary interest in spirituality reflects a *dramaturgical rationality,* which serves the postmodern need to encourage individuals to establish their own freedom and identity in a society that has lost faith in the possibility of anything other than localized solutions to its spiritual fragmentation.

Generally speaking, the hermeneutics of contemporary religious education pre-packages and forecloses the problem of religious truth and imposes its solutions on the lifeworlds of pupils. Its understanding of religious truth is a flexible one, capable of being restated to meet the developing needs of society: truth is that which Christians know to be true and seek to persuade you to believe; or truth is found in the comprehensive liberal consensus that treats all belief systems as equally valid and makes the realization of freedom and tolerance its fundamental goal; or truth has to do with the postmodern affirmation that reality is created by individuals according to their personal desires and preferences. Thus religious education itself cannot be abstracted from the power structures that impose ideological representations: it functions instrumentally to construct and apply models and interpretations of religion that distort the issue of religious truth in the service of benign forms of social and psychological engineering.

8.3 The hermeneutics of critical religious education

The rich tradition of hermeneutical theory offers a means of conceptualizing the process and nature of understanding in religious education; to date, this tradition is only implicit in religious education, or at best engages with it in a relatively unsystematic manner. This section will attempt to begin to redress the balance. The hermeneutics of religious education will vary according to context, and our particular concern is for a critical hermeneutic committed to addressing questions of truth and truthfulness in an environment in which both are deeply contested matters. We have already seen that the primary bearers of ultimate truth claims are discrete religious traditions, and in particular, the propositions and worldviews through which their adherents seek to organize their lives. The central task of the religious education teacher is to enable pupils to grapple with disputed claims about the ultimate order-of-things and orientate their lives appropriately in response to their emergent understanding. Such responses should be both procedural and substantial. The procedural response, mirroring the concerns of comprehensive liberalism, requires pupils to cultivate the twin virtues of freedom and tolerance insofar as this is morally and intellectually possible. The substantial response, mirroring the concerns of political liberalism, requires them to cultivate appropriate levels of religious literacy, so that they can own their core beliefs and modify their behaviour in an appropriate and responsible manner.

The crucial hermeneutical question to be resolved concerns the proper object of study. One increasingly popular candidate, particularly amongst those committed to spiritual and contextual approaches to religious education, is the *empirical realm* of the immediate experiences of pupils. Although there is no disputing the importance of enabling pupils to make sense of their experiences as they relate to questions of ultimate truth, the fact remains that their horizons of meaning are necessarily limited. Hence, a key task of religious education is to expand the horizons of pupils by developing their awareness of the *actual realm* beyond their immediate experience, in particular the actuality of religious traditions as they engagewith ultimate questions. Such discrete traditions are ambiguous entities: insider and outsider alike contest their identities, the truth of their worldviews, and the validity of the lifeworlds they sustain. If pupils are to begin to make sense of such traditions, they must learn to look beyond external phenomena and penetrate into the *real realm* of the structures and forces that drive such traditions. This entails taking seriously their truth claims, together with the arguments of those who deny the veracity of such claims. Since religious traditions make truth claims about ultimate reality, it is the question of the reality and nature of the transcendent order-of-things that constitutes the basic object of understanding for critical religious education.

Access to the actual world and the forces and structures that organize reality is only possible through our own experiences: when we encounter new phenomena that expand our horizon of understanding, we necessarily do so from our own unique perspectives. As Gadamer demonstrates clearly, such pre-experience will inevitably affect the process of understanding, and as such, recognition of the prepositions pupils bring with to the classroom is a prerequisite for any depth of understanding. Hence, religious education *must* empower pupils to recognize and claim ownership of their prior experiences, understandings, prejudices, beliefs and worldviews. Since such presuppositions may be implicit or incoherent, we cannot necessarily assume their presence in the focal awareness of pupils, and may therefore need to be proactive in encouraging appropriate levels of self-reflection and self-awareness. Such pre-understanding is far richer than mere attitude and emotive preference. On a general level, religious education should be concerned with those experiences that relate directly to the central object of religious understanding, namely transcendent reality; this suggests that pupils need to develop an appreciation of the particular worldviews within which, however implicitly, they live out their lives. On a more specific level, pupils will also need to identify their presuppositions about the actual traditions, themes and issues explored in the classroom. Recognition of prejudice is the necessary basis for approaching the study of religion with an open mind; self-conscious ownership of their presuppositions will enable pupils to formulate questions about religious traditions and their truth claims, anticipate the results of their questioning, reassess their understanding in the light of their expanding knowledge, and revise their own beliefs, actions and worldviews where necessary.

If the understanding that pupils bring with them to the classroom constitutes one of the two principle horizons of meaning in the hermeneutics of religious education, the second horizon is that of transcendent reality itself. With the possible exception of some forms of mystical experience, the ebb and flow of culture necessarily mediates our understanding of ultimate reality, especially through discrete religious traditions. There is a constant danger, in attending to these traditions, of allowing our understanding to be filtered through the secular presuppositions of recent Western thought, and thereby focusing on the horizontal plane of religions as cultural phenomena, rather than the vertical plane of religions as vehicles through which we (potentially) engage with the divine or transcendent. Religious education must cultivate appropriate forms of autonomy and tolerance, not as ends in themselves but as a means to the greater end of grappling with questions of ultimate truth. Hence, the key task of critical religious education is to present the horizon of the world's religions to pupils in a manner in which their transcendent truth claims take centre stage. Pupils need to feel the force of such claims and learn to respond to them in an appropriate manner.

In approaching the horizon of religion, it is necessary to recognize the basic dialectical principle of the hermeneutical circle, whereby the whole of a phenomenon illuminates the parts, and the parts illuminate the whole in a reciprocal manner. This means that exploration of the worldview of a religion – its meta-narrative, basic questions, symbols and praxis – constitute a necessary, although insufficient, aspect of the hermeneutical process. We need to supplement such overviews with contextual investigations of the ways in which actual individuals and local communities live out that worldview. Similarly, understanding of the core meaning and truth claims of a tradition must draw the attention to the beliefs of actual adherents, of community gatekeepers and official representatives, and of academic commentators – both 'insiders' and 'outsiders'. Since such beliefs are likely to be contested, it will be necessary to introduce pupils, in appropriate ways, to the nature of such contestation, rather than seek any premature resolution prior to the start of the learning process. Such dialectic will seek to illuminate the prototypical heart of a tradition, thereby avoiding the extremes of imposing some reified essential identity or deconstructing the tradition into the arbitrary sum of its atomistic parts. Recognition of a religion's prototypical identity must not avoid the disputed nature of the tradition and, consequently, attention must be paid to the way its identity is contested both internally (e.g. disputes between conservative and liberal Anglicans) and externally (e.g. disputes between Islam and Western secularism). In addition, attention must be paid to those individuals and communities living on the borderlands between traditions, whose worldviews claim not to recognize boundary markers between discrete religious and secular traditions.

The basic hermeneutical model that I am proposing is, then, one based broadly on Gadamer's notion of the critical engagement of the horizons of the interpreter and the object of interpretation. It takes the horizon of meaning of the pupil seriously by seeking to first identify it, and then transform and enrich it. However, in doing so, it is not content to allow pupils merely to express personal or communal preferences along the lines of reader-response theory, nor does it limit understanding to the level of a romanticized empathy for religious believers. Although their instinctive responses and capacity for empathetic engagement are important dimensions of the experience of pupils, they are not in themselves a sufficient basis for a potentially transformative engagement with religion. We need to hold out the possibility that the pre-understanding of pupils may be misplaced, inappropriate or even simply wrong. In the same way, empathetic engagement with a religious adherent is not necessarily a sign of deep religious understanding. Hence the model seeks to take the horizon of pupils seriously by enabling them to recognize, articulate and reflect critically on their core beliefs and worldviews, and empowering them to place their experiences within a broader framework of meaning. The model also seeks to take the horizon of the religions seriously, by refusing to reduce them to mere cultural phenomena, projecting some artificial essence, or deconstructing them down to their atomistic parts. The authenticity of religious life derives from the fact that adherents believe certain things about the real world, and attempt to live their lives in harmony with their beliefs. To take the horizon of religion seriously is to take the possibility that religious adherents might be right to think and act in that way seriously; in which case, pupils deserve access to such truth claims and life styles in order to evaluate them for themselves.

The framework departs from Gadamer with its rejection of his notion of the fusion of the horizons of interpreter and the object of interpretation. Given the contingency of our knowledge, and contested nature of our beliefs, such a utopian vision is best read as an eschatological hope rather than present reality. If we did hold beliefs and live lives in complete harmony with the ultimate order-of-things, then our quest for truth would be over. Although subscribers to a particular religious or secular tradition may hold firmly to their beliefs and are justified in doing so, provided that they have thought them through, all but the most committed fundamentalist would accept that their knowledge is never complete and their attempts to live fruitful lives only partially successful. This is best understood not as an excuse for scepticism, but for the recognition that we hold fast to our beliefs on the model of faith seeking understanding. Hence the engagement of our two horizons of meaning constitutes an ongoing process in which it is possible to achieve success and move forward, although the journey – for the present at least – is far from complete. The primary task of religious education is to support and guide the ongoing pilgrimage towards a final goal, rather than allow pupils to engage in some random nomadic wandering or to refuse the journey on the grounds that they have already reached their destination.

This suggests that the role of the teacher stands somewhere between the extremes of the expert who imparts pre-packaged knowledge into the minds of the pupils and the facilitator who is content to draw out that which pupils already implicitly know. In a liberal context, in which religious truth claims are the subject of fundamental dispute, there can be no role for a teacher who seeks to act confessionally by imposing one particular (contested) understanding of religion. There can be no place for imposing the perspective of a particular religious tradition, of some form of secular humanism, or of comprehensive liberalism that treats religious truth claims as purely private affairs. At the same time, there can be no role for a teacher who imposes the narrowly conceived ideology that the inner experiences of the pupil are necessarily authentic, and hence limits the task of education to that of drawing out the innate potential of the individual pupil. In such cases, the teacher must choose between two unpalatable options.

Either, she must trust the initial instincts of the child and assume their authenticity, in which case she will have no option but to nurture attitudes such as racism and homophobia. Or, she must affirm that the authentic experiences of the pupil lie buried beneath the surface, in which case she will seek to draw out the values that she herself deems to be valid and consequently mould pupils into her own pre-conceived notion of authenticity. Between these two extremes stands the notion of the teacher as expert facilitator. First, she will be an acknowledged expert on the kind of responses to religion that are reasonable, responsible and above crass superstition as well as on appropriate ways of conducting the pursuit of ultimate truth. Second, she will be a facilitator, determined to draw out the potential of her pupils by broadening and deepening their limited range of experiences, specifically by drawing them into potentially transformative conversations with new religious horizons of meaning.

8.4 Conclusion

Having previously identified discrete religious traditions as primary bearers of transcendent truth claims, and suggested that such claims are revealed in communal narratives and worldviews, the present chapter sought to reflect on the nature and process of understanding through which pupils might encounter and respond to such truth claims. I distinguished two broad trajectories within contemporary hermeneutical theory: one flowing from romanticism and culminating in postmodern reader-response theory, the other rooted in the critical hermeneutics of Gadamer and Habermas. A consideration of the fragmented nature of hermeneutical reflection in liberal religious education revealed a tendency to draw on the former of these trajectories, and drew the conclusion that it is unable to support a rigorous quest for truth. I then offered my own critical framework for religious education, drawing largely, although not exclusively, on the critical hermeneutics of Gadamer and Habermas. I suggested that a critical engagement between pupils' horizons of meaning and those of discrete religious traditions and oriented towards the contested issue of transcendent truth, offers a more viable hermeneutical framework for critical religious education. The discussion implied that mere understanding of a worldview or truth claim is not enough. Since it is possible to understand truth claims that may be true or false, critical religious education must attend to the process of making informed critical judgements between conflicting truth claims: it is to this issue that we must now turn.

9

Epistemology: wrestling with truth

We have envisaged critical religious education as a series of conversations between pupils' horizons of meaning and the worldviews of a range of discrete religious traditions; conversations designed to enable them to make informed judgements between competing truth claims and thereby take responsibility for their own beliefs and actions. This is not an especially original objective; as we noted in Chapter 5, it was at the heart of the original vision of liberal education, and it remains an aspiration for many contemporary religious educators. Thus, Michael Grimmitt recognizes the importance of evaluating truth claims and relating them to personal beliefs, and has called for the development of a critical awareness of various ideological structures present in society (Grimmitt, 1987, pp. 224ff, 1994). Similarly, Robert Jackson insists that 'young people should have the right to study and reflect on *different* views of truth represented within and across religious traditions as well as considering the functions of religious activity in people's lives' (Jackson, 1997, p. 126). However, this vision has not been realized in any systematic or sustained manner and a major reason for this is, I suggest, epistemological: the absence of any coherent understanding of the epistemic basis of religion and of the relationship between faith and reason. Hence the opening two sections of this chapter will explore the issue of the rationality of religious belief in the light of two contrasting epistemological models: foundationalism and contextualism. I will defend a critical form of contextualism and argue that, for a set of beliefs to be genuinely rational, it is necessary to survey the available evidence, make informed critical judgements between competing truth claims, and seek to live out our beliefs as consistently as possible in ordinary life. These issues will be the focus of the final three sections.

9.1 Foundational epistemology

Foundational epistemology seeks to establish a secure basis for knowledge. Paul Hirst distinguished between primitive and sophisticated forms of education: the former transmits subjective opinion, the later objective knowledge (Hirst, 1972). Education, if it is to avoid slipping into subjectivity, must establish an indubitable foundation for knowledge. Hence Hirst appealed to distinctive 'forms of knowledge' – mathematical, scientific, historical, philosophical, etc. – each of which contains a network of distinctive concepts that generate truth claims whose veracity is testable against experience (Shone, 1973). Although Hirst accepted that religions employ distinctive concepts, he denied that these are testable against experience, and concluded that there is 'no reason why anyone should take such religious claims seriously' (Hirst, 1972, p. 9). It follows that an education concerned to transmit religious truth will necessarily be primitive, and that the best a sophisticated education can hope to achieve is to utilize the social sciences to teach objectively *about* religion as a cultural phenomenon. Hence Hirst's challenge to critical religious education: either demonstrate secure rational foundations for religious truth claims or justify a non-foundationalist approach to the teaching of religious truth.

Foundationalists seek to establish knowledge on the basis of self-evident data, claiming to be able to identify 'foundational or basic beliefs which guarantee their own truth' and 'are accessible to any rational person, irrespective of their historical or cultural contexts' (McGrath, 2002, p. 21). Modern foundationalism has its roots in Rene Descartes' search for certainty: aware of 'multitude of errors that [he] had accepted as true . . . and the dubiousness of the whole superstructure', and fearful that he may be deluded about reality, he embarked on a 'quest for some fixed point, some stable rock upon which we can secure our lives against the vicissitudes that constantly threaten us' (Descartes, 1970, p. 61; Bernstein, 1983, p. 18). He proceeded, via a hermeneutic of suspicion, to doubt everything he formerly took for granted – his received cultural heritage, his sense experience, his faith of the truths of logic, even his own sanity – in the hope of finding epistemological security. He expressed the result of his search in the self-evident dictum *cogito ergo sum*, 'I think, therefore I am' – 'this proposition "I am",

"I exist", whenever I utter it or conceive it in my mind, is necessarily true' (Descartes, 1970, p. 67). From this vantage point, Descartes retraces his sceptical path and, in the light of this newfound self-understanding, reconstructs his knowledge of the world; it is no longer dependent on the vagaries of habit or arbitrary authority, but rather rests on the secure foundation of his immediate self-consciousness.

Foundational epistemology distinguishes between first-order basic beliefs and second-order 'mediate or non-basic beliefs . . . derived from these immediate or basic beliefs' (McGrath, 2002, p. 21). Basic beliefs are self-evident and need no further justification: they might include sense experience, a logical premise, immediately apprehended moral truth, or – in Descartes' case – the incontrovertible fact that he exists. Non-basic beliefs consist of knowledge built upon the foundations of such basic beliefs via empirical verification, logical deduction, rational argument, etc. Modern philosophy has tended to identify three main candidates for self-evident basic beliefs. First, *empirical observation* grounds first-tier knowledge in immediate sense experience: my experience of an object that is black, warm and makes a purring sound enables me to construct second-tier knowledge of the domestic cat. Second, *idealistic reflection* grounds first-tier knowledge in innate ideas and logical concepts: the concept of God as a perfect being, coupled with the notion that it is a greater perfection to exist than not to exist, enables me to affirm second-tier knowledge of the existence of God. Third, *romantic intuition* grounds first-tier knowledge in immediate aesthetic, moral and spiritual apprehension: I know a sunset to be beautiful simply because I experience its beauty immediately and unreflectively.

It is tempting to assume that religious belief requires some form of secure foundation. Appeals to sacred scripture, religious experience and the teachings of various institutional authorities certainly suggest a dependence on some primary self-evident source of religious knowledge. Indeed, Nicholas Wolterstorff suggests that, due largely to the influence of Aristotle, foundationalism 'has been the reigning theory . . . in the west since the high middle ages . . . among Christians as well as among non-Christians' (Wolterstorff, 1999, p. 30). However, the relative absence of foundationalism in the patristic era of Christianity is noteworthy. The early church was keenly aware that its knowledge of the Trinitarian God was dependent on divine revelation *mediated* through the witness of the Biblical writers and church tradition. The belief that there could be no direct and indubitably self-evident encounter with God meant that there is little in patristic literature resembling modern notions of biblical or papal infallibility. Scripture required detailed exegesis in order to reveal its meaning, and the nature and results of such exegesis were matters of ongoing debate; experiences of the Holy Spirit needed to be carefully scrutinized and tested in the light of biblical teaching and received tradition; and the Church's creedal formulations constituted attempts to give authentic expression to the heritage of faith, rather than provide its infallible foundation. Knowledge of God was always indirect rather than direct, mediated rather than unmediated. The combination of a strong sense of the otherness, holiness and mystery of God, coupled with a deep awareness of human fallibility, meant that 'faith seeking understanding' always took precedence over 'understanding seeking faith'. Since nobody has ever seen God directly, the early church never claimed access to infallible first-tier data: the Christian life always proceeds *from* and *through* faith – 'For now we see in a mirror, dimly, but then we will see face to face. Now I know only in part; then I will know fully' (1 Corinthians 13: 12).

In the modern era, attempts to justify Christianity to an increasingly sceptical public meant that forms of foundationalism gradually came to dominate theological epistemology. Why put one's faith in Christianity rather than a host of other religious and secular alternatives? Why trust the Bible rather than the Qur'an or Bhagavadgita? The failure to provide positive answers to such questions encouraged forms of fideism in which 'the decision to "believe" is made on "non-rational" factors' (Markham, 1998, p. 1). Fearful of slipping into circular arguments in which Christianity was justified on Christian grounds, some theologians resorted to the epistemic dependence thesis, 'according to which the primary criteria for deciding about the truth of Christian beliefs ... must not themselves be distinctively Christian' (Marshall, 2000, p. 50). Hence, rather than appeal to the integrity of the Christian faith itself, they sought some external foundation on which to ground Christian truth claims.

The primary candidates for such foundations were those previously established by secular philosophers: empirical observation, idealistic reflection, and romantic intuition. First, appeals to empirical observation sought to pass from first-tier observation of the natural order to a second-tier inference of the existence of a divine creator. Thus Cleanthes, in David Hume's *Dialogues Concerning Natural Religion*:

> The curious adapting of means to ends, throughout all nature, resembles exactly, though it much exceeds, the productions of human contrivance; of human design, thought, wisdom and intelligence. Since, therefore the effects resemble each other, we are led to infer, by all the rules of analogy, that the causes also resemble; and that the Author of nature is somewhat similar to the mind of man; though possessed of much larger faculties, proportioned to the grandeur of the work, which he has executed.
>
> (Hume, 1947, p. 143)

Second, appeals to idealistic reflection sought to deduce second-tier knowledge of God from first-tier self-evident rational premises. As we have already seen, versions of Anselm's ontological argument sought to deduce God's existence from the idea of a perfect being: given that existence is a mode of perfection, the idea of the all-perfect being logically entails its existence. Third, appeals to romantic intuition sought to ground belief in religious experience. According to Freidrich Schleiermacher, Christianity is rooted in the 'consciousness of being absolutely dependent, or, which is the same thing, of being in relation with God' (Schleiermacher, 1976, p. 12). This constitutes a classic example of the interiority thesis, 'according to which Christian beliefs are justified to the extent that they adequately express certain inner experiences' (Marshall, 2000, p. 50). Such appeals to self-evident spiritual experience appealed equally to liberal Christians' experience of God as the ground of being and evangelical Christians' experience of the redemptive power of Christ.

Such attempts to interpret religious belief foundationally fall short on two counts. First, the illegitimacy of the passage from first-tier foundations to second-tier faith: the order inherent in the universe does not necessarily warrant a theological explanation, it is not clear that existence is a mode of perfection, and personal spiritual experience is open to a vast range of different interpretations. Second, there is no obvious relationship between the kind of deity deduced from empirical observation, rational reflection and spiritual experience, and the specific God worshipped by particular

religious communities. At the very least, such philosophical foundations need supplementing by appeals to theological knowledge
available through revelation. This, however, simply reopens the
question of the legitimacy of appeals to revelation. Ironically, such
appeals increasingly embraced foundationalist assumptions: treating
scripture and creed as the indubitable grounds of faith led directly
to forms of biblical fundamentalism and assertions of the infallibility
of ecclesiastical teaching. Thus, attempts to establish the legitimacy
of religious faith on foundationalist grounds tend to generate
reductive accounts of religious belief systems, fail to offer adequate
protection against scepticism, and still require some form of appeal
to sources of revelation whose authority is far from self-evident.
This being the case, Hirst's claim that the transmission of religious
truth claims necessarily constitutes a primitive form of education
appears to be well founded.

9.2   Contextual epistemology

Contextual epistemology emerged in response to three fundamental
problems faced by foundationalism. First, there is no agreement
about the nature and extent of the supposedly 'self-evident' first-
tier foundations of knowledge. Second, the transition from first-
tier principles to more complex second-tier knowledge has not
produced the desired level of objectivity, since it has proved
possible to build a variety of different knowledge systems on the
same foundational principles. Third, the assumption that the only
alternative to certain knowledge is a thoroughgoing scepticism has
proved unfounded. Although much of our knowledge is limited
and fallible, we nevertheless retain a relatively secure understanding
of many aspects of reality and subscribe to many reasonable beliefs
– genocide is evil, Mozart a master musician – whose truth we
cannot demonstrate with absolute certainty. The nature of the
reality we seek to understand, together with the diverse methods
through which we engage with it, are so complex and multifaceted
that the simplistic vision of certain knowledge constructed on secure
foundations has proved nothing more than an intellectual mirage.
Given the incoherence permeating foundationalism, we would do
well to reject it should an alternative epistemological framework
show itself to possess greater explanatory power. Such is the case,
I suggest, with contextual epistemology.

Descartes' strategy of systematically bracketing-out his existing knowledge in the search for certainty constitutes a radically de-contextualized epistemology that seeks to establish an idealized god's eye 'view from nowhere' (Nagel, 1986). In sharp contrast, contextual epistemology proceeds from the understanding of the world that we inherit from our communities and traditions: the basic epistemological task is to scrutinize and revise that which we believe we already know, rather than build afresh from first principles. There is no vantage point 'from which we can view and evaluate our beliefs' other than 'our already existing beliefs' (McGrath, 2002, p. 35). Thus, Thomas Kuhn claims that we learn science not by artificially abstracting ourselves from the scientific community, but by immersing ourselves in it (Kuhn, 1970). Similarly, Michael Polanyi argues that the process of formulating, testing and evaluating hypotheses is dependent on our personal engagement with that which we seek to understand (Polanyi, 1958). And, as we have already noted, Hans-Georg Gadamer insists that knowledge necessarily proceeds from our pre-understanding and prejudice (Gadamer, 1979, p. 245). In a famous analogy, Otto Neurath suggests that:

> We are like sailors who on the open sea must reconstruct their ship but are never able to start afresh from the bottom. Where a beam is taken away a new one must at once be put there, and for this reason the rest of the ship is used as support. In this way, by using the old beams and drift-wood, the ship can be shaped entirely anew, but only by gradual reconstruction.
>
> (McGrath, 2002, pp. 34f)

Knowledge proceeds from the worldviews, conceptual structures, theories and beliefs that are already familiar to us. By reflecting on them, identifying their strengths and weaknesses, and addressing inconsistencies and unresolved problems, we gradually work our way towards a deeper and more coherent understanding of reality. According to contextualism, the legitimacy of our beliefs is not dependent on any single item but on the way in which the parts connect together in a coherent whole. Knowledge is more like a rope than a chain: where a chain is only as strong as its weakest link, a rope is far sturdier than its constituent threads (Wittgenstein, 1968, p. 32). 'Both in science and in everyday knowledge we approach the truth by correcting an existing body of partly erroneous "knowledge", not by preserving the deliverances of an infallible source' (Collier, 2003, p. 66).

For some, the suggestion that at 'the foundation of well-founded belief lies belief that is not founded' leads directly to relativism (Wittgenstein, 1975, p. 33). On this view, contextualism describes the way we come to hold our beliefs but has nothing positive to say about their justification. In the absence of universally valid foundations, knowledge rests on the dubious claims and counter-claims generated in a variety of local contexts. In such a situation, it is better to assume that truth claims are relative to the communities that make them, than to claim one specific tradition enjoys privileged access to truth. There are two basic reasons for questioning such relativism. The first is that we regularly 'judge between competing theories on the basis of their intrinsic merits as explanations of reality' (McGrath, 2002, p. 192). This is simply an extension of the kind of judgements we make in everyday life: thus, when boarding an aircraft, we tacitly assume that scientists understand the natural world better than astrologers. The second is that relativism makes precisely the kind of judgement between contrasting belief systems that it claims to be illegitimate: the suggestion that we have no access to universally justifiable beliefs actually constitutes a cross-cultural judgement claiming universal validity. It is clear then, that the rejection of foundationalism 'does not necessarily entail a rejection of realism, or give intellectual legitimation to any such slide into a freewheeling relativism' (p. 33). Judgements between conflicting truth claims rarely take the form of logical proof or direct empirical verification; rather they are analogous to the deliberations of a jury in a court if law, faced with the task of drawing appropriate conclusions in the light of the available evidence. Responsible judgement requires 'receptivity to data, skill in reasoning, and yearning for truth' (Quine and Ullian, 1978, p. 4). The alternative to absolute certainty is not arbitrary choice, but informed judgement measured against the standard of 'reasonable doubt'.

The pursuit of knowledge proceeds from a raft of normative beliefs, assumptions and expectation, and – given the fallibility of human beings – the results will normally be contingent and subject to further revision. The initial task is to gather as much evidence as possible, since the greater the extent, depth and quality of the available data, the more likely we are to make appropriate judgements. Our search also requires appropriate tools, skills, procedural principles and criterion for judgement, all of which are subject to refinement in the light of the realities we encounter. Although some data will be available through first-hand experience, most will be mediated through tradition and testimony. Further, the relevant evidence will normally present itself in the form of holistic perceptions rather than isolated atomistic facts: we tend to understand reality through noetic apprehension, immediately recognizing meaningful patterns of experience rather than constructing them from individual items of sense data – thus, we perceive a cat directly rather than construe the presence of a cat from its colour, shape, sound and movement.

At its most basic, the pursuit of truth involves nothing more complex than an ongoing dialogue between authority and experience (Collier, 2003). The evidence placed before us takes the form of a range of authorities, each offering particular understandings of reality. Since not all authorities are equally trustworthy, we must be prepared to make critical judgements whenever tensions arise between conflicting truth claims: each 'authority must prove itself at the bar of reason, suspicion and . . . experience' (p. 79). Our judgements rarely follow any strictly enforceable rational or empirical procedures; rather they involve the looser process of weighing up of available options in order to establish the most likely implications of the evidence. Few of us lay claim to the extremes of absolute certainty or thoroughgoing relativism; rather, we recognize that our beliefs generally enable us to make good sense of the world, while accepting that we can be mistaken about many things. If we feel the need to revise certain beliefs because they no longer enable us to make sense of experience, we rarely use this as a trigger for systematically questioning everything. This is the case even in radical shifts in belief: loss of religious faith, for example, is unlikely to result in any questioning of the status of science.

This suggests that the basic criteria for true belief is not the extent to which it conforms to some pre-established foundational principle, but rather the coherence and explanatory power of the overall tapestry of an entire belief system. It follows that we do not need to be able to justify all of our individual beliefs separately in order to claim that our worldview is rational. This holistic model has the advantage of allowing beliefs that we hold fast to, but that we cannot yet fully justify, play an appropriate role in our overall web of understanding. Thus it is entirely rational to believe that genocide is evil and to act in accordance with that belief, despite being unable to explain the *precise* reasons for subscribing to this belief. We embrace a complex web of knowledge and seek to live in accordance with it until such time as a more authoritative, fruitful and coherent belief system gives us cause to consider revising it.

In asserting the epistemic primacy of faith in this manner, I am not suggesting that suspicion has no place in the epistemological process, although it is important to distinguish between critical scrutiny and thoroughgoing scepticism. All authorities should be open to question, and it is necessary to be aware of the power structures that will inevitably impinge on our judgements. Contra some postmodern thinkers, the fact that the pursuit of knowledge is inevitable bound up with such structures does not warrant a simplistic identification of knowledge with power, although it certainly makes the practice of making informed judgements more difficult. It is only by identifying power structures and taking them into consideration when making judgements that we are able to distinguish between legitimate knowledge and illegitimate force.

9.3 Knowledge and reasonable belief

To draw relativistic conclusions from the fact that religious belief possesses no indubitably certain foundation is to generate an account of religion that is unacceptable to mainstream religious adherents. As Collier points out, so long as 'the religious language game is meaningful only to the religious, one use of religious language ceases to make any sense at all: evangelism, the use of words to persuade a non-believer to believe' (p. 90). Attempts to isolate religious language games from other forms of discourse and deny their realistic commitments reflect the comprehensive liberal desire to 'live and let live'. Defenders of such a view act 'in the spirit of an anthropologist who wants to preserve the quaint customs of "primitive" people and does not care for them enough to tell them what he holds to be true' (p. 90). As a Christian, Collier finds such attitudes 'peculiarly insulting', especially when compared to the respect afforded his beliefs by the 'honest antagonism' of atheists (p. 90).

Collier's response to such unsolicited patronage is to claim a close affinity between religious knowledge and other forms of knowledge. He accepts that there are variations between different types of knowledge: scientific knowledge is different from practical 'know-how', which in turn is different from interpersonal understanding. It is no surprise, then, to find that religious knowledge has its own peculiarities; nevertheless, such peculiarities do not make it qualitatively different from other types of knowledge: all knowledge 'claims to be true about something, and is mistaken if what it is about does not exist or is different from how it is conceived' (p. 77). Further, the basic epistemological procedures of all types of knowledge are identical: the testing of various sources of authority against experience. In attempting to make sense of the world, we inevitably start out from a web of belief that constitutes either a religious or a secular worldview. There is no neutral ground or faith-free default position to fall back on: we all start out from a set of faith commitments that we can hold either rationally or irrationally. Although there are many beliefs held in common across different belief systems, worldviews as a whole tend to be mutually exclusive; if one is true, all others are false.

According to Torrance, theology constitutes a science operating in the public sphere in the same manner as other sciences. In 'any branch of knowledge we begin within the knowledge relation where we actually are, and seek to move forward by clarifying and testing what we already know and by seeking to deepen and enlarge its content' (Torrance, 1978, p. 2). Following Barth, he recognizes that Christian theology must focus upon its proper object 'in such a way that it might be consistently faithful to the concrete act of God in Jesus Christ' (p. 7). A genuinely scientific Christian theology must 'begin with the actual knowledge of God' possessed by the Christian community and 'seek to test and clarify this knowledge by inquiring carefully into the relation between our knowing of God and God Himself in His being and nature' (p. 7). As such, theology is no arbitrary process: it is restricted in what it may legitimately say by the evidence of Christian revelation. If rationality consists of 'our ability to relate our thought and our action appropriately to objective intelligible entities', then theology is as much a rational endeavour as any other academic discipline (p. 11). Its epistemological procedures parallel the way in which the physical and social sciences generate belief. Scientific theology

218 Critical Religious Education and Multiculturalism

has no exclusive access to truth, and does not depend on any fideistic assertions: the data of Christian revelation is located firmly in the public sphere, where it is open to rational debate and discussion. 'As a science, theology is only a human endeavour in quest of the truth' (p. 281). Like other academic disciplines, theology is a process of inquiry that respects objectivity, utilizes a technical vocabulary, does not operate within any *preconceived* metaphysical framework, and recognizes that its investigations ultimately 'come up against a line beyond which they cannot penetrate' (p. 290).

Since all knowledge flows from prior commitment, the basic outlook of contextual epistemological is that of faith, whether religious or secular, seeking understanding. It follows that it is epistemically permissible to uphold the 'unrestricted epistemic primacy' of a set of beliefs without prior justification: this is simply something we all do (Marshall, 2000, p. 145). However, this 'does not mean that we can believe whatever we like' (p. 145). This is highly significant for any defence of the rationality of religious belief: the assumption that the religious adherents necessarily believe 'testimony in the face of strong contrary evidence' reflects the assumptions of modern foundationalism in general, and the positivist criteria of verification in particular (Quine and Ullian, 1978, p. 59). From a foundationalist perspective, Kierkegaard's notion of the 'leap of faith' and Tertullian's assertion that 'I believe because it is absurd' invite the equation of religious belief with Lewis Carroll's Queen, who believes 'as many as six impossible things before breakfast' (p. 60). However, such a view is mistaken on two counts. First, Kierkegaard and Tertullian are, on this issue at least, unrepresentative of mainstream Christian thought, which has always insisted on the rationality of Christianity. Second, the act of religious faith is not a departure from some secular norm since *all* beliefs – both religious and secular – are faith driven. The crucial issue for both groups is to avoid the 'whiff of fideism' by testing faith through critical reflection on the best available evidence (Marshall, 2000, p. 141). Although this does not 'require that we be able to give reasons for every one of our beliefs', our 'epistemic responsibilities do seem to require that we be open to changing any one of our beliefs if given sufficient reason to do so' (p. 145). Whatever our worldview, we cannot claim to hold it rationally unless we are willing to subject it to critical reflection in the light of alternatives: defending it where possible, refining it where necessary, and even abandoning it if convinced that there are reasonable grounds for doing so (pp. 141ff).

Basil Mitchell has addressed the task of justifying large-scale beliefs, arguing that it is possible to make out a rationally grounded cumulative case for Christianity and, by implication, other world-views (Mitchell, 1973). He points out how cumulative judgements operate in other spheres of human knowledge, citing literary exegesis and historical investigation as examples. 'Given a range of possible meanings' of a poem, 'the critic is justified in selecting that meaning which, in the light of the poem as a whole (and any other relevant evidence), makes the best sense' (p. 51). Such judgement is based on the 'culmination of probabilities, independent of each other, arising out of the nature and circumstances of the case which is under review' (p. 51; cf. Newman, 1979, p. 230). Since judgement across widely differing conceptual schemes regularly takes place in the spheres of science and philosophy, it is also possible between different holistic paradigms, including large-scale belief systems and worldviews. This is so in the disputes between realism and anti-realism, Newtonian and post-Einsteinian science, and Islam and secular humanism. In a post-foundational context, it is not possible to specify precise rules when we come to make such decisions, rather we have to rely on broad criteria such as consistency, coherence, simplicity, elegance, explanatory power and fertility. The result is not absolutely certainty, but reasonable belief, provided that we make choices with appropriate care and competence (Mitchell, 1973, p. 95). Although it is natural to desire greater certainty than this, it is a brute fact that reality constitutes a deep mystery to us: we have no god's-eye perspective on the ultimate order-of-things, and must reconcile ourselves to achieving what we can with our limited resources.

This account of the rational nature of religious and secular worldviews raises two issues that we must deal with in greater depth: we will explore criteria for rational judgement in the next section, and the relationship between faith and reason in the final one.

9.4   Criteria for critical judgement

Daniel Hardy chastises the 1975 Birmingham Agreed Syllabus for its failure 'to face the task of training and assisting the student in his task of choosing responsibly' between a range of different life stances (Hardy, 1975, p. 13). By default, it 'encourages the student to think that he is the sole judge of what is true, that what he finds to be true for him *is* true' (p. 13). This raises the question of the criteria against which to assess worldviews. The minimum requirement for considering a worldview rationale is, as we have seen, that we have reasonable grounds for believing in its probable truthfulness when compared with alternatives. Ultimately our judgements will be rooted in forms of authority: just as we trust the authority of scientists, so religious adherents acknowledge the authority of religious teachers, prophets, visionaries and saints. Because both scientific and religious authorities are capable of being mistaken, we must choose our authorities wisely: better to listen to Einstein than an undergraduate physics student, to attend to Mohammed than a recent convert to Islam, to trust an acknowledged authority on church history than the author of *The Da Vinci Code* (Brown, 2004; cf. Wright, N. T., 2005). We reject authorities not because they are authorities per se, but because we judge them to be wrong; and we judge the veracity of their truth claims by exercising reason in testing them against our own experience of life. In this section, I offer five general criteria for adjudicating between worldviews: congruence, coherence, fertility, simplicity and depth (Mitchell, 1973, p. 95; Poole, 1995, p. 47).

a) *Congruence.* A worldview is more likely to be true if it is congruent with our life experience. A Christian seeing a vision of the Virgin Mary will relate her experience to the patterns of meaning provided by the Christian story, whereas an atheist will interpret the experience very differently. The crucial issue is whether the patterns of meaning that inform our lives are congruent with our experience of the way the world really is. Imagine two complete strangers who happen to stumble across one another, fall in love, and try to account for their meeting: was it purely accidental ('a chance in a million'), fate ('written in the stars'), or due to divine providence ('the will of God')? Their initial answers will draw directly to their worldviews, be they naturalistic, astrological or theistic. However, it may be that – for example – their original naturalistic interpretation is incongruent with their sense that were somehow 'meant' to meet; in which case, they may be tempted to reconsider their original beliefs in the light of the testimony of religious believers who experience the active presence of God in their lives. Similarly, the experience of the death of a child may force a parent to reconsider their belief in an all-loving and all-powerful God. The greater the harmony between our beliefs and experiences, the more reasonable it is for us to assume that our beliefs are true; the greater the discord, the more we are justified in considering other possibilities. Since we have no vantage point beyond the interplay of belief and experience, our judgements are necessarily circular and wrapped up with some form of 'doxastic' practice (Alston, 1989). We interpret our experiences in the light of our beliefs and our beliefs in the light of our experiences: the reasoning may be necessarily circular but, as such, excels the arbitrary expression of preference.

b) *Coherence.* Since most of our knowledge is of entities that we do not experience directly, the coherence of our accounts of reality is a more basic criterion than their convergence with our sense experience. At the micro-level, we affirm the truth value of the formula H_2O not by tasting hydrogen and oxygen, but by considering the coherence of the basic vocabulary of chemistry. At the macro-level, we reject anti-realistic accounts of science in the light of the greater coherence of realistic ones, since if 'the theoretical claims of the natural sciences were not correct, their massive empirical success would appear to be totally accidental, or at best a stunning concatenation of coincidences' (McGrath, 2001, p. 73). Similarly, the belief in a benevolent, all-powerful and all-knowing God appears incoherent in the light of the prevalence of suffering in the world; hence the theist must either reject belief in God or offer a theodicy that is more coherent than any atheistic alternative (Wright, N. T., 2006). A worldview is more likely to be coherent if it has been the subject of sustained critical examination over a long period of time and thereby achieved 'classic' status. Thus, Islam has undergone intense philosophical and theological scrutiny, whereas similar examination of astrology is notable either through its absence or through the paucity of its positive results (Seymour, 2004). In the fields of art, music and literature the 'classic' status of Rembrandt, Beethoven and Shakespeare is widely acknowledged; similarly, some religious texts and traditions are recognized classics, having stood the test of rigorous scrutiny both within and beyond the communities that own them (Tracey, 1981, pp. 99ff).

c) *Fertility.* A worldview is fertile if it is able to 'permit the acceptance of alien beliefs when its holders meet with good reasons to hold them true' without compromising its integrity (Marshall, 2000, p. 147). Take, for example, the Christian doctrine of creation. Refusal of assimilate the fruits of modern physics and literary criticism by appealing to a literalistic reading of the book of Genesis casts considerable doubt on the worldview of Christian creationists. At the same time, the willingness of the most Christians to embrace such insights suggests a fertile and robust worldview. Both pre-modern Christians who assert that it is God 'who holds the flat earth still and moves round it the heavenly lights', and contemporary Christians who affirm that whatever 'the true scientific description of the world, it is God who brings about that state of affairs', maintain the integrity of the doctrine of creation (Swinburne, 1983, p. 181). However, only the latter view allows for an accept-ance of the insights of modern science, and Christianity is more likely to be true if it embraces, rather than rejects, science. The Christian doctrine of the resurrection poses problems that are more complex: the claim 'that although Christ was killed on the cross, he subsequently came back to life' constitutes 'a clear case of a violation of a natural law' (p. 189). One of the key functions of the doctrine is to assert the power of God over nature, thereby establishing eternal life rather than physical death as the ultimate destiny of humankind: 'If Christ has not been raised, your faith is futile' (1 Corinthians 15: 17). In this case, assimilation of the alien belief that the natural order is inviolate seriously compromises the coherence of Christianity, thereby making it less likely to be true. This leave Christians with the task of justifying belief in miracles by arguing, for example, that 'if there is a God who is responsible for the whole order of nature, including its conformity to natural laws', then it is perfectly rational to accept that he 'can on occasion suspend the normal operation of natural laws' (p. 188). A fertile Christianity, committed to preserving belief in resurrection yet willing to assimilate the insights of contemporary cosmology, is more likely to be true than either a sterile Christian liberalism that fails to preserve its belief in the sovereignty of God or a barren Christian fundamentalism that remains closed to modern science.

d) *Simplicity.* The principle of Occam's razor, that the simplest explanation is normally the best, suggests that the more straightforward the aesthetic beauty and moral integrity of a worldview, the more likely it is to be true. A good scientific theory 'calls attention to its own beauty and partly relies on it for claiming to represent empirical reality' (Polanyi, 1958, p. 133). Whenever our experiences mesh with our explanations, we find ourselves responding to the inherent beauty and order of the emerging patterns of meaning. Such simplicity is necessarily relative to the complexity of the reality it seeks to describe: as Nobel Prize winner Sheldon Glashow wryly observes, 'string theorists have a theory that appears to be consistent and is very beautiful, very complex, and I don't understand it' (Glashow, 2005). Newman places moral integrity alongside aesthetic beauty, arguing that possession of an appropriate temperament is necessary if we are to connect with the values inherent in the universe (Dulles, 2002, p. 39). This assumes, quite correctly, that value is an inherent part of reality: even the naturalist who claims that the natural world is morally neutral is attributing a specific moral value to it (Collier, 1999). Marshall urges caution at this point, drawing attention to the relatively even distribution of virtue across different belief systems (Marshall, 2000, pp. 182ff). Nevertheless, the kind of people a worldview tends to generate can be significant, since we do not normally 'believe people who habitually lie or contradict themselves or show great credulity, or use manipulative techniques, or have a financial interest in convincing you, or turn their converts into zombies' (Collier, 2003, p. 84). The ethical structure of a belief system, as opposed to the relative goodness of its adherents, also needs to be taken into account. Contrast, for example, a Christian morality predicated on the notion of original sin and a secular humanist morality predicated on the natural goodness of humanity: the former anticipates a world in which all is not well and a church full of wicked people living under God's grace, the latter a world in which goodness predominates through human effort. It is possible to test both set of beliefs against our own experience of the world.

e) *Depth.* A worldview is more likely to be true by virtue of its superior illuminatory depth. It may be that we encounter an account of reality that, so to speak, 'trumps' our own by presenting us with a richer and more profound vision of the order-of-things. An analogy with the realm of art and literature will help shed light on this final criterion. Many novels, paintings, films and musical compositions contain a richness of intellectual, moral, aesthetic and spiritual insight, and others do not. The former are more than mere entertainments: they reveal ways of understanding the world that would not otherwise be available us, and as such warrant repeated exposure and detailed exploration. Television soap operas tend to function on the level of entertainment, designed to enable us to relax for a while and forget the tedium and challenges of ordinary life. They lack illuminatory depth because their plots are obvious, leading characters stereotyped, and responses to moral dilemmas overly simplistic. However, occasionally we find ourselves watching films and documentaries that transcend mere entertainment: rather than allow us to withdraw from the world for a while, they bring us face to face with reality, forcing us to reconsider our cherished assumptions and beliefs, and providing us with an illuminatory depth of insight that reveals them to be profound works of art. It is often difficult to anticipate such encounters in advance, and equally difficult to explain precisely why we responded in the way we do. To introduce a religious analogy, an 'entertainment' functions as a mirror, reflecting the already familiar back to us in an enjoyable manner; great art, on the other hand, functions as an icon, opening our eyes to new visions of reality and illuminating ways of being in the world previously unavailable to us. The basic difference between entertainment and art is that the latter possesses a depth of spiritual insight absent in the former: Shakespeare's insights into the human condition have an authority that forces us to rethink our understanding of humanity, in a manner that, say, a Jeffrey Archer novel does not. By analogy, a worldview manifesting such illuminatory depth is more likely to be a vehicle for truth, and hence more worthy of serious attention, than one that merely skates the surface of reality.

9.5   Faith and reason

Does this account of the rationality of belief do justice to the nature of religious faith as practices by adherents? As Mitchell points out, 'conversion from one system to another is rarely effected by rational argument alone, as it involves the believer's entire personality and his whole way of perceiving and responding to the world' (Mitchell, 1973, p. 134). Faith, that is to say, entails far more than merely a rational choice between conflicting worldviews. In setting out a set of criteria through which to judge between conflicting worldviews, I may well have given a number of false impressions: first, that I am advocating a narrowly rationalistic approach to religious understanding; second, that I seek to allow pupils to make objective selections from a range of possible options set out on the shelves of the religious education supermarket; third, that my insistence that our knowledge is necessarily limited leaves no room for the whole-hearted commitment of faith.

a) *Rationalism.* Is the pursuit of truth in religious education excessively academic? Does it sidestep the personal nature of faith? Reflecting on what he perceives as the 'heavy rationalism' of my approach to religious education, Jackson comments that I seem 'so concerned that the expression of feeling might lead to error that the emotions do not appear to figure in [my vision of] classroom education' (Jackson, 2004, p. 84). He goes on to suggest I regard 'any spiritual practice or exploration of emotions . . . [as] potentially misleading', and imply that 'emotional expression must *follow* intellectual clarification' (p. 85, my italics). This, he argues,

> is rather like being told that one must go through the discipline of learning chords in jazz before being allowed to play or sing, or having to do a course in the history of art before one's enjoyment of a picture can be authentic.
>
> (p. 85).

Jackson here assumes a distinction between reason and emotion that I wish to undermine. It is not a matter of putting reason before emotion or emotion before reason, but of seeing them as twin aspects of a single process. In the same way, thought and action need to be seen as intimately linked: we ought not to 'think then act' or 'act then think', but 'think *as* we act'. This combination of reason, feeling, thought and action draws on the Aristotelian notion of *phronesis* or 'practical wisdom' that, I have argued elsewhere, ought to be at the heart of critical religious education (Wright, 2003c; cf. Dunne, 1997). Jackson acknowledges that I have responded to my critics by 'pointing out that [my] method involves not only a quest for knowledge and truth, but also the search for wisdom' (p. 84). However, it would be more precise to say that I am concerned to affirm the *identity* of the two: since truth and truthfulness are simply two sides of the same coin, there can be no quest for knowledge and truth without the search for wisdom.

We pursue truth both in our everyday lives and in educational settings: there is no fundamental difference between the two, other than that the latter is normally more focused and intentional. A saxophonist will become more accomplished with her instrument whether she is performing in a jazz club, playing alone for pleasure, or receiving instruction from her teacher. In the latter case, she will deliberately seek to develop her ability by focusing on specific skills and techniques, learning chords, taking time to understand musical theory, and attending to the playing of acknowledged masters of her instrument – Lester Young, Charlie Parker, John Coltrane, for example. By analogy, while there is no basic difference between wrestling with ultimate questions of meaning and truth in the contexts of ordinary life and the classroom, the deliberate pursuit of truth in a rigorous academic setting is an extremely valuable undertaking. In both settings, our encounters with, and exploration of, religion 'should not be a passionless affair, since it engages with fundamental existential concerns of immediate relevance to us all' (p. 84; cf. Wright, 2003c, p. 288).

b) *Choice.* What then of the 'parody of religious education as offering fully autonomous pupils choices of religions, as if from the supermarket shelf'? (Jackson, 1997, p. 130). The pervasiveness of contemporary consumerism, when coupled with the liberal commitment to personal autonomy, means that the individual is 'more likely to confront culture and the sacred cosmos as a "buyer"' (Luckman, 1967, p. 99). My insistence on a critical engagement with questions of ultimate truth is not an attempt to return to the much derided 'shopping trolley' model of religious education, in which the wares of different religious and secular traditions are set out before pupils in the expectation that they will 'purchase' the one that suits them best. The notion of pupils as consumers making critical selections from various belief systems resonates strongly with rational choice theory, which is primarily concerned with the political and economic implications of the choices made by autonomous citizens between their own self-interest and the collective needs of society as a whole. At its most basic, the theory contends that individuals will tend to make choices that appear to them to be most likely to maximize personal gain and minimize personal cost rather than act altruistically. In the background stands the assumption that the best way to make key decisions in life – about core beliefs, long-term relationships, ultimate goals and so forth – is by stepping back and carefully weighing options and likely outcomes in an impersonal and disinterested manner. Transferred into the classroom, such an approach to decision making in the field of religious belief would, to say the least, be artificial and contrived; the net result would be the over rationalization of belief and would leave little room for feeling, emotion and commitment.

A recent collection of essays has identified four key problems with the assumptions underlying rational choice theory, to which I will add a fifth (Tritter and Archer, 2000). First, the notion of objective rationality is inadequate, since many other factors, such as emotional attitude, cultural context and personal history, influence our decisions. Second, the notion of autonomous decision making ignores the fact that decisions are often collective affairs, made by couples, families, groups, nations and even the international community. Third, the notion that decisions normally flow from the careful evaluation of clear and unambiguous evidence is naive, since our judgements are frequently dependent on partial and even inadequate information. Fourth, the notion that our decisions take place in a neutral context ignores the various power structures that inform or impinge on them. Fifth, it seems to me that the suggestion that we make decisions for selfish rather than altruistic reasons entails an unnecessarily pessimistic evaluation of human nature.

As I argued in the last chapter, the appropriate model for the pursuit of truth is not of rational individuals making objective choices between a range of available worldviews, but of pupils exploring their given beliefs and commitments in the light of various alternatives: to reiterate, the basic pattern is not of understanding seeking faith, but of faith seeking understanding. The use of the criteria outlined above for making judgements between conflicting worldviews ought to operate in this latter context. This is not to say that there is no place for critical reflection, merely that such reflection will inevitably take place within the ebb and flow of our ongoing struggle to make sense of ourselves and or place in the grand scheme of things.

c) *Commitment.* What then of the relationship between the total commitment demanded of religious believers and the limited and provisional nature of our knowledge? Cardinal Newman's celebrated *Essay in Aid of a Grammar of Assent* offers a potential solution to this dilemma (Newman, 1979). His discussion of the relationship between faith and knowledge begins with a critique of Locke's evidentialism, which sought to base knowledge on deductive reason by building on the raw material of immediate sense-experience. According to Locke, only such evidential knowledge could provide the knower with objective certainty. To pass beyond knowledge into sphere of belief required acceptance of the uncertainties of faith, defined as 'Assent to any Proposition, not thus made out by the Deduction of Reason' (Locke, 1975, p. 689). Locke placed two important restrictions on faith. First, 'nothing that is contrary to, and inconsistent with the clear and self-evident Dictates of Reason, has a Right to be urged, or assented to, as a Matter of Faith' (p. 696). Second, the level of assent to a particular belief must not extend beyond the warranted evidence. Newman offered four key objections to Locke's account of faith. First, it fails to account for the fact that most religious believers do not ground their faith on rational proof. Second, empirical evidence rarely causes people to alter their core commitments. Third, religious faith is more than mere intellectual assent, but rather involves the commitment of the whole person. Fourth, although faith entails certitude for most religious adherents, such certitude is unavailable when people assent to evidence-based religious beliefs (Dulles, 2002, pp. 34ff).

Newman rejects Locke's notion of faith as a response to the world that seeks to go beyond reason but nevertheless has a duty to conform to it, in favour of a notion of the fundamental unity of faith and reason: that is to say, the act of faith is itself an exercise in reason. We understand the world not by constructing knowledge out of the atomistic parts of sense experience, but through a holistic engagement with it. Knowledge flows from the concrete experiences of the whole person. Through such experiences, we acquire what Newman terms 'antecedent expectations' – tacit knowledge, presuppositions, assumptions, etc. – that enable us make responsible judgements in the absence of rigorous demonstration. We respond to the world rationally and instinctively in and through faith. Newman coined the term 'illative sense' to refer to this holistic capacity to respond intelligently to the experiences life throws at us. The farmer who is weatherwise can accurately predict when the rain will fall, and the lover can tell at a glance whether the beloved is troubled or content: both are entirely justified in whole-heartedly committing to their beliefs, even although it is unlikely that either will be able to assign logical grounds to their knowledge (Newman, 1979, pp. 270ff). In such cases, we can never be certain that our beliefs are correct since we can never offer indubitable proof of our core beliefs. Nevertheless, we are entirely justified to act on the assumption that our sense of how things are in the world is indeed correct. Indeed this is a familiar feature of life: the feminist, the gay rights campaigner, the political activist, the religious believer, all make faith commitments that could possibly be misplaced, but which they are entirely justified to pursue with total commitment, given their illative sense that they *must* be right.

According to Locke, such thinking is deeply misplaced: it is precisely the fact that we act on our beliefs as if they were true that gives birth to fanaticism, engenders intolerance and breeds violence. However, the crucial issue is not whether we respond to our deepest held beliefs in a wholehearted manner, but whether our beliefs are actually true. If it is true that genocide is a great evil, then a person who holds that belief is perfectly justified to do all in her power to bring about the downfall of governments that practice genocide. Similarly, those whose faith stance causes them to commit acts of genocide are wrong to do so, not because they are fanatics but because genocide is wrong. An act of faith is not a provisional commitment to a set of beliefs that are so uncertain that it is improper to respond wholeheartedly to them. Rather, it is an act of saying something like the following:

> *This is how I see the world. I am aware of the possibility that I may be wrong, but I feel in the depth of my being that I must somehow be right, or at least that I am close to being right. I have considered other options and found them wanting, although I will continue to listen to them. However, for the present, and for the foreseeable future, I can do nothing more than say, with Martin Luther, 'Here I stand, I can do no other'.*

This, or something like this, is simply the way the vast majority of us actually conduct our day-to-day existence, whether theist, atheist or agnostic. I suggest that we are quite justified to do so, even if for no other reason than that the alternative of a laissez faire agnostic passivity itself constitutes a deeply held commitment to a particular faith stance.

9.6 Conclusion

Prior to the start of this chapter, I argued that critical education's primary concern should be for discrete religious traditions as bearers of ultimate truth claims; that such claims are expressed in the propositional truth claims and worldviews of such traditions; and that the appropriate way of engaging with them is through a dialogue between their various horizons of meaning and the horizons of meaning of the pupils. In this chapter, I addressed ways of judging between conflicting truth claims. I argued that, given the inadequacy of various forms of foundational epistemology, we should approach this issue from the perspective of a critical contextual epistemology. This entails weighing up a raft of probabilities by attending to a range of different authorities and, to this end, I identified five criteria through which judgements might be made. I concluded by suggesting that a holistic model of faith-seeking understanding, combining reason, feeling, thought and action in a unified practical wisdom, constitutes the appropriate milieu in which such criteria should be drawn upon.

Part IV
Theory and Practice

10

The pedagogy of learning

The final chapter of this study is concerned with the pedagogy of religious education. Pedagogy, the science of teaching and learning, has both a theoretical and practical dimension. In the British context, 'pedagogy' tends to refer to practical issues of teaching rather than to theories of learning; 'in the traditions of continental Europe', on the other hand, 'pedagogy is a discipline devoted to scholarship and research in the field of that phenomenon' (Marton and Booth, 1997, pp. 167f). In this chapter, I suggest that the pedagogy of religious education cannot be reduced to the pragmatic task of bridging theory and practice. Practical teaching issues need to be brought into dialogue with fundamental theoretical questions about the nature of learning, and it is only by answering such questions that religious education can hope to have any lasting impact on pupils. Consequently, this chapter does not set out to offer practical guidance to teachers: although such guidance is important, it raises issues about the professional development of teachers that are beyond the scope of this book, which restricts itself to developing a theory of critical religious education (Wright and Brandom, 2000). I begin by offering a résumé of the argument of the previous chapters; in the following section, I sketch a pedagogic theory structured around the Variation Theory of Learning and phenomenography; in the final section, I apply this theory directly to religious education.

10.1 Towards a pedagogy of critical religious education

In Part I, I set out two guiding principles for critical religious education. The first was that religious education should be fundamentally concerned with the *pursuit of truth and truthfulness*. I identified four key dimensions of this process: that 'truth' is simply the totality of all that exists regardless of our ability to apprehend it; that whether reality includes a transcendent or divine dimension is a matter of dispute; that since reality clearly possesses some kind of order, it is reasonable to assume it possesses some kind of ultimate meaning, which is rooted, perhaps, in God, the natural order or human values; and that to act truthfully is to live in harmony with the ultimate order-of-things. The second guiding principle was that of political liberalism. I argued that liberalism responds to the challenge of pluralism in two fundamentally different ways. Comprehensive liberalism identifies freedom and tolerance as ontologically normative, tends to be indifferent to contested truth claims, and functions confessionally in seeking to transmit its particular worldview. Political liberalism, on the other hand, views the principles of freedom and tolerance as a pragmatic means of establishing the necessary conditions for the pursuit of truth and truthful living in a plural society. As such, it has the potential to host an inclusive education system in which people from many different traditions can pursue contested questions of truth and truthfulness in a climate of freedom and tolerance.

In Part II, I set out to justify the centrality of the pursuit of truth and cultivation of truthfulness in religious education. I began by drawing attention to the fact that classical religious education tended to focus on the pursuit of ultimate truth and sought to enable pupils to live truthful lives in harmony with the actual order-of-things. I went out to show how some forms of liberal religious education have effectively marginalized questions of truth and truthfulness, in the process transforming the subject into a form of moral education designed merely to nurture the twin principles of freedom and tolerance by inducting pupils into a closed comprehensive liberal worldview. I sought to counter this tendency by proposing a critical religious education whose primary focus is simultaneously on the truth claims of religion and the implications of such truth claims for the task of living the good life. Such an approach, I argued, should be inherently inclusive, willing to listen to the voices of adherents of any possible worldview and address their truth claims.

In Part III, I set out to map the contours of an inclusive heuristic framework for critical religious education, one designed to help organize and focus the pursuit of truth in a liberal context. I suggested that the primary focus of such a framework should be ontological, and that religious education should begin by examining the primary bearers of transcendent truth claims: discrete religious traditions. However, if we are to understand these traditions adequately, it is necessary to place them in the wider contexts of the ordinary lives of religious adherents, universal accounts of religion, and secular alternatives to religion. I then suggested that religious language constitutes our main means of accessing transcendent truth claims, and that consequently we must pay attention both to the various forms of religious discourse (propositional, metaphoric, narrative, etc.) and to the various ways in which such discourse functions to establish, maintain and renew specific worldviews and practices. I then presented a hermeneutical framework, predicated on the notion of transformative dialoguebetween different horizons of meaning. Finally, I set out the case for organizing religious education around a contextual epistemology that seeks not definitive proof but reasoned and responsible judgement between conflicting truth claims. I suggested that such judgement must always precede from and through faith, and proposed a set of criteria to aid this process.

This vision of critical religious education raises important pedagogical questions. Theories of contemporary religious education tend to begin by identifying either a disciplinary (e.g. phenomenological, ethnographic) or ideological (e.g. romantic, postmodern) perspective as the basis on which to generate specific visions of the nature of the subject The pedagogic task is envisaged as that of finding practical ways of realizing such visions in the classroom. This has lead to the creation of a variety of pedagogies of religious education that are, for the most part, mutually exclusive (Grimmitt, 2000). Consequently, religious education in Britain has become the site of a series of 'curriculum wars', in which religious educators compete with one another to establish the dominance of their particular vision of the subject at the expense of others. One of the concerns of this book is to try to break this mould. I am increasingly convinced that religious educators have much more in common than they like to think, and that the subject would benefit enormously from a new era of consensus. To this end, I have presented a vision of religious education that seeks to be as inclusive of alternative viewpoints as possible and demonstrated its essential harmony with both current legislation and the emerging national

236 Critical Religious Education and Multiculturalism

consensus presented in the National Framework. Although the critical realism upon which this vision of religious education is based certainly contains both disciplinary and ideological features, it retains a fundamental openness to a range of different theological, philosophical and disciplinary perspectives and seeks to function heuristically by drawing such perspectives into a mutually beneficial conversation. The intention is that the exploration of the contested nature of religion, and of the various ideological perspectives and academic disciplines that seek to shed light on religion, should take place *in the classroom itself*. Instead of a series of conflicting visions of religious education, each offering a particular solution to the contested nature of religion, we need to move towards a single vision of religious education in which the contested nature of religion is explored within a common framework.

Practical issues of classroom teaching, linked to the professional development of teachers, are beyond the scope of this book; nevertheless, a few brief comments will help place the argument of this chapter in context. Robert Jackson notes the 'feeling of distance from the classroom (especially in relation to young or less able pupils) that comes across in [my] writings' (Jackson, 2004, p. 86). This is not a reference to the scholarly nature of my work: few would dispute that we should theorize religious education at the highest possible intellectual level, and that the practical needs of teachers do not require us to dumb-down the intellectual rigour with which we explore the subject. To this end it is important to distinguish the tasks of theoretical reflection and the professional development of teachers: although there is an intimate reciprocal relationship between the two, one cannot be allowed to dominate the other. From the point of view of the classroom teacher, Jackson's remarks are partly justified: there is indeed a need to show how we might actualize the theory of critical religious education in the classroom. In doing so, however, we should avoid mystifying the transition from theory to practice, especially as it applies to the pursuit of truth: all subjects in the curriculum deal with contested meanings and do so by employing standard teaching strategies that are transferable across different subject areas. The intellectual complexity of a subject is no bar to teaching it, at an appropriate level, in the classroom: we can reasonably expect most pupils in mainstream education to have at least an embryonic understanding of the Big Bang despite the highly complex nature of astrophysics.

The task facing critical religious education does not differ in any fundamental way from the common educational task of enabling pupils to become intelligent about complex issues. Jackson suggests that it would be 'instructive to see the results of a project in which Wright collaborated with primary and secondary teachers so that they could develop strategies to adapt his ideas to particular situations' (p. 86). There has already been some work in this area: an action research project directed by Susanna Hookway and based at King's College London worked alongside teachers and pupils to construct a pedagogy focused on the pursuit of truth in religious education (Hookway, 2002, 2004). Although there is potential for extending this project, the task is beyond the scope of the present book.

With these observations in mind, we can turn to the task of theorizing the pedagogy of critical religious education. I have some reservations about Jackson's focus on the pedagogy of teaching, which seems to me to be in danger of moving too quickly from the task of theorizing the subject to that of addressing practical questions of teaching methodology. The core argument of the present chapter is that a focus on the *pedagogy of teaching* needs to be proceeded by a focus on the *pedagogy of learning*. Before asking questions about how teaching might achieve our curricular aims, we need to address the fundamental issue of how pupils learn. In addressing this issue, I will draw on work pioneered by Ference Marton, Professor of Education at Gothenburg University, and developed by an international network of scholars that identifies pedagogy as a field of academic research and scholarship in its own right rather than merely a pragmatic means of traversing the gap between theory and practice. The focus of this research trajectory is two-fold: on the Variation Theory of Learning and on phenomenography.

10.2   The Variation Theory of Learning and phenomenography

Marton and his colleagues argue that the pedagogy of learning has logical priority over the pedagogy of teaching: we have to understand how pupils learn before asking how best to teach them. We cannot assume that the conditions necessary for effectively learning are automatically in place and put all our efforts into the task of teaching in the belief that perfecting that task will enable us to teach 'all things to all men' (Marton, Runesson and Tsui, 2004, p. 35). Instead, we should proceed by 'taking learning as the point of departure and exploring the conditions that might be conducive to bringing that learning about' (p. 35). This is not to imply 'that it does not matter whether the teaching is whole class, or whether pupils work in groups; whether pupils are engaged in task-based or problem solving learning, or in project work' (p. 39). Differences in the way that teachers actually teach will constrain or facilitate learning; however, before addressing such issues we must establish an appropriate 'space of learning' in which pupils can engage with whatever the teacher intends them to learn. If teacher and pupils do not work together to constitute an appropriate space of learning, the conditions necessary for effective learning will not be established, whatever the teaching methods adopted by the teacher (p. 39).

The Variation Theory of Learning claims that learning brings about a change in our awareness: to acquire knowledge is 'to see the world, or aspects of the world, in particular ways' (Marton and Booth, 1997, p. vii). We all experience the world differently, and changes in our experience bring about the expansion of our knowledge and enable us to respond to the world in new ways. In order to learn, we must *experience variation* by encountering objects, events, ideas and 'ways of seeing the world' that were previously unavailable to us.

Meno's paradox asserts 'the impossibility of learning something because the learner either must already know the stuff or is otherwise unable to recognize it when encountered' (p. 178; Plato, 1961, pp. 353ff). You cannot look for something unless you know what you are looking for, since you will not know where to look and will not be able to recognize it should you do happen to stumble across it; however, if you already know what you are looking for, there is no point in looking for it. The paradox assumes a gulf between the knower and the object of knowledge: replacing such a person–world dualism with a non-dualistic model, in which person and world occupy the same ontological space, immediately dissolves the paradox. Since we indwell the world, the pursuit of knowledge is not a quest for some mysterious object 'out there', but rather a process of expanding, enriching and deepening our experiences of that with which we are already – in one way or another – engaged. Thus, a child will inevitable perceive the night sky as an aspect of her environment; she may gaze up at the stars and wonder whether space goes on for ever, or whether there is a brick wall at the end of the universe; when she is introduced to the concept 'God', her questions about the infinity of space will be expanded through the introduction of the notion of transcendence. Hence her understanding of God is not arrived at by encountering a *totally* alien concept, but by the gradual expansion of that which she already knows. The quest for knowledge involves 'taking the experiences of people seriously and exploring the physical, the social, the cultural world they experience' (Marton and Booth, 1997, p. 13). We neither construct the world nor have it imposed on us, but rather experience it by virtue of the fact that we indwell it and are part of it. There is 'not a real world out there and a subjective world in here', just one reality constituted by the interrelationship between the world and the learner (p. 13). 'The world we deal with is the world as experienced by people, by learners . . . the people, the learners, we deal with are people experiencing aspects of the world' (p. 13).

Despite the fact that there is only one world, we all experience it differently and our experiences are always partial. Learning entails coming to experience the world in a different way: new experiences of the world 'transcend the learner's life-world' and enable her to understand the world in deeper ways, thereby expanding her knowledge and enabling her to act more competently (p. 202). Since 'one way of experiencing the world can be judged to be better than another way', it follows that 'some people must have become better at experiencing the world – or have experienced the world in a better way, or have gained better knowledge – than others' (p. 13). The notion of 'better' is understood in terms of that which the teacher intends pupils to learn; in the context of critical religious education, this means learning more about ultimate truth and developing competencies for truthful living. Learning, as a rule, is not a process of acquiring basic facts and building them up into complex wholes; rather, it proceeds 'from an undifferentiated and poorly integrated understanding of the whole to an increased differentiation and integration of the whole and its parts' (p. viii). The learner starts out with some partial knowledge of the object of study, in the form of 'undifferentiated and unintegrated wholes' that 'are likely to appear confused and erroneous when judged against the criteria of received wisdom' (p. viii). Nevertheless, such partial experiences 'are the seeds from which valid knowledge can grow' (p. viii). Learning is always learning about *something*: a process of seeing a particular aspect of the world in a new way. People perceive situations in a limited number of qualitatively different ways, and by experiencing variation in their perceptions they will be better able to recognize patterns of meaningful experience and hence respond to new situations in more effective ways (pp. 14ff). Thus, a novice angler may struggle to spear a fish, whereas a practised angler with previous experience of the effects of the refraction of light on water is far more likely to achieve her goal.

In principle, it is possible to gain unlimited knowledge of a particular situation by viewing it from an infinite number of perspectives. However, only an omniscient God can possibly achieve this; our modest ability to process information means that we are necessarily selective, attending to certain aspects of a situation at the expense of others. We discern things by attending to what we take to be their most critical aspects. In doing so, we perceive them as similar to, or different from, other things; seeing an object 'in terms of its part-whole structure means . . . seeing what the parts and whole *are* and what they *are not*' (Marton and Tsui, 2004, p. 9). This is important, since a pupil's inability to see the topic or problem in a particular way, or to attend to its relevant aspects, is often a cause of their inability to learn. Hence, learning to experience the world in a better, or more truthful, way involves discernment, variation and simultaneity.

a) *Discernment* entails pupils identifying central features of the object under investigation and recognizing how they vary with respect to other features. It requires recognition of wholes in their context (a deer in a forest), of parts within wholes (body, head, antlers), and of the relation of wholes to their context (is the deer motionless or running?). To understand Islam in the modern world, it is necessary to place it in the context of Western liberalism (wholes in their context), the beliefs and practices of Muslims (parts within wholes), and the various responses of Islam to the global hegemony of Western liberalism (the relation of wholes to their context). Since alternative ways of discerning the object of study may not be readily apparent to pupils, one task of the teacher is to provide access to them. As it is possible to perceive an object in an infinite number of ways, the teacher must focus on those dimensions of variation most significant for the particular understanding aimed for in the lesson.

b) *Variation* is basic to learning: we cannot properly appreciate the colour blue without experience of other colours, and can know relatively little about the distinctiveness of our country until we have visited another. A person seeking to appreciate the symphony will learn more by listening to more than one Mozart symphony, more still by contrasting them with symphonies by Brahms and Lutoslawski, and more again by comparing them with string quartets and piano sonatas. Some dimensions of variation are significant for understanding, others less so: thus knowledge of the styles of dress of each composer has little significance for understanding their symphonies (I write with memories of my own music lessons indelibly, etched on my mind). Similarly, a lesson spent meticulously drawing the positions adopted by Muslims when praying is likely to be less valuable than one that contrasts a life lived in submission to the will of Allah with a life in which God has no role to play.

c) *Simultaneity* involves the learner focusing on different dimensions of variation simultaneously. The foreground of our awareness is ever changing: we are constantly filtering aspects of our awareness into the background, and can only be focally aware of a limited range of experiences at any one time. Effective learning requires pupils to hold significant experiences in focal awareness at the same time. We recognize a tall person when we see one because we are simultaneously aware – whether through immediate observation or recollection – of our experience of people of short and average height. Similarly, we recognize an act of kindness because we respond to it by bringing our own experiences of acts of kindness and cruelty into focal awareness.

According to Variation Theory, education is concerned to increase pupils' knowledge and experience of the world. Teachers generally identify a normative way of experiencing the object of study, which they assume is lacking in pupils and that they aim to make available to them. 'Some ways of experiencing [the object of knowledge] are more complex, more inclusive, or more specific than others, and they coincide to a greater or lesser extent with those considered to be crucial for further educational development' (p. 126). Variation Theory is more than mere philosophical speculation: it is rooted in, and is constantly being refined by, empirical research conducted across a range of subject areas and age groups in many different cultural contexts. Much of this empirical study utilizes the research specialization 'phenomenography'.

Phenomenography is not primarily a research methodology or a theory of experience, but rather an approach to 'identifying, formulating and tackling certain sorts of research questions, a specialization that is particularly aimed at questions of relevance to learning and understanding in an educational setting' (Marton and Booth, 1997, p. 111). Neither is phenomenography a branch of empirical psychology: it has no interest in 'describing mental representations, short- or long-term memory, retrieval processes, and the rest of the conceptual apparatus of the cognitivists' (p. 113). The focus is not on what is going on inside the mind, but on the ways in which we *interact* with the world. Further, phenomenography is not a branch of phenomenology. Thought they have a shared interest in our experience of the world, phenomenography stands apart from both the philosophy and methodology of phenomenology. It is not concerned to reveal the essence of any given phenomena, but to explore the *relationship* between the world we indwell and ourselves. Hence, phenomenographic research focuses

> on ways of experiencing different phenomena, ways of seeing them, knowing about them, and having skills related to them . . . Whereas the phenomenologist might ask, 'How does the person experience the world?' the phenomenographer would ask something more like, 'What are the critical aspects of ways of experiencing the world that make people able to handle it in more or less efficient ways?'
>
> (p. 117)

At its most basic, phenomenography aims to identify the critical variation that exists within any given groups experience of a phenomenon. Its central concern is to discern the various ways in which pupils experience the object of study and thereby identify how their experiences need modification if they are to achieve the learning outcomes intended by the teacher. In order to make such experiences available to them, it is vital that the teacher take account of the critical variation in the experience of the object of study that pupils bring with them to the classroom prior to the commencement of the formal learning process. Thus, phenomenography provides teachers with a means of identifying the prior experience of pupils, and thereby helps them organize the learning space in such a way as to ensure they are exposed to the significant variations in experience that they currently lack.

Phenomenography is concerned to map the various 'ways in which the people being studied experience the phenomenon of interest' (p. 129). The basic unit of phenomenographic research is the internal relationship between those who experience and that which they experience. The observation that the world can be experienced in an infinite number of ways, coupled with the recognition that some ways of experiencing the world are clearly better than others, opens up the possibility of identifying 'critical differences in people's capabilities of experiencing the phenomena in which we are interested' (p. 123). Such variation in the ways of experiencing the world stems from the fact that we encounter phenomenon in a limited number of qualitatively different ways, and can be focally aware of only a limited number of aspects of our experience at any one time. Although we can hold some aspects of a phenomenon in our focal awareness, we will relegate others to our background awareness – perhaps because we take them for granted, or assume they have no critical significance for our understanding – and there will always be other potential experiences not yet encountered. The aim of phenomenography is to identify the critical variation in the ways that a selected group experience a particular phenomenon. The researcher attempts to engage with the group's experiences of the phenomenon vicariously (p. 121). Phenomenographic descriptions are accounts of the 'internal relationship between persons and phenomena: ways in which persons experience a given phenomena and ways in which a phenomena is experienced by persons' (p. 122). 'At the root of phenomenography lies an interest in describing the phenomena in the world as others see them, and in revealing and describing the variation therein, especially in an educational context' (p. 111).

Phenomenography seeks to depict the ways in which a given group experiences the object of interest. Marton and his colleagues refer to descriptions of the various ways in which a group

244 Critical Religious Education and Multiculturalism

experiences an object as the 'outcome space'. Accounts of the outcome space are developed at a collective level: the focus is not on individual experiences, but on the totality of experiences within the group. The phenomenographer is interested in critical variation in the way an object is perceived, regardless of whether such variation exists within the group as a whole, within a subset of the group, or within the experiences of an individual group member. It seeks to identify specific categories of variation and describe the logical relationship between them. As a rule, there is a hierarchical relationship between critical variations in experience: some are more advanced, intricate and significant than others. Hence, the outcome space takes the form of a grid of increasing complexity: different ways of experiencing an object constitute 'subsets of the component parts and relationships within more inclusive or complex ways of seeing the phenomenon' (p. 125). There is no attempt to offer a comprehensive description of the totality of ways of experiencing an object – given the infinite number of potential ways, such a task is impossible – merely to identify critical variation in the experiences of the group under investigation. The categories of phenomenological description identified by the research must have a clear relationship to the phenomenon under investigation, stand in a logical and normally hierarchical relationship to one another, and be limited to the minimum required to capture the critical variation revealed by the data (p. 125).

The outcome space reveals both the actuality and potentiality of the group's experience, and as such directs the teacher's attention to the dimensions of variation that she will need to introduce in the classroom. In phenomenography, data collection and data analysis are inseparable. In describing the variation in experience present in the group, the researcher will certainly seek to be true to the available data. However, she will also seek to interpret it in the light of her particular understanding of the phenomenon and of the way it is experienced by others outside the group, especially 'the phenomenon's treatment in other research traditions: how it appears in literature, in treatises and in textbooks or how it has been handled in the past and in different cultures' (p. 129). This dialectical process effectively brings variation in the experiences of the pupils – and variation in the experiences of those professional and academic experts whose experiences the teacher will try to introduce them to – into conversation with one another. By mapping the various ways in which pupils experience the object of study, phenomenography provides the teacher with valuable information as she seeks to establish an appropriate learning space.

Returning to Variation Theory, Marton and his colleagues are clear that specific learning conditions must be established if particular learning outcomes are to be achieved. Although there are many different ways of teaching the same topic, and it is never possible to guarantee that learning will take place, learning is unlikely to occur unless the teacher recognizes that 'whatever you are trying to learn, there are certain necessary conditions for succeeding' (Marton and Tsui, 2004, p. ix). Hence the need to focus on 'the sort of pedagogical situations in which a pupil or pupil is engaged in an effort to learn (gain knowledge) about some aspect of his or her world in collaboration with a teacher, instructor, or equivalent substitute' (Marton and Booth, 1997, p. 178). The key to effective teaching is to organize the learning space in a manner that establishes the necessary conditions for pupils' experience of the world to be expanded and deepened in ways appropriate to the learning targets. The process of 'finding out what these conditions are, and bringing them about, should be the teacher's primary professional task' (Marton and Tsui, 2004, p. ix).

Advocates of Variation Theory rehabilitate the notion of the teacher as an 'expert' responsible for transmitting knowledge from generation to generation. She 'can be seen as one who, as a member of an older generation with a status grounded in an experience of aspects of the world and an experience of transmitting it to members of the younger generation, is accorded the task of transforming ignorant youths into experienced maturity' (Marton and Booth, 1997, p. 167). It is the teacher's responsibility to define the object of learning in the light of the prescribed curriculum. However, she can only transmit this object if she can first relate it to the experiences of her pupils. Hence, there needs to be an empathetic relationship between teacher and class, based on mutual exchange of their experiences of the world: 'the essential feature is that the *teacher takes the part of the learner*, sees the experience through the learner's eyes, becomes aware of the experience through the learner's awareness' (p. 179).

The object of learning possesses certain features that pupils must discern if they are to achieve the prescribed learning outcomes. Hence, the teacher must construct the lesson around the most significant dimensions of variation. A distinction is made between the 'intended', 'enacted' and 'lived' objects of learning: the intended object is that which the teacher intends pupils to learn; the enacted object is that which she presents to pupils in the classroom; the lived object is that which they actually learn. Effective learning requires continuity between what teachers intend to teach, what they actually teach, and what pupils end up learning. Such continuity is dependent, at least in part, on the teacher successfully identifying both the significant features of the object of study presented in the curriculum and the critical features of the pupils' prior understanding of the object that they bring with them to the classroom. By identifying the experiences that pupils already possess, together with the experiences that she intends them to possess, she can constitute the space of learning in a manner designed to expanding their experience of the object of study in appropriate ways. The teacher derives her understanding of the significant features of the object of study from the curriculum, interpreted in the light of the received wisdom of society, especially the received wisdom of fellow professionals, academics and other experts. She derives her understanding of the critical features of the object of study *as discerned by pupils* from empirical observation at the start of the learning process: ideally, from detailed phenomenographic research; more practically, from her working knowledge of her pupils reinforced by initial questioning.

Learning is always learning about something: it 'takes place as part of the ongoing exploration of the world' as pupils learn to experience the world in new ways (p. 138). That which we learn becomes part of our knowledge, part of our experience of the world and, as such, it changes us by altering our relationship with the world we indwell. Our experience is normally mediated experience: we gain most of our knowledge not by experiencing objects directly, but be attending to authorities that enable us to encounter them at second-hand. Such knowledge tends to be communal rather than individualistic: we experience the world through the experiences of others, based on a common language that articulates shared patterns of meaning. Hence 'our own world becomes increasingly the world of others as well, and the latter world as already experienced, is a constitutive force in learning' (p. 139). Our new experiences are never unique; rather there is always some level of continuity with our previous experiences. Thus, for example, a theist encountering a non-theistic religion for the first time will experience variation in their previous experience of religion. 'Genuine learning always relates to the learner's reality, the world as already experienced' (p. 140). It follows that learning is normally a process of 'developing more detailed knowledge of phenomena we experience in certain ways' and, as such, seeks to bring about a qualitative change in a person's experience of that phenomena (p. 139). When learning takes place, the relationship between the learner and the object of study changes:

> The learner has become capable of discerning aspects of the phenomena other than those she had been capable of discerning before, and she had become capable of being simultaneously and focally aware of other aspects, or more aspects, of the phenomena than was previously the case.
>
> (p. 142)

As this relationship changes, so the pupils themselves change, becoming more aware of the world they indwell and better able to interact appropriately with it.

Variation theorists distinguish between surface and deep awareness within the learning process. Surface approaches to learning are relatively superficial, tend to sidestep dimensions of variation, and focus directly on the learning task itself. Deep approaches to learning tend to be more profound, engage directly with critical variation, and focus directly on the object of study. That is why attempts to develop depth learning through staged questions, which seek to point pupils towards significant features in the object of study, frequently fail: the progressive sequence of questions focuses attention on the learning *task*, rather than the *object of study* itself. In contrast, approaches that present pupils with the object of study as a whole, and invite them to identify its critical features in the light of contrasting interpretations, tend to be more successful, precisely because they deflect attention away from the task onto the object of study. The defining features of deep learning identified by advocates of Variation Theory can be summarized thus:

> Pupils should intend to understand the material for themselves, rather than simply reproduce the curricular content . . . interact critically, rather than passively accept ideas and information . . . relate their learning to previous knowledge and experience, rather than concentrate on the

assessment requirements . . . use organizing principles to integrate their ideas, rather than think unsystematically . . . relate evidence to conclusions, rather than simply memorize facts.

(Hella and Wright, 2008, p. 11)

At the heart of effective learning is the teacher's ability to work with students to establish the *relevance structure* of the space of learning. The enactment of learning in the classroom must be related to both the pupils' prior experiences of the object of study, and the experiences the teacher intends them to encounter: pupils must be able to perceive the connection and variation between both sets of experience. If the relevance structure is in place, then it is possible for the pupil not just to experience something new, but to experience it in the manner necessary for an appropriate understanding of the object of study. If effective learning is to take place, 'it is necessary that something varies, some aspect of the situation that surrounds the person' (Marton and Booth, 1997, p. 145). 'By learning, our experience of the world, or our experienced world, gets more differentiated and more integrated. Our world grows richer, we become more enlightened' (p. 158).

10.3 Religious education and the pedagogy of learning

I have argued that religious education should seek to enable pupils to learn simultaneously from and about religion, and that it should do so by focusing on the heart of the world's religious traditions, namely their concern to enable adherents to live authentic lives in harmony with the ultimate order-of-things. Variation Theory is committed to a relational, non-dualistic, ontology: the fact that we indwell the world that we seek to understand means that we cannot reduce learning to mere self-expression or impose knowledge from outside pupils' actual experiences. Instead, learning begins from the current experiences of pupils and develops via the introduction of variation into these experiences. Learning is always an expansion and deepening of that which the pupils already know; in theological terms, learning always proceeds from and through faith.

The religious education teacher is in the position of expert authority: it is her responsibility, in the light of curricular requirements, to introduce appropriate variation into her pupils' experiences of religion. Religious education sets out to change pupils' understanding of religion and of their place in the ultimate order-of-things: there is no point in teaching the subject if there is no aspiration that they change, or if the aspiration is purely arbitrary – change for the sake of change. Hence, the teacher needs a clear vision of the ways in which she wants her pupils to develop and this, in turn, means she must identify the significant experiences they must encounter if they are to change in the way she intends. It is important to recognize that this notion of educationally norm-ative ways of experiencing need not be overly prescriptive: thus, a teacher may judge that pupils ought to experience how to make appropriate judgements between conflicting points of view. The central feature of religion is its concern to understand the trans-cendent nature of reality and to enable human beings to live life in harmony with the ultimate order-of-things. In a plural setting, the contested nature of religion makes it imperative that pupils experience variation between different accounts of ultimate reality – variation within religions, variation between religions, and variation between religious and secular accounts of reality. The task of the teacher is to work with pupils to construct the learning space so that the heart of religion – namely its concern for truth and truthfulness in the light of transcendent claims about the ultimate nature of reality – comes to the fore. This will enable religious education to cultivate appropriate levels of religious literacy; that is to say, develop pupils' competence to reason, feel and act wisely with regard to religious accounts of the ultimate order-of-things.

Because pupils already indwell the world they seek to understand, they bring to the space of learning a set of experiences related to questions of transcendence. These may be implicit or explicit, coherent or confused, reasonable or irrational, clearly articulated or vaguely expressed, and may be held with varying degrees of intelligence. The important thing is that they already relate to the object of study in some way; consequently, effective learning entails the qualitative expansion and deepening to pupils' experiences of the world as these relate to questions of ultimate truth and truthful behaviour. If the first task of the teacher is to identify the significant aspects of religion as the primary object of study, then the second task is to identify the critical aspects of the pupils' understanding that they bring with them to the space of learning.

Based on her knowledge of these features, the teacher must identify the dimensions of variation that pupils need to encounter if they are to move from a relatively meagre and superficial range of experiences to a qualitatively richer and deeper set. In doing so, it is crucial that she identifies the most significant dimensions of variation: submission to Allah may be more significant than Muslim dress codes, the concept of incarnation more significant than church architecture, and so forth. It is only when this preliminary work in the field of the pedagogy of learning is complete, and the significant aspects of the object of study identified, that attention can turn to the pedagogy of teaching and important questions about classroom organization, grouping, task setting, resources, teaching methods and so forth can be addressed.

One final comment, before we focus on the potential use of phenomenography in religious education. Earlier, I identified learning from and learning about religion as dual aims for religious education, and suggested that they are twin aspects of a single process. It should now be clear that the unity of learning about and from religion ultimately has an ontological basis: pupils should learn *about* the ontological dimension of religion by focusing on ultimate truth claims; they should learn *from* religion by addressing the question of their own existential relationship to the ultimate ontological structures of reality (Hella and Wright, 2008). When we experience variation in our understanding of ultimate reality, we necessarily experience a shift in our own personal relationship to it. We do not learn facts and values about religion and then ask what their implications are for our own spiritual lives. Rather, we develop knowledge and insight only by reorienting ourselves, through the gradual expansion and deepening of our experience, towards the realities – putative or real – witnessed to by religious traditions and their adherents. This reorientation necessarily brings about a change in the pupil, one that constitutes a single movement: a change in our knowledge about ultimate reality is simultaneously a change in our existential orientation towards ultimate reality – it is impossible to have one without the other.

Turning then to phenomenographic research, the first thing to note is that, to date, it has had relatively little impact in the field of religious education, although some important studies have been undertaken (Hella, 2008, pp. 6f). Here we will focus, by way of a case study, on Elina Hella's research into Finnish upper secondary school pupils' understanding of Lutheranism.

Although the majority of the Finnish population belong to the Evangelical Lutheran Church of Finland, characteristically for northern Europe there are relatively high levels of nominal allegiance. Finnish religious education, despite retaining vestiges of its confessional past, is broadly liberal in outlook. Hella detected a level of ambiguity here, with the subject hovering between a liberal future and confessional past, and suggested this reflects a broader ambiguity about the place of Lutheranism within Finnish society – an ambiguity that provides the context for her research. The study set out to explore variation in the way pupils conceptualize their understanding of Lutheranism: specifically, it aimed to establish which particular aspects of their experience are critical and to identify dimensions of variation in their discernment. Hella's wider goal was to explore ways in which the results of this empirical research might enable teachers to enhance Lutheran pupils' learning about their own religion in relation to others.

Hella's data consisted of 63 responses to a projective writing task: pupils were asked to imagine making friends with a Spanish teen-ager while visiting Santiago de Compostela and to respond to the following question: 'I know that there is Lutheranism in America, Germany and Scandinavia, but I have never really understood what Lutheranism is about. Could you tell me how you understand Lutheranism?' (pp. 7f). She undertook complementary interviews with eleven pupils, inviting them to comment on their essays and clarify their statements. Her data analysis followed the phenomenographic principles and procedures established by Marton. Each of the emergent categories of description included two analytical aspects: the overall holistic meaning of Lutheranism as discerned by pupils, and the derivation of such wholes from the internal parts of Lutheranism and its differentiation from other aspects of experience. The outcome of this phenomenographic analysis was the identification of five categories of variation in pupils' understanding of Lutheranism, hierarchically ordered according to their increasing complexity.

Category 1: Lutheranism as a religion

At the lowest level pupils draw on fragmented pieces of information (hymns, the name 'Luther', church attendance, etc.) to identify

Lutheranism as a religion alongside other religions, such as Islam. As one respondent put it, 'Lutheranism is one of the religions, for which organ music is played' (p. 10).

Category 2: Lutheranism as the Finnish Christian way of life

Pupils discern Lutheranism as one of a number of Christian denominations and differentiate it from non-Christian religions. They relate the external features of Lutheran practise to its cultural function as part of the Finnish way of life, and view the church as a public institution. 'It is our religion that includes baptism, wedding and funeral, and you can go to church if you want, but you do not have to' (p. 12).

Category 3: Lutheranism as nominal Christians and real believers

Pupils distinguish between the external trappings of Lutheranism and inner faith. They identify faith as a private matter not always visible to the observer, and recognize that celebration of the principle rites of passage – including confirmation – may possess only cultural value for many Lutherans. Nevertheless, some pupils perceived nominal allegiance to retain spiritual value:

> Lutheranism just is part of me. It is not very big part, but so big that I would not want to live without it either. I can admit that I am Christian out of habit. I only go to church on Christmas, besides celebrations, I pray seldom. I hold on into Lutheranism when I can benefit from it. It means security to me.
>
> (p. 15)

Category 4: Lutheranism as a personal relationship with God

Pupils describe Lutheranism in terms of their personal relationship with God and their ongoing wrestling with this relationship: 'I have almost lost my faith in God and believe only in the existence of 'goodness' and 'evil'' (p. 16). The discussion tends to adopt theological categories broadly resonant with mainstream Lutheran theology: 'Are God and Christ or Jesus Christ the same or not . . . And who is the Holy Spirit? I personally cannot understand those three as one: Father, Son and Eternal Spirit' (p. 16).

Category 5: Lutheranism as faith in salvation as the gift of God

In this final category, the ambiguity of pupils' personal relationship with God is resolved through the recognition of the sovereignty of grace: at the heart of Lutheranism is the proclamation of a merciful and forgiving God, and of faith as a divine gift. They relate the central meaning of Lutheranism to a range of interconnected theological concepts: salvation, mercy, death, hell, eternal life, etc. 'The basic idea of Lutheranism is that the human being is saved because of God's mercy' (p. 17).

Hella's data reveals critical variation in pupils' understandings of Lutheranism: they experience Lutheranism as a religion, as an aspect of Finnish cultural life, as a tradition that embraces nominal and committed adherents, as a means of access to a personal relationship with God, and as a vehicle mediating divine grace. Each category connects to the others in a hierarchical sequence: none is necessarily wrong in itself, but each category progressively reveals deeper and more authentic understandings of Lutheranism.

How might the results of this study enable the teacher to teach more effectively? The crucial issue is that of the relationship between the pupils' experiences and the experiences she wishes them to grapple with. Phenomenographic description does not claim to make an 'ought' out of an 'is': the fact that pupils experience different ways of understanding Lutheranism does not mean that they are incapable, given the appropriate experience, of thinking in categories other than those identified in the research. The first task facing the teacher is to identify the experiences necessary to fulfil the aims of the curriculum. Thus the teacher, guided by the curriculum and her knowledge of Lutheran theology, may decide that the deepest and most profound way of experiencing Lutheranism is that of the fifth category: Lutheranism as faith in salvation as the gift of God. If none of the pupil group had identified that particular category, it would still constitute an appropriate lesson aim. It is important to note, in passing, that experience of Lutheranism as faith in salvation as the gift of God is not necessarily the same as embracing that faith for oneself. Indeed, one of the pupils who described Lutheranism in terms of the final category was explicit that their description was not that of a member of the Lutheran church, but of a sympathetic outsider. Whatever their personal response to

Lutheranism, a deep understanding of that tradition requires pupils to understand that at the heart of the self-understanding of Lutheranism is a belief in the grace of God. The second task facing the teacher is to relate the significant aspects of Lutheranism identified by the curriculum, and those aspects pupils themselves identify as critical. If appropriate learning is to take place, it is imperative that pupils experience the variation between these aspects for themselves. Pupils who only view Lutheranism as a religion need to experience, in a progressive manner, the other four aspects if they are to reach the level of discernment that some of their classmates have already achieved.

Debate about the pedagogy of religious education tends to focus on teaching styles and ways of approaching a topic. Should we start with phenomenological description, or spiritual self-expression? Should we deal with religions thematically, or in terms of discrete traditions? Should we focus on religious language, or feelings and emotions? If the aim of the lesson is to bring pupils to a deep understanding of the core of Lutheran faith, then the simple answer is that many different approaches and teaching styles have the potential to be effective. However, none is likely to be effective unless the pupils are enabled to experience significant variation in the critical understanding that they bring with them to the classroom. No amount of creative writing, or attending to the voices of ordinary Lutherans, or phenomenological descriptions of Lutheran worship, or theological 'concept-cracking' will enable pupils to understand the core of Lutheranism unless such activities enable pupils to discern significant differences between various understandings of Lutheranism.

Of course, the results of such phenomenographic research will not always be available to teachers and, in any case, will only reveal the critical experiences of the particular group under investigation. How then might teachers apply Variation Theory in the classroom in the absence of such research? In seeking to answer this question, we will conduct a brief thought experiment.

Let us imagine a teacher setting out to teach a course on Christian Belief at lower secondary level. The basic curricular aim is to enable pupils to explore the core truth claims of Christianity. From her prior knowledge of the make-up of the class, the teacher has already decided that the basic dimension of variation driving the course will be between Christian theism and secular naturalism. The first course unit prescribed by the syllabus requires her to explore the Christian doctrine of creation through a study of the creation myth in the first chapter of Genesis. She recognizes that a deep understanding of the doctrine requires its integration within the Christian worldview as a whole, and so accepts that this initial unit will form the start of a longer journey. With this in mind, she decides that her basic aim in this initial unit is for pupils to experience the intellectual rigour with which many Christians embrace the Genesis myth, and recognize that it offers a true account of the origins of the universe for many rational people.

At the planning stage, her study of the place of the myth in Christian theology reveals three potentially significant dimensions of variation. First, the nature of God: Christians believe God is personal and created the universe for a purpose, and consequently reject deistic belief in God as the impersonal first cause of a mechanistic universe as well as the pantheistic identification of God with the universe. Second, faith and reason: the basic variation here is between rational proof of the existence of a creator God, faith as a groundless leap in the dark, and faith as reflective assent in the light of experience. Third, theology and science: the central variation here is between the mythological account of creation in Genesis and scientific accounts of the origin of the universe. At this initial stage of lesson preparation, the teacher suspects that one or other of these three sets of variation may offer a valuable means of organizing the learning space. Her preliminary thoughts have also identified other dimensions of variation that she does *not* anticipate having a significant role to play. In particular, she sees little value in any of the following: literary and historical criticism focused on the origins and development of the myth; comparative study of other creation myths; creative responses through poetry and art; and consideration of ecological and environmental issues. Although she suspects that some of these – especially the last two – will quickly engage the interest of pupils, she does not anticipate them enabling pupils to grapple with the truth claims embedded in the myth in any depth.

Let us now imagine that, prior to the start of the course, the teacher has a preliminary discussion with her pupils about the Genesis myth and supplements this with a written homework assignment. She discovers that the class has a basic knowledge of the myth and recognize that it is a story about the origins of the universe. They assume that God is a personal being, show surprisingly little interest in epistemological questions of faith and reason, and focus instead on issues raised by modern science, especially the Big Bang and evolution. Although they have some awareness of the difference between literal and metaphorical readings of the Genesis myth, their ability to reflect on its relationship with the dominant scientific theory of the origins of the universe is, for the most part, limited to an assumption that it is necessary to make and either/or choice between the two – although a few pupils do attempt to defend the reciprocal truth of both accounts. Hence the teacher arrives at a hierarchical map of the critical variation in experience that her pupils will bring with them to the classroom. The Genesis myth tells the story of a personal creator God; people read it either literally or metaphorically; science offers an alternative theory of the origins of the universe; some people choose to accept one of the accounts and exclude the other; others see them as complementary accounts of the same event. None of these variations in understanding is actually wrong, but all but the last fall short of the depth and breadth of experience the teacher intends her pupils to achieve.

It is now apparent to the teacher that she should focus on the variation between theological and scientific accounts of the origin of the universe and, with this in mind, identifies a number of crucial theological issues embedded in mainstream Christianity. First, that the literal reading of Genesis employed by Christian creationists is a modern phenomenon. When the fifteenth-century scholar John Collet 'expressed the opinion that the story of creation was a 'poetic figment' used by Moses to explain the divine purpose to a primitive people', he was merely reflecting longstanding exegetical practice: the first Christian theologians employed a standard distinction between literal, allegorical, typological and spiritual readings of Scripture (Mackie, 1972, p. 243). Second, Christian theologians have consistently sought to respect science and work with it. Thus, towards the end of the fourth century, Augustine insisted that 'Scripture must be interpreted in a way that is not contradicted by established scientific conclusions' (Hodgson, 2005, p. 26). Indeed, he held it to be a

> disgraceful and dangerous thing for an infidel to hear a Christian talking nonsense on these topics, and we should take all means to prevent such an embarrassing spectacle in which people see vast ignorance in a Christian and laugh it to scorn.

(p. 27)

Third, the suggestion that the Christian belief that the world 'is good, rational, contingent and open to the human mind' provides science with the basic ontological presuppositions upon which it depends, receives considerable support from philosophers of science (p. 11). Fourth, mainstream theologians recognize that science and scripture engage with the world in qualitatively different ways. As Pope John Paul II insisted, the Bible 'does not concern itself with the details of the physical world'; there are 'two realms of knowledge, one that has its source in revelation and one that reason can discover by its own power' (p. 12). Fifth, these qualitatively different ways of experiencing the world are complementary rather than mutually exclusive: 'the methodologies proper to each makes it possible to bring out different aspects of reality' (p. 12). As the early-sixth-century theologian John Philoponus pointed out, 'Genesis was written for spiritual and not scientific instruction' (p. 27). Creationists who claim that fossils are not millions of years old, but were created by God just a few thousand years ago to 'trick' secular scientists 'do indeed recognize the power of the creator, but do so in a way that is both radically unscientific and also insulting to God's integrity' (p. 13). As Peter Hodgson points out, it is 'vital to hold together both truths, namely the creation of all by God, and the scientific discoveries that have shown us how the world has developed over the ages' (p. 13; Peacock, 1993).

With these theological observations in mind, it becomes clear to our teacher that the significant dimension of variation lacking in the current experience of most of her pupils is that of the possibility that the dominant scientific account of the origin of the universe and the Genesis account of creation together constitute distinctive but mutually compatible truth claims. This decision resonates with our earlier identification of fertility – the ability to incorporate alien beliefs into a belief system provided that adherents have good reason for doing – as an important indicator of potential truth. Since her basic aim is for pupils to recognize that belief in the truth of the Genesis myth can be entirely rational (which is not the same as necessarily accepting it as true), enabling them to recognize the two discourses as mutually compatible becomes the focus of her teaching.

In the first of four dimensions of variation, she introduces pupils to the contrast between stories that make no claims about reality, stories that make literal truth claims, and stories that make non-literal truth claims. She presents them with an extract from a romantic novel written merely to entertain, an anecdotal account of the occasion when her window cleaner fell off his ladder and broke his leg, the myth of Icarus, and the Genesis myth itself. By identifying variation between each story, she invites pupils to explore the proposition that the novel tells us nothing substantial about the world, that the anecdote tells us literal truth, and that the two myths deal with non-literal truth. The myth of Icarus tells us that it is important to be aware of our limitations, although there was never an actual Icarus who flew too close to the sun; the Genesis myth tells us that God created the world, although there was not an actual seven-day period of creation.

The second dimension of variation focuses on the fact that different forms of discourse engage with reality in different ways. With the distinction between literal and non-literal meaning fresh in their minds, she introduces pupils to a partisan account of a football match, a recipe for chocolate cake, a love poem, and a scientific description of the Big Bang. By asking pupils to focus on the different kinds of speech act involved in each example, she invites them to explore the proposition that each text engages truthfully with reality, but in different ways and for different reasons.

The third dimension of variation addresses the notion that different discourses are capable of providing equally valid descriptions of the same phenomena. With the previous variation in mind, she invites pupils to explore different ways of describing a Hollywood actor. How might a physicist, a chemist, a biologist, a psychologist, a poet, a painter, a fan, a close friend, a gossip columnist, a politician or a theologian undertake the task? Are there any descriptions that do not provide knowledge and insight? Are some descriptions more important or valuable than others? Are there any descriptions that exclude others? In what ways might the descriptions be mutually compatible?

Introducing these three sets of variation, selected with the pupils' previous experiences and voices of the theologians in mind, provides the necessary context for the fourth and final dimension of variation. The teacher intends pupils to explore the proposition that the scientific account of the Big Bang and the Genesis myth are mutually compatible. The former is more 'literal' than the latter, despite employing metaphorical language, and seeks to offer an accurate description of the physical events through which our universe came into being. The latter offers a non-literal account of the transcendent cause of the Big Bang, and seeks to nurture and guide spiritual development. Pupils are asked to consider the Genesis myth and an account of the Big Bang in the light of three contrasting and mutually incompatible positions: first, the creationist claim that the Genesis myth is literally true and the scientific account false; second, the atheistic claim that the scientific account is essentially complete and the Genesis myth redundant; third, the orthodox Christian claim that the texts are equally true, and hence offer entirely compatible and complementary accounts of the origins and source of the universe.

My intention, in describing this imaginary scenario, is to shed light on the suggestion that the pedagogy of learning, guided by Variation Theory and phenomenography, constitutes a crucial stage in the process of enabling pupils to grapple with questions of truth and truthfulness in the classroom. I will conclude by making five further observations. First, none of the four dimensions of variation identified by our hypothetical teacher carries substantial implications about the teaching styles and methods required to enact the intended object of learning in the classroom: teachers are free to select from a range of different options. Second, although the lessons described would be challenging, a glance that the intellectual demands made on lower secondary school pupils in other subject areas suggests that, provided the lesson is taught well, there is nothing that ought to be beyond their intellectual capacities. Third, it may appear that the discussion focused on the process of learning about religion, to the detriment of that of learning from religion. However, as I have sought to stress throughout this book, the two tasks are inseparable. One of the key spiritual questions that pupils must ask is whether they live in a purposeful universe created by a gracious and loving God, or in a world driven by impersonal natural forces. The answer they give will have a direct impact on their understanding of themselves and their place in the universe. The recognition that many highly intelligent people believe the Genesis myth to be true inevitably contributes to their learning from religion. Fourth, none of this implies a return to confessionalism, since to understand that rational people believe in the myth is not the same as believing it for oneself. Pupils should be aware that rational people believe in the truth of the Genesis myth – to think otherwise is to possess an inadequate understanding of Christianity – and begin to understand the implications of that fact for their own lives. Fifth, the learning sequence developed by our teacher had little sympathy for the claims of creationists. This is entirely appropriate, since creationism is built on foundations that are intellectually and spiritually unsustainable. The task of critical religious education is not to strive for a relativistic balance between all traditions, opinions and schools of thought, but rather to strive to produce an informed, intelligent and religiously literate society.

10.4   Conclusion

In this final chapter, I considered the pedagogical implications of making the pursuit of truth and cultivation of truthfulness central to religious education. In doing so, I challenged the model of a direct transition from theory to practice. There are important theoretical reflections that teachers need to make about the nature of pedagogy in religious education: in particular, the need to recognize that the pedagogy of learning has logical priority over the pedagogy of teaching. The pedagogy of learning in religious education, I suggested, has much to learn from Variation Theory and phenomenography: only by expanding the present experience of pupils in a manner that enables them to address issues central to the concerns of the world's religions will it be possible to develop appropriate levels of religious literacy through which they can explore issues of ultimate truth and truthfulness in a critical and potentially life-changing manner.

References

All biblical quotations are taken from the New Revised Standard Version (Anglicized Edition).

Allen, D. (1987). 'Phenomenology of religion', in Eliade, M. (ed.) *The Encyclopaedia of Religion, Volume 11*, London: Collier-Macmillan, pp. 272–285.

Alston, W. P. (1996) *A Realist Conception of Truth*, Ithaca, NY: Cornell University Press.

Alston, W. P. (1989) 'A doxastic practice approach to epistemology', in Clay, M. and Lehrer, K. (eds) *Knowledge and Skepticism*, Boulder, CO: Westview Press.

Alter, R. (1981) *The Art of Biblical Narrative*, Scrantan, PA: Basic Books.

Archer, M. S., Collier, A., and Porpora, D. V. (2004) *Transcendence: Critical Realism and God*, London: Routledge.

Aristotle (1962) *The Politics*, Harmondsworth, Middlesex: Penguin Books.

Armstrong, K. (2001) *The Battle for God: Fundamentalism in Judaism, Christianity and Islam*, London: HarperCollins.

Arnold, M. (1994) *Culture and Anarchy*, New Haven, CT: Yale University Press.

Astley, J. (2002) *Ordinary Theology: Looking, Listening and Learning in Theology*, Aldershot, Hampshire: Ashgate.

Auerbach, E. (2003) *Mimesis: The Representation of Reality in Western Literature*, Princeton, NJ: Princeton University Press.

Austin, J. L. (1976) *How to Do Things with Words*, Oxford: Oxford University Press.

Ayer, A. J. (1971) *Language, Truth and Logic*, Harmondsworth, Middlesex: Penguin Books.

Barrett, C. K. (1955) *The Gospel According to St John: An Introduction with Commentary and Notes on the Greek Text*, London: SPCK.

Barth, K. (1956) *Church Dogmatics. Volume One: The Doctrine of the Word of God, Part Two*, Edinburgh: T. & T. Clark.

Barth, K. (1957) *Church Dogmatics. Volume Two: The Doctrine of God, Part One*, Edinburgh: T. & T. Clark.

Baudrillard, J. (2001) *Selected Writings*, Cambridge: Polity Press.

BBC News (2004) *Profile: Rocco Buttiglione*, *http://news.bbc.co.uk/2/hi/europe/3718210.stm*, accessed 21 October 2004.

BBC News (2006) *Cartoon Protest Slogans Condemned*, *http://news.bbc.co.uk/1/hi/uk/4682262.stm*, accessed 5 February 2006.

Berlin, I. (2000) *The Proper Study of Mankind*, New York: Farrar, Straus & Giroux.

Bernstein, R. J. (1983) *Beyond Objectivism and Relativism: Science, Hermeneutics and Praxis*, Oxford: Blackwell.

Bhaskar, R. (1977) *A Realist Theory of Science*, London: Verso.

Bhaskar, R. (1998) *The Possibility of Naturalism: A Philosophical Critique of the Contemporary Human Sciences*, London: Routledge.

Bleicher, J. (1980) *Contemporary Hermeneutics: Hermeneutics as Method, Philosophy and Critique*, London: Routledge & Kegan Paul.

Bright, J. (1967) *The Authority of the Old Testament*, Nashville, TN: Abingdon.

Bromiley, G. W. (1979) *Introduction to the Theology of Karl Barth*, Edinburgh: T. & T. Clark.

Brown, D. (2004) *The Da Vinci Code*, London: Corgi.

Brown, T. L. (2003) *Making Truth: Metaphor in Science*, Champaign, IL: University of Illinois Press.

Brueggemann, W. A. (1972) *In Man We Trust: The Neglected Side of Biblical Faith*, Atlanta, GA: John Knox.

Bultmann, R. (1971) *The Gospel of John*, Oxford: Blackwell.

Bush, G. W. (2004) *President Bush Discusses Early Transfer of Iraqi Sovereignty*, *http://www.whitehouse.gov/news/releases/2004/06/20040628-9.html*, accessed 15 November 2004.

Byrne, P. (2003) *God and Realism*, Aldershot, Hants.: Ashgate.

Cantle Report (2001) *Community Cohesion: A Report of the Independent Review Team Chaired by Ted Cantle*, London: HMSO.

Cassirer, E. (1951) *The Philosophy of the Enlightenment*, Princeton, NJ: Princeton University Press.

Childs, B. S. (1992) *Biblical Theology of the Old and New Testaments: Theological Reflection on the Christian Bible*, London: SCM.

City of Birmingham District Council Education Committee (1975) *Living Together: A Teacher's Handbook of Suggestions for Religious Education*, Birmingham: City of Birmingham District Council Education Committee.

City of Birmingham Education Committee (1975) *Agreed Syllabus of Religious Instruction*, Birmingham: City of Birmingham Education Committee.

Clement of Alexandria (1994a) 'The Instructor', in Roberts, A. and Donaldson, J. (eds) *Ante-Nicene Fathers. Volume Two: Fathers of the Second Century*, Peabody, MA: Hendrickson, pp. 207–298.

Clement of Alexandria (1994b) 'The stroma, or miscellanies', in Roberts, A. and Donaldson, J. (eds) *Ante-Nicene Fathers. Volume Two: Fathers of the Second Century*, Peabody, MA: Hendrickson, pp. 299–568.

Clements, R. E. (1983) *A Century of Old Testament Study*, Guildford, Surrey: Lutterworth Press.

Collier, A. (1994) *Critical Realism: An Introduction to Roy Bhaskar's Philosophy*, London: Verso.

Collier, A. (1999) *Being and Worth*, London: Routledge.

Collier, A. (2003) *On Christian Belief: A Defence of a Cognitive Conception of Religious Belief in a Christian Context*, London: Routledge.

Cooling, T. (1994) *A Christian Vision for State Education: Reflections on the Theology of Education*, London: SPCK.

Cooling, T. (2000) 'Pupil learning', in Wright, A. and Brandom, A.-M. (eds) *Learning to Teach Religious Education in the Secondary School: A Companion to School Experience*, London: RoutledgeFalmer, pp. 71–87.

Copleston, F. (1946) *A History of Philosophy. Volume One: Greece and Rome*, Westminster, MD: The Newman Press.

Cormier, H. (2001) *The Truth is What Works: William James, Pragmatism, and the Seed of Death*, Lanham, MD: Rowman & Littlefield.

Cowdell, S. (1988) *Atheist Priest? Don Cupitt and Christianity*, London: SCM.

Cox, E. (1966) *Changing Aims in Religious Education*, London: Routledge & Kegan Paul.

Cox, E. (1983) 'Understanding religion and religious understanding', *British Journal of Religious Education*, 6: 1, pp. 3–7.

Cox, E. and Cairns, J. (1989) *Reforming Religious Education: the Religious Clauses of the 1988 Education Reform Act*, London: Kogan Page.

Crites, S. (1989) 'The narrative quality of experience', in Hauerwas, S. and Jones, L. G. (eds) *Why Narrative? Readings in Narrative Theology*, Grand Rapids, MI: William B. Eerdmans, pp. 65–88.

Cupitt, D. (1980) *Taking Leave of God*, London: SCM.

Cupitt, D. (1991) *What is a Story?* London: SCM.

Danermark, B., Ekstrom, M., et al. (2002) *Explaining Society: Critical Realism in the Social Sciences*, London: Routledge.

Day, D. (1985) 'Religious education 40 years on: a permanent identity crisis?', *British Journal of Religious Education*, 7: 2, pp. 55–63.

DES/HMI (1977) *Supplement to Curriculum 11–16*, London: HMSO.

D'Costa, G. (ed.) (1990) *Christian Uniqueness Reconsidered: The Myth of a Pluralistic Theology of Religions*, Maryknoll, NY: Orbis Books.

D'Costa, G. (2000) *The Meeting of Religions and the Trinity*, Edinburgh: T. and T. Clark.

Descartes, R. (1970) *Philosophical Writings*, London: Nelson.

Devitt, M. (1997) *Realism and Truth*, Princeton, NJ: Princeton University Press.

DfEE/QCA (1999) *National Curriculum Handbook for Teachers*, London: QCA.

DfES/QCA (2004) *Religious Education: The Non-Statutory National Framework*, London: QCA.

Dostoyevsky, F. M. (1958) *The Brothers Karamazov*, Harmondsworth, Middlesex: Penguin Books.

Dulles, A. (2002) *Newman*, London: Continuum.

Dunne, J. (1997) *Back to the Rough Ground: Practical Judgment and the Lure of Technique*, Notre Dame, IN: University of Notre Dame Press.

Eco, U. (1981) *The Role of the Reader: Explorations in the Semiotics of Texts*, London: Hutchinson.

Eliade, M. (1987) *The Sacred and Profane: The Nature of Religion*, San Diego, CA: Harcourt Brace.

Erricker, C. (2001) 'Shall we dance? Authority, representation and voice: the place of spirituality in religious education', *Religious Education*, 96: 1, pp. 20–35.

Erricker, C., and Erricker, J. (2000) *Reconstructing Religious, Spiritual and Moral Education*, London: Routledge.

Evans-Pritchard, E. E. (1976) *Witchcraft, Oracles, and Magic among the Azande*, Oxford: Clarendon Press.

Fish, S. (1980) *Is There a Text in this Class? The Authority of Interpretative Communities*, Cambridge, MA: Harvard University Press.

Fish, S. (1999) *The Trouble with Principle*, Cambridge, MA: Harvard University Press.

Flood, G. (1996) *An Introduction to Hinduism*, Cambridge: Cambridge University Press.

Flood, G. (1999) *Beyond Phenomenology: Rethinking the Study of Religion*, London: Cassell.

Foucault, M. (1974) *The Order of Things: An Archaeology of the Human Sciences*, London: Tavistock/Routledge.

Foucault, M. (1989) *The Archaeology of Knowledge*, London: Routledge.

Foucault, M. (1990) *The History of Sexuality. Volume One: An Introduction*, Harmondsworth, Middlesex: Penguin Books.

Frei, H. W. (1974) *The Eclipse of Biblical Narrative: A Study of Eighteenth and Nineteenth Century Hermeneutics*, New Haven, CT: Yale University Press.

Gadamer, H.-G. (1979) *Truth and Method*, London: Sheed & Ward.

Gearon, L. (2004) *Citizenship through Secondary Religious Education*, London: RoutledgeFalmer.

Gerson, L. P. (1994) *God and Greek Philosophy: Studies in the Early History of Natural Theology*, London: Routledge.

Gilson, E. (1955) *History of Christian Philosophy in the Middle Ages*, London: Sheed & Ward.

Glashow, S. (2005) *The Elegant Universe: Viewpoints on String Theory, http://www.pbs.org/wgbh/nova/elegant/view-glashow.html*, accessed 2 December 2005.

Goldman, R. (1964) *Religious Thinking from Childhood to Adolescence*, London: Routledge & Kegan Paul.

Gray, J. (2003) *Al Qaeda and What it Means to be Modern*, London: Faber & Faber.

Grimmitt, M. (1973) *What Can I Do in RE?* Great Wakering, Essex: Mayhew-McCrimmon.

Grimmitt, M. (1987) *Religious Education and Human Development: The Relationship Between Studying Religious and Personal, Social and Moral Development*, Great Wakering, Essex: McCrimmons.

Grimmitt, M. (1994) 'Religious education and the ideology of pluralism', *British Journal of Religious Education*, 16: 3, pp. 133–47.

Grimmitt, M. (ed.) (2000) *Pedagogies of Religious Education: Case Studies in the Research and Development of Good Pedagogic Practice in RE*, Great Wakering, Essex: McCrimmons.

Groome, T. H. (1980) *Christian Religious Education: Sharing Our Story and Vision*, San Francisco, CA: Jossey-Bass.

Gunton, C. E. (1983) *Yesterday and Today: A Study of Continuities in Christology*, London: Darton, Longman & Todd.

Gunton, C. E. (1985) *Enlightenment and Alienation: An Essay Towards a Trinitarian Theology*, Basingstoke: Marshall, Morgan & Scott.

Gunton, C. E. (1995) *A Brief Theology of Revelation*, Edinburgh: T. & T. Clark.

Habermas, J. (1989) *The Theory of Communicative Action. Volume Two: Lifeworld and System – A Critique of Functionalist Reason*, London: Polity Press.

Habermas, J. (1991) *The Theory of Communicative Action. Volume One: Reason and the Rationalization of Society*, Cambridge, Polity Press.

Hamidullah, M. (1979) *Introduction to Islam*, London: MWH.

Hammond, J., Hay, D., et al. (1990) *New Methods in R. E. Teaching*, Harlow, Essex: Oliver & Boyd.

Hanfling, O. (ed.) (1992) *Philosophical Aesthetics: An Introduction*, Oxford: Blackwell.

Hardy, D. W. (1975) 'Teaching religion: a theological critique', *Learning for Living*, 15: 1, pp. 10–16.

Hardy, D. W. (1976) 'The implications of pluralism for religious education', *Learning for Living*, 16: 2, pp. 56–62.

Hardy, D. W. (1982) 'Truth in religious education: further reflections on the implications of pluralism', in Hull, J. (ed.) *New Directions in Religious Education*, Lewes, Sussex: Falmer Press, pp. 109–18.

Hart, K. (1991) *The Trespass of the Sign. Deconstruction: Theology and Philosophy*, Cambridge: Cambridge University Press.

Hauerwas, S. (1981) *A Community of Character: Toward a Constructive Christian Social Ethic*, Notre Dame, IN: University of Notre Dame Press.

Hay, D. (1982a) 'Teaching the science of the spirit', in Priestley, J. G. (ed.) *Religion, Spirituality and Schools*, Exeter: University of Exeter School of Education, pp. 37–53.

Hay, D. (1982b) *Exploring Inner Space: Is God Still Possible in the Twentieth Century?* Harmondsworth, Middlesex: Penguin Books.

Hay, D. (1985) 'Suspicion of the spiritual: teaching religion in a world of secular experience', *British Journal of Religious Education*, 7: 3, pp. 140–7.

Hay, D. (with Nye, R.) (1998) *The Spirit of the Child*, London: Harper Collins.

Haydon, G. (1997) *Teaching about Values: A New Approach*, London: Cassell.

Heelas, P. (1996) *The New Age Movement: The Celebration of the Self and the Sacralization of Modernity*, Oxford: Blackwell.

Heimbrock, H.-G., Scheilke, C. Th. and Schreiner, P. (2001) *Towards Religious Competence: Diversity as a Challenge for Education in Europe*, Munster: Lit.

Hella, E. (2008) 'Variation in Finnish students' understanding of Lutheranism and its implications for religious education: a phenomenographic study', *British Journal of Religious Education*, forthcoming.

Hella, E. and Wright, A. (2008) 'Learning "about" and "from" religion: phenomenography, the variation theory of learning and religious education in Finland and the UK', *British Journal of Religious Education*, forthcoming.

Heraclitus (2003) *Fragments*, Harmondsworth, Middlesex: Penguin Books.

Hick, J. (1977) *God and the Universe of Faith*, London: Collins.

Hick, J. (1989) *An Interpretation of Religion: Human Responses to the Transcendent*, London: Macmillan.

Hick, J. and Knitter, P. F. (eds) (1987) *The Myth of Christian Uniqueness*, London: SCM.

Hirst, P. (1965) 'Liberal education and the nature of knowledge', in Archambault, R. D. (ed.) *Philosophical Analysis and Education*, London: Routledge & Kegan Paul, pp. 113–38.

Hirst, P. (1972) 'Christian education: a contradiction in terms?', *Learning for Living*, 11: 4, pp. 6–11.

Hirst, P. (1974) *Knowledge and the Curriculum*, London: Routledge & Kegan Paul.

HMSO (1944) *Education Act*, London: HMSO.

HMSO (1988) *Education Reform Act*, London: HMSO.

Hodgson, P. E. (2005) *Theology and Modern Physics*, Aldershot, Hampshire: Ashgate.

Holley, R. (1978) *Religious Education and Religious Understanding: An Introduction to the Philosophy of Religious Education*, London: Routledge & Kegan Paul.

Hookway, S. (2002) 'Mirrors, windows, conversations: RE for the millennial generation', *British Journal of Religious Education*, 24: 2, pp. 99–110.

Hookway, S. R. (2004) *Questions of Truth: Developing Critical Thinking Skills in Secondary Religious Education*, Norwich, Norfolk: Religious and Moral Education Press.

Houlden, L. (2002) *The Strange Story of the Gospels: Finding Doctrine through Narrative*, London: SPCK.

Hudson, W. D. (1975) *Wittgenstein and Religious Belief*, London: Macmillan.

Hull, J. M. (1984) *Studies in Religion and Education*, Lewes, Sussex: Falmer Press.

Hull, J. M. (1992) 'Editorial: the transmission of religious prejudice', *British Journal of Religious Education*, 14: 2, pp. 69–72.

Hull, J. M. (1998) *Utopian Whispers: Moral, Religious and Spiritual Values in Schools*, Norwich, Norfolk: Religious and Moral Education Press.

Hume, D. (1947) *Dialogues Concerning Natural Religion*, Indianapolis, IN: Bobbs-Merill.

Hume, D. (2000) *A Treatise of Human Nature*, Oxford: Oxford University Press.

Husserl, E. (1976) *Logical Investigations, 2 Volumes*, London: Routledge & Kegan Paul.

Ingram, D. (1987) *Habermas and the Dialectic of Reason*, New Haven, CT: Yale University Press.

Jackson, R. (1997) *Religious Education: An Interpretative Approach*, London: Hodder & Stoughton.

Jackson, R. (2001) 'Creative pedagogy in religious education: case studies in interpretation', in Heimbrock, H.-G., Scheilke, C. T. and Schreiner, P. (eds) *Towards Religious Competence: Diversity as a Challenge for Education in Europe*, Munster: Lit, pp. 34–52.

Jackson, R. (2004) *Rethinking Religious Education and Plurality: Issues in Diversity and Pedagogy*, London and New York: RoutledgeFalmer.

Jackson, R. and Nesbitt, E. (1993) *Hindu Children in Britain*, Stoke-on-Trent: Trentham.

Jaeger, W. (1961) *Early Christianity and Greek Paideia*, Cambridge, MA: Belknap/Harvard University Press.

Jaeger, W. (1986) *Paideia: The Ideals of Greek Culture, 3 Volumes*, New York: Oxford University Press.

James, W. (1978) *Pragmatism and the Meaning of Truth*, Cambridge, MA: Harvard University Press.

Jones, M. V. (1976) *Dostoyevsky: The Novel of Discord*, London: Paul Elek.

Kant, I. (1959) *What is Enlightenment?* New York: Bobbs-Merrill.

Kant, I. (1998) *Groundwork of the Metaphysics of Morals*, Cambridge: Cambridge University Press.

Kavanagh, A. (1984) *On Liturgical Theology*, New York: Pueblo Publishing.

Kee, A. (1985) *The Way of Transcendence: Christian Faith without Belief in God*, London: SCM.

Kekes, J. (1999) *Against Liberalism*, New York: Cornell University Press.

Kelly, J. N. D. (1950) *Early Christian Creeds*, London: Longmans, Green and Co.

Kelsey, D. H. (1992) *To Understand God Truly: What's Theological about a Theological School?* Louisville, KY: Westminster/John Knox Press.

Kerferd, G. B. (2003) 'The Sophists', in Taylor, C. C. W. (ed.) *Routledge History of Philosophy. Volume One: From the Beginning to Plato*, London: Routledge, pp. 244–70.

Kierkegaard, S. (1967) *Philosophical Fragments*, Princeton, NJ: Princeton University Press.

King, U. (1995) 'Historical and phenomenological approaches' in, Whaling, F. (ed.) *Theory and Method in Religious Studies: Contemporary Approaches to the Study of Religion*, London: Mouton de Gruyter, pp. 41–176.

Kraft, F. (2004) 'Theologisieren mit kindern: ein neues didaktisches leitbild für den religionsunterricht der grundschule?, *Theologische Beiträge*, 35, pp. 81–91.

Kuhn, T. S. (1970) *The Structure of Scientific Revolutions*, Chicago, IL: University of Chicago Press.

Kung, H. (1980) *Does God Exist? An Answer for Today*, London: Collins.

Kung, H. (1992) *Judaism: The Religious Situation of Our Time*, London: SCM.

Kymlicka, W. (1995) *Multicultural Citizenship: A Liberal Theory of Minority Rights*, Oxford: Oxford University Press.

Lakoff, G. (1987) *Women, Fire and Dangerous Things: What Categories Reveal About the Mind*, Chicago, IL: University of Chicago Press.

Lakoff, G. and Johnson, M. (1980) *Metaphors We Live By*, Chicago, IL: University of Chicago Press.

Lampe, G. W. H. (1997) 'Christian theology in the patristic period', in Cunliffe-Jones, H. (ed.) *A History of Christian Doctrine*, Edinburgh: T. & T. Clark, pp. 21–180.

Leganger-Krogstad, H. (2001) 'Religious education in a global perspective: a contextual approach', in Heimbrock, H.-G., Scheilke, C. Th. and Schreiner, P. (eds) *Towards Religious Competence: Diversity as a Challenge for Education in Europe*, Munster: Lit, pp. 53–73.

Lindbeck, G. A. (1984) *The Nature of Doctrine: Religion and Theology in a Postliberal Age*, Philadelphia, PA: Westminster Press.

Locke, J. (1975) *An Essay Concerning Human Understanding*, Oxford: Clarendon Press.

Locke, J. (1993) *Political Writings*, Harmondsworth, Middlesex: Penguin Books.

Locke, J. (2000) *Some Thoughts Concerning Education*, Oxford: Oxford University Press.

London County Council (1947) *The London Syllabus for Religious Education*, London: London County Council.

Loughlin, G. (1996) *Telling God's Story: Bible, Church and Narrative Theology*, Cambridge: Cambridge University Press.

Loukes, H. (1961) *Teenage Religion: An Enquiry into Attitudes and Possibilities Among British Boys and Girls in Secondary Modern Schools*, London: SCM.

Loukes, H. (1965) *New Ground in Christian Education*, London: SCM.

Luckman, T. (1967) *The Invisible Religion*, London: Macmillan.

MacIntyre, A. (1985) *After Virtue: A Study of Moral Theory*, London: Duckworth.

MacIntyre, A. (1988) *Whose Justice? Whose Rationality?* London: Duckworth.

Mackie, J. D. (1972) *The Earlier Tudors 1485–1558*, Oxford: Clarendon Press.

Markham, I. (1998) *Truth and the Reality of God: An Essay in Natural Theology*, Edinburgh: T. & T. Clark.

Marshall, B. D. (2000) *Trinity and Truth*, Cambridge: Cambridge University Press.

Martines, L. (2006) *Scourge and Fire: Savonarola and Renaissance Florence*, London: Jonathan Cape.

Marton, F. and Booth, S. (1997) *Learning and Awareness*, Mahwah, NJ: Lawrence Erlbaum Associates.

Marton, F., Runesson, U. and Tsui, A. B. M. (2004) 'The space of learning', in Marton, F. and Tsui, A. B. M. (eds) *Classroom Discourse and the Space of Learning*, Mahwah, NJ: Lawrence Erlbaum Associates, pp. 3–42.

Marton, F. and Tsui, A. B. M. (eds) (2004) *Classroom Discourse and the Space of Learning*, Mahwah, NJ: Lawrence Erlbaum Associates.

Martos, J. (2001) *Doors to the Sacred: A Historical Introduction to the Sacraments in the Catholic Church*, Liguori, MO: Liguori/Triumph.

Marvell, J. (1976) 'Phenomenology and the future of religious education', *Learning for Living*, 16: 1, pp. 4–8.

McCarthy, T. (1978) *The Critical Theory of Jurgen Habermas*, Cambridge, MA: MIT Press.

McFague, S. (1982) *Metaphorical Theology: Models of God in Religious Language*, London: SCM.

McGrath, A. E. (1994) *Christian Theology: An Introduction*, Oxford: Blackwell.

McGrath, A. E. (2001) *A Scientific Theology. Volume One: Nature*, Edinburgh: T. & T. Clark.

McGrath, A. E. (2002) *A Scientific Theology. Volume Two: Reality*, Edinburgh: T. & T. Clark.

McGrath, A. E. (2003) *A Scientific Theology. Volume Three: Theory*, Edinburgh: T. & T. Clark.

McGrath, A. E. (2004) *The Twilight of Atheism: The Rose and Fall of Disbelief in the Modern World*, London: Rider.

Melchert, C. F. (1994) 'What is religious education?', in Astley, J. and Francis, L. J. (eds) *Critical Perspectives on Christian Education: A Reader on the Aims, Principles and Philosophy of Christian Education*, Leominster: Gracewing, pp. 48–60.

Melchert, C. F. (1998) *Wise Teaching: Biblical Wisdom and Educational Ministry*, Harrisburg, PA: Tinity Press International.

Mill, J. S. (1978) *On Liberty*, Indianapolis, IN: Hackett Publishing.

Mitchell, B. (1973) *The Justification of Religious Belief*, London: Macmillan.

Moore, A. (2003) *Realism and Christian Faith: God, Grammar and Meaning*, Cambridge: Cambridge University Press.

Mueller-Vollmer, K. (ed.) (1986) *The Hermeneutics Reader*, Oxford: Basil Blackwell.

Murdoch, I. (1970) *The Sovereignty of Good*, London: Routledge & Kegan Paul.

Nagel, T. (1986) *The View from Nowhere*, Oxford: Oxford University Press.

Newbigin, L. (1982) 'Teaching religion in a secular plural society', in Hull, J. (ed.) *New Directions in Religious Education*, Basingstoke: Falmer Press, pp. 97–107.

Newman, J. H. (1979) *An Essay in Aid of a Grammar of Assent*, Notre Dame, IN: University of Notre Dame Press.

Newman, J. H. (1982) *The Idea of a University Defined and Illustrated*, Notre Dame, IN: University of Notre Dame Press.

Noble, P. R. (1994) 'Hermeneutics and Post-Modernism: can we have a radical reader-response theory? Part I', *Religious Studies*, 30: 4, pp. 419–36.

Noble, P. R. (1995) 'Hermeneutics and Post-Modernism: can we have a radical reader-response theory? Part II', *Religious Studies*, 31: 1, pp. 1–22.

O'Connor, D. J. (1952) *John Locke*, Harmondsworth, Middlesex: Penguin Books.

Otto, R. (1931) *The Idea of the Holy: An Inquiry into the Non-Rational Factor in the Idea of the Divine and its Relation to the Rational*, Oxford: Oxford University Press.

Palmer, R. E. (1969) *Hermeneutics*, Evanston, IL: Northwestern University Press.

Pannenberg, W. (1976) *Theology and the Philosophy of Science*, London: Darton, Longman & Todd.

Pannenberg, W. (1994) *Systematic Theology, Volume Two*, Edinburgh: T. & T. Clark.

Parmenides (1984) *Fragments*, Toronto: University of Toronto Press.

Patterson, S. (1999) *Realist Christian Theology in a Postmodern Age*, Cambridge: Cambridge University Press.

Peacocke, A. (1993) *Theology for a Scientific Age: Being and Becoming – Natural, Divine and Human*, London: SCM Press.

Phillips, D. Z. (1976) *Religion without Explanation*, Oxford: Basil Blackwell.

Placher, W. C. (1998) 'Postliberal Theology', in Ford, D. F. (ed.) *The Modern Theologians: An Introduction to Christian Theology in the Twentieth Century*, Oxford: Blackwell, pp. 343–56.

Plato (1961) *The Collected Dialogues of Plato*, Princeton, NJ: Princeton University Press.

Polanyi, M. (1958) *Personal Knowledge: Towards a Post-Critical Philosophy*, London: Routledge & Kegan Paul.

Poole, M. W. (1995) *Beliefs and Values in Science Education*, Buckingham: Open University Press.

Popkin, R. H. (1964) *The History of Scepticism: From Erasmus to Descartes*, New York: Harper & Row.

Popper, K. (1966) *The Open Society and its Enemies. Volume One: Plato*, London: Routledge & Kegan Paul.

Porpora, D. V. (2001) *Landscapes of the Soul: The Loss of Moral Meaning in American Life*, New York: Oxford Universiy Press.

Pritchard, J. B. (ed.) (1958) *The Ancient Near East: An Anthology of Texts and Pictures, Volume One*, Princeton, NJ: Princeton University Press.

Quine, W. V. and Ullian, J. S. (1978) *The Web of Belief*, New York: McGraw-Hill.

Rawls, J. (1971) *A Theory of Justice*, Cambridge, MA: Belknap/Harvard University Press.

Rawls, J. (1993) *Political Liberalism*, New York: Columbia University Press.

Ricoeur, P. (1976) *Interpretative Theory: Discourse and the Surplus of Meaning*, Fort Worth, TX: Texas Christian University Press.

Ricoeur, P. (1977) *The Rule of Metaphor: Multi-Disciplinary Studies of the Creation of Meaning in Language*, Toronto: University of Toronto Press.

Ricoeur, P. (1991) 'Life in quest of narrative', in Wood, D. (ed.) *On Paul Ricoeur: Narrative and Interpretation*, London: Routledge, pp. 20–33.

Robinson, J. A. T. (1963) *Honest to God*, London: SCM.

Rorty, R. (1980) *Philosophy and the Mirror of Nature*, Oxford: Basil Blackwell.

Rorty, R. (1982) *The Consequences of Pragmatism (Essays: 1972–1980)*, Minneapolis, MN: University of Minnesota Press.

Rorty, R. (1989) *Contingency, Irony and Solidarity*, Cambridge: Cambridge University Press.

Rousseau, J.-J. (1986) *Emile*, London: Dent.

Rummel, E. (2004) *Erasmus*, London: Continuum.

Sacks, A. (2003) *The Dignity of Difference: How to Avoid the Clash of Civilisations*, London: Continuum.

Said, E. (1978) *Orientalism*, London: Routledge & Kegan Paul.

Said, E. (1993) *Culture and Imperialism*, London: Chatto & Windus.

Sayer, A. (2000) *Realism and Social Science*, London: Sage.

SCAA (1994) *Model Syllabuses for Religious Education*, London: SCAA.

Schleiermacher, F. D. E. (1958) *On Religion: Speeches to its Cultured Despisers*, London: Harper & Row.

Schleiermacher, F. D. E. (1976) *The Christian Faith*, Edinburgh: T. & T. Clark.

Schleiermacher, F. D. E. (1977) *Hermeneutics: The Handwritten Manuscripts*, Missoula, MT: Scholars Press.

Schools Council (1971) *Religious Education in Secondary Schools: Schools Council Working Paper 36*, London: Evans/Methuen Educational.

Schwöbel, C. (1995) 'Imago Libertatis: human and divine freedom', in Gunton, C. (ed.) *God and Freedom: Essays in Historical and Systematic Theology*, Edinburgh: T. & T. Clark, pp. 57–81.

Searle, J. R. (1996) *The Construction of Social Reality*, Harmondsworth, Middlesex: Penguin Books.

Seymour, P. (2004) *The Scientific Proof of Astrology: A Scientific Investigation of How the Stars Influence Human Life*, London: Quantum.

Sharpe, E. J. (1975) 'The phenomenology of religion', *Learning for Living*, 15: 1, pp. 4–9.

Sharpe, E. J. (1986) *Comparative Religion: A History*, London: Duckworth.

Shone, R. (1973) 'Religion: a form of knowledge?', *Learning for Living*, 12: 4, pp. 5–8.

Simon, U. (1978) *A Theology of Auschwitz*, London: SPCK.

Smart, N. (1968) *Secular Education and the Logic of Religion*, London: Faber & Faber.

Smart, N. (1978) 'What is religion?', in Smart, N. and Horder, D. (eds) *New Movements in Religious Education*, London: Temple Smith, pp. 13–22.

Smart, N. (1995) 'The scientific study of religion in its plurality', in Whaling, F. (ed.) *Theory and Method in Religious Studies: Contemporary*

Approaches to the Study of Religion, London: Mouton de Gruyter, pp. 177–190.

Smith, J. W. D. (1969) *Religious Education in a Secular Setting*, London: SCM.

Smith, W. C. (1991) *The Meaning and End of Religion*, Minneapolis: Fortress Press.

Soskice, J. M. (1985) *Metaphor and Religious Language*, Oxford: Oxford University Press.

Spellman, W. M. (1988) *John Locke and the Problem of Depravity*, Oxford: Clarendon Press.

Star Trek (2005) *Scripts: Star Treck the Motion Picture*, *http://www.geocities.com/ussmunchkin7/Star_Trek_I.htm*, accessed 17 May 2005.

Strawson, P. (1952) *Introduction to Logical Theory*, London: Methuen.

Stiver, D. R. (2001) *Theology after Ricoeur: New Directions in Hermeneutical Theology*, Louisville, KY: Westminster John Knox Press.

Surin, K. (1980) 'Can the experiential and the phenomenological approaches be reconciled?', *British Journal of Religious Education*, 2: 3, pp. 99–103.

Sutherland, S. (1984) *Faith and Ambiguity*, London: SCM.

Swann Report (1985) *Education for All: The Report of the Commission of Inquiry into the Education of Children from Ethnic Minority Groups*, London: HMSO.

Swinburne, R. (1983) *Faith and Reason*, Oxford: Clarendon Press.

Taylor, C. (1992) *Sources of the Self: The Making of the Modern Identity*, Cambridge: Cambridge University Press.

Taylor, M. C. (1982) *Deconstructing Theology*, New York: Crossroad Publishing.

Taylor, M. C. (1984) *Erring: A Postmodern A/theology*, Chicago, IL: University of Chicago Press.

Temple, W. (1942) *Christianity and Social Order*, Harmondsworth, Middlesex: Penguin Books.

Thiselton, A. (1992) *New Horizons in Hermeneutics: The Theory and Practice of Transforming Biblical Reading*, London: HarperCollins.

Thompson, D. (ed.) (1995) *The Concise Oxford Dictionary*, Oxford: Clarendon Press.

Tillich, P. (1951) *Systematic Theology. Volume One: Reason and Revelation, and Being and God*, London: SCM.

Torrance, T. F. (1978) *Theological Science*, Oxford: Oxford University Press.

Torrance, T. F. (1995) *Divine Meaning: Studies in Patristic Hermeneutics*. Edinburgh: T. & T. Clark.

Torrance, T. F. (2002) *Karl Barth: An Introduction to His Early Theology 1910–1931*, Edinburgh: T. & T. Clark.

Tracey, D. (1981) *The Analogical Imagination: Christian Theology and the Culture of Pluralism*, London: SCM.

Tritter, J. Q. and Archer, M. S. (eds) (2000) *Rational Choice Theory: A Critique*, London: Routledge.

Van der Leeuw, G. (1992) *Religion in Essence and Manifestation*, Princeton, NJ: Princeton University Press.

Von Balthasar, H. U. (1984). *The Glory of the Lord, A Theological Aesthetics. Volume Four: Studies in Theological Style – Clerical Styles*. Edinburgh: T. & T. Clark.

Von Rad, G. (1972) *Wisdom in Israel*, London: SCM.

Walker, A. and Wright, A. (2004) 'A Christian university imagined: recovering paideia in a broken world', in Astley, J., Francis, L. J., et al. (eds) The *Idea of a Christian University: Essays on Theology and Higher Education*, Milton Keynes: Paternoster, pp. 56–74.

Ward, G. (1996) *Theology and Contemporary Critical Theory*, London: Macmillan.

Warnke, G. (1987) *Gadamer: Hermeneutics, Tradition and Reason*, Cambridge: Polity Press.

Weinsheimer, J. C. (1985) *Gadamer's Hermeneutics: A Reading of Truth and Method*, New Haven, CT: Yale University Press.

White, J. (2004a) 'Introduction', in White, J. (ed.) *Rethinking the School Curriculum: Values, Aims and Purposes*, London: RoutledgeFalmer, pp. 1–19.

White, J. (2004b) 'Should religious education be a compulsory school subject?', *British Journal of Religious Education*, 26: 2, pp. 151–164.

White, J. (2005) 'Religious education as a compulsory subject in English and Welsh schools: reply to Andrew Wright', *British Journal of Religious Education*, 27: 1, pp. 21–4.

Wiggershaus, R. (1995) *The Frankfurt School: Its History, Theories and Political Significance*, Cambridge: Polity Press.

Williams, B. (2002) *Truth and Truthfulness: An Essay in Genealogy*, Princeton, NJ: Princeton University Press.

Wilson, G. H. (1997) 'Wisdom', in VanGeneren, W. A. (gen. ed.) *New International Dictionary of Old Testament Theology and Exegesis, Volume Four*, Carlisle, Cumbria: Paternoster Publishing, pp. 1276–85.

Wilson, J. (1971) *Education in Religion and the Emotions*, London: Heinemann Educational.

Winch, P. (1964) 'Understanding a primitive society', *American Philosophical Quarterly*, 1: 4, pp. 307–24.

Winch, P. (1990) *The Idea of a Social Science and Its Relation to Philosophy*, London: Routledge.

Wittgenstein, L. (1968) *Philosophical Investigations*, Oxford: Blackwell.

Wittgenstein, L. (1974) *Tractatus Logico-Philosophicus*, London: Routledge & Kegan Paul.

Wittgenstein, L. (1975) *On Certainty*, Oxford: Basil Blackwell.

Wolterstorff, N. (1996) *John Locke and the Ethics of Belief*, Cambridge: Cambridge University Press.

Wolterstorff, N. (1999) *Reason within the Bounds of Religion*, Grand Rapids, MI: William B. Eerdmans.

Wright, A. (1993) *Religious Education in the Secondary School: Prospects for Religious Literacy*, London: David Fulton.

Wright, A. (1997) 'Hermeneutics and religious understanding. Part one: The hermeneutics of modern religious education', *Journal of Beliefs and Values*, 18: 2, pp. 203–16.

Wright, A. (1998a) *Spiritual Pedagogy. A Survey, Critique and Reconstruction of Contemporary Spiritual Education in England and Wales*, Abingdon, Oxon.: Culham College Institute.

Wright, A. (1998b) 'Hermeneutics and religious understanding. Part two: Towards a critical theory for religious education', *Journal of Beliefs and Values*, 19: 1, pp. 59–70.

Wright, A. (1999) *Discerning the Spirit: Teaching Spirituality in the Religious Education Classroom*, Abingdon, Oxon.: Culham College Institute.

Wright, A. (2000) *Spirituality and Education*, London: RoutledgeFalmer.

Wright, A. (2001a) 'Religious education, religious literacy and democratic citizenship', in Francis, L. J., Astley, J. and Robbins, M. (eds) *The Fourth R for the Third Millennium: Education in Religion and Values for the Global Future*, Dublin: Lindisfarne, pp. 201–219.

Wright, A. (2001b) 'Dancing in the fire: a deconstruction of Clive Erricker's post-modern spiritual pedagogy', *Religious Education*, 96: 1, pp. 120–35.

Wright, A. (2003a) 'Freedom, equality, fraternity? Towards a liberal defence of faith community schools', *British Journal of Religious Education*, 25: 2, pp. 142–52.

Wright, A. (2003b) 'Context, competence and cultural diversity: religious education in a European setting', *Journal of Beliefs and Values*, 24: 1, pp. 111–17.

Wright, A. (2003c) 'The contours of critical religious education: knowledge, wisdom, truth', *British Journal of Religious Education*, 25: 4, pp. 279–91.

Wright, A. (2004a) *Religion, Education and Post-modernity*, London: RoutledgeFalmer.

Wright, A. (2004b) 'The justification of compulsory religious education: a response to Professor White', *British Journal of Religious Education*, 26: 2, pp. 165–74.

Wright, A. (2005) 'On the intrinsic value of religious education', *British Journal of Religious Education*, 27: 1, pp. 25–8.

Wright, A. (2007a) 'Hospitality and the voice of the other: confronting the economy of violence through religious education', in Astley, J.,

Robins, M. and Francis, L. J. (eds) *Peace or Violence: The Ends of Religion and Education?* Cardiff: University of Wales Press.

Wright, A. (2007b) 'Critical realism as a tool for the interpretation of cultural diversity in liberal religious education', in de Souza, M., Engebretson, K., et al. (eds) *International Handbook of the Religious, Moral and Spiritual Dimensions of Education,* The Netherlands: Springer Academic Publishers.

Wright, A. (2008) 'Contextual religious education and the actuality of religions', *British Journal of Religious Education,* forthcoming.

Wright, A. and Brandom, A.-M. (eds) (2000) *Learning to Teach Religious Education in the Secondary School: A Companion to School Experience,* London: RoutledgeFalmer.

Wright, G. E. (1952) *God Who Acts,* London: SCM.

Wright, N. T. (1992) *Christian Origins and the Question of God. Volume One: The New Testament and People of God,* London: SPCK.

Wright, N. T. (2005) *Decoding the Da Vinci Code: The Challenge of Historic Christianity to Post-Modern Fantasy, http://www.spu.edu/depts/uc/response/summer2k5/features/davincicode.asp,* accessed 10 May 2006.

Wright, N. T. (2006) *Evil, and the Justice of God,* London: SPCK.

Yates, P. (1988) 'Religious education: an anthropological view', *British Journal of Religious Education,* 10: 3, pp. 135–44.

Index

provisional nature of 177; of the
reality of God 62; reasonable
belief and 216–19; Variation
Theory of Learning and 238–40,
241, 246; wisdom and 60
Kuhn, Thomas 213

Lakoff, George 155
Lampe, G. W. H. 75
language, hermeneutics and
188–90
language, picture theory of 159
language, religious *see* religious
language
language and reality 11–12, 17,
24
language games 163, 164, 165
learning, object of 245–6; *see also*
pedagogy of critical religious
education; pedagogy of learning
and religious education;
phenomenography; Variation
Theory of Learning
learning about religion and
learning from religion 81,
86–7, 107–8, 250, 259
Leganger-Krogstad, H. 119
liberal education 31, 46, 48
liberalism 3, 4, 29–30; education
and 46–51; egalitarian 45;
liberal education and 31;
Renaissance humanism as
background to 30–1; as
worldview 32–3; *see also*
comprehensive liberalism;
political liberalism
liberal politics *see* political
liberalism
liberal religious education 3, 4,
79–81, 234; ascendancy of
truthfulness in 94–7; from
confessionalism to liberalism
81–6; eclipse of truth in 90–3;
hermeneutics of 191–200;

political liberalism and 97–103;
truth and truthfulness in
86–90
liberal society, distinction
between liberal morality and
40–1
liberty, negative and positive
43–5; *see also* freedom
life stances, distinction between
religious and secular 133
lifeworlds 189; of individual
religious adherents 151–2, 157;
liberal religious education and
pupils' 192, 196
Lindbeck, George 173, 174
Locke, John 32, 41–3, 167–8,
228, 229
logical positivism 10
*London Agreed Syllabus for
Religious Education* 82
London County Council 82–3
Loughlin, G. 171, 174
Loukes, Harold 83, 192
love 71, 124, 160
Luckman, T. 226
Lutheranism, study of pupils'
understanding of 251–4

McGrath, A. E. 108–9, 140, 154,
221; contextual epistemology
213, 214; foundational
epistemology 208, 209
MacIntyre, Alasdair 2, 43,
171–2
Mackie, J. D. 256
Markham, I. 132, 210
Marshall, B. D. 210, 211, 218,
222
Marton, Ference 233;
phenomenography 242–5;
Variation Theory of Learning
237–42, 245–8
Martos, J. 140
matter 18–19

reductionist interpretations
135–40
reflective living 43–4
relationships 40, 117, 120, 242,
243
relativism 138, 164, 166, 214;
epistemic 7, 8, 12–13, 131;
theological 100–1
relevance structure 248
religionism 109, 112, 144, 147
religions, definition of 155
religious education: in ancient
Israel 55–64; British
Government's National
Framework 48–50; in the early
church 72–8; Platonic 65–72;
see also critical religious
education; liberal religious
education; National
Framework; pedagogy of
learning and religious education
*Religious Education in Secondary
Schools: Schools Council Working
Paper 36* (Smart) 84–6
*Religious Education: The Non-
Statutory National Framework*
(DfES/QCA) 48–50, 86–7,
104–8, 111, 118, 141, 236
religious language 134, 135,
137–8, 145, 235; belief and
216; creeds and propositions
158–62; experiential-expressive
model of 92–3, 192–3;
hermeneutics and 182;
metaphor 133–4, 160, 167–70,
180; narrative and story 170–6;
religious and secular worldviews
176–80; religious speech acts
162–7
religious life stances, connection
between religious beliefs and
149–50
religious particularity, challenge
posed by 90–3

religious practice 149
religious principles 34
religious truth claims 80, 81, 138,
194, 235; in British religious
education 82, 84, 85; challenge
posed by 91–3; compatibility of
scientific truth claims and
257–9; creeds and propositions
158–62
religious understanding,
distinction between
understanding religion and 88
Renaissance humanism 30
Republic 68–9
respect 33, 34
revelation 143, 212, 257
Ricoeur, Paul 170, 171
Robinson, John 134
Roman Catholicism 34, 115; *see
also* Christianity
Romans 6: 1 63
Romantic ideas: freedom 39;
hermeneutics 182–3, 186–7,
205; metaphor 168
romantic intuition 209, 210, 211
Rorty, Richard 24–5, 168, 198
Rousseau, J.-J. 32, 37, 119
Russell, Bertrand 139

salvation 141–2
salvific communities 132, 148–56
Savonarola 30
scepticism 12–13, 15, 23, 66, 100
Scheilke, C. Th. 119, 135–6
Schleiermacher, Friedrich 92,
182–3, 211
schools, faith-based 115
Schools Curriculum and
Assessment Authority (SCAA)
87
Schwöbel, C. 39
science 2, 12, 13, 16, 17, 19–20,
154; Christianity's acceptance
of 222; coherence of 221;